DRAWING (IN) THE FEMININE

STUDIES IN COMICS AND CARTOONS
Jared Gardner, Charles Hatfield, and Rebecca Wanzo, Series Editors

DRAWING (IN) THE FEMININE

Bande Dessinée and Women

Edited by Margaret C. Flinn

THE OHIO STATE UNIVERSITY PRESS
COLUMBUS

Copyright © 2024 by The Ohio State University.
All rights reserved.

The various characters, logos, and other trademarks appearing in this book are the property of their respective owners and are presented here strictly for scholarly analysis. No infringement is intended or should be implied.

This book is freely available in an open access edition thanks to The Ohio State University Libraries' Billy Ireland Cartoon Library & Museum and generous support provided by a grant from The Ohio State Energy Partners (OSEP). OSEP is a joint venture between ENGIE North America and Axium Infrastructure.

Library of Congress Cataloging-in-Publication Data
Names: Flinn, Margaret C., editor.
Title: Drawing (in) the feminine : bande dessinée and women / edited by Margaret C. Flinn.
Other titles: Studies in comics and cartoons.
Description: Columbus : The Ohio State University Press, [2024] | Series: Studies in comics and cartoons | Includes bibliographical references and index. | Summary: "Examines the variety and impact of contemporary women's production in French and Francophone comics art and also considers historical bande dessinée output to illuminate the contributions of women creators"— Provided by publisher.
Identifiers: LCCN 2023044275 | ISBN 9780814215142 (hardback) | ISBN 0814215149 (hardback) | ISBN 9780814283332 (ebook) | ISBN 0814283330 (ebook)
Subjects: LCSH: Women in comics. | Women cartoonists. | Women and literature. | Comic books, strips, etc.—France—History and criticism. | Comic books, strips, etc.—French-speaking countries—History and criticism.
Classification: LCC PN6745 .D73 2024 | DDC 741.5944—dc23/eng/20231226
LC record available at https://lccn.loc.gov/2023044275

Other identifiers: ISBN 9780814259009 (paperback) | ISBN 0814259006 (paperback)

Cover design by Sarah Flood-Baumann
Text compositions by Stuart Rodriguez
Type set in Palatino Linotype

CONTENTS

List of Illustrations   vii

List of Tables   ix

Editor's Acknowledgments   xi

INTRODUCTION   MARGARET C. FLINN   1

PART 1 • INDUSTRY, AUDIENCE, AND PLATFORMS

CHAPTER 1   Women Cartoonists: A New Avenue for Understanding a Little-Known Profession?
JESSICA KOHN   21

CHAPTER 2   Women in Color: Comics Artists and the Ninth Art in France
SYLVAIN LESAGE   37

CHAPTER 3   Between *Ah! Nana* and *Okapi*: Nicole Claveloux at the Crossroads
BENOÎT CRUCIFIX   53

CHAPTER 4   Gender Equality? *Hshouma!* Women, Sexuality, and Comics Activism in Morocco
JENNIFER HOWELL   75

PART 2 • GEOGRAPHIES OF IDENTITY

CHAPTER 5   Graphic Entanglements: Images of Women, Nature, and Brittany in Contemporary Comics
ARMELLE BLIN-ROLLAND   97

CHAPTER 6   The Feminine Plural in Africa and the Diaspora: Quartets of Women in *Aya de Yopougon* and *La vie d'Ebène Duta*
MICHELLE BUMATAY   124

CHAPTER 7   Revolutionary Comics: Samandal's Feminist Topography of Resistance
ALEXANDRA GUEYDAN-TUREK   142

CHAPTER 8   Unveiling IVG: Representations of Women's Experiences of Abortion in the *Bande Dessinée*
CATRIONA MACLEOD   160

PART 3 • REPRESENTATIONS AND HISTORY (HERSTORIES)

CHAPTER 9   The Face of Women in Early *Bandes Dessinées*: Töpffer, Cham, Musset, Gustave Doré
JACQUES DÜRRENMATT   181

CHAPTER 10   The Amazons of Dahomey in French and African Comics
MARK MCKINNEY   198

CHAPTER 11   Catel: Portrait of the Twenty-First-Century Feminist Artist and Author of Drawn Biography
ISABELLE DELORME   222

CHAPTER 12   The Women behind the Woman behind the Man: Women Drawing Plural Collective Voices onto the Page in Emilie Plateau's *Noire*
VÉRONIQUE BRAGARD   239

List of Contributors   253

Index   257

ILLUSTRATIONS

FIGURE 0.1	Sophie Labelle, *Assignée garçon* #156	3
FIGURE 3.1	Nicole Claveloux, *Les aventures d'Alice au pays des merveilles*	63
FIGURE 3.2	Nicole Claveloux, "L'insupportable Grabote et le lion Léonidas," *Okapi*, no. 30	65
FIGURE 3.3	Nicole Claveloux, "L'insupportable Grabote et le lion Léonidas," *Okapi*, no. 42	67
FIGURE 3.4	Nicole Claveloux, *Go, Go, Go, Grabote!*	68
FIGURE 4.1	Girl on a bus, Zainab Fasiki, *Hshouma: Corps et sexualité au Maroc*	78
FIGURE 4.2	The female body shown in anatomical position, Zainab Fasiki, *Hshouma: Corps et sexualité au Maroc*	88
FIGURE 5.1	Roland Michon and Laëtitia Rouxel, *Brigande! Marion du Faouët: Vie, amours et mort*	104
FIGURE 5.2	Delphine Le Lay and Alexis Horellou, *Plogoff*	110
FIGURE 6.1	Marguerite Abouet and Clément Oubrerie, *Aya de Yopougon*	130
FIGURE 6.2	Elyon's, *La Vie d'Ebène Duta*	134

FIGURE 7.1	Lena Merhej, "Éditorial/Al-iftitāḥiyyah"	147
FIGURE 7.2	Nour Hifaoui Fakhouri, "Ahed wa Karīm / Ahed et Karim / Ahed and Karim"	153
FIGURE 8.1	Désirée Frappier and Alain Frappier, *Le choix*	167
FIGURE 8.2	Aude Mermilliod, *Il fallait que je vous le dise*, p. 33	172
FIGURE 8.3	Aude Mermilliod, *Il fallait que je vous le dise*, p. 52	174
FIGURE 9.1	Anne Simon, *Gousse & Gigot*	190
FIGURE 9.2	Gustave Doré, *Des-agréments d'un voyage d'agrément*	194
FIGURE 10.1	Lucien Lefèvre, *Théâtre de la Porte St. Martin*	201
FIGURE 10.2	Front cover of *Le petit journal*	204
FIGURE 10.3	Pat Masioni and Sylvia Serbin, *Les femmes soldats du Dahomey*	217
FIGURE 11.1	Catel Muller and José-Louis Bocquet, *Kiki de Montparnasse*	230
FIGURE 12.1	Emilie Plateau, *Noire: La vie méconnue de Claudette Colvin*, p. 10	245
FIGURE 12.2	Emilie Plateau, *Noire: La vie méconnue de Claudette Colvin*, p. 75	250

TABLES

TABLE 1.1	Women *bédéiste*'s generation according to their date of birth and the start of their drawing work (professional activity)	28
TABLE 1.2	Geographic origin of *bédéistes* according to their generation	28
TABLE 1.3	Geographic origin of women *bédéistes* according to their generation	28
TABLE 1.4	Gender of *bédéistes* according to their training	29
TABLE 1.5	Type of periodical according to the generation of *bédéiste*	33
TABLE 1.6	Type of periodical according to the gender of *bédéiste*	33

EDITOR'S ACKNOWLEDGMENTS

I am immensely grateful for the patience and support of Ana Jimenez-Moreno and the staff at The Ohio State University Press, without whom such a beautiful object could not have become part of the world, as well as the editorial assistance of Morgan Podraza for carrying us over the finish line and Holly Engel for completing the index. This volume would not have been conceived without the encouragement of Jenny Robb, nor come into being without the enthusiastic welcome of series editors Jared Gardner and Charles Hatfield, and astute readings by the press's peer reviewers. Financial support for this project was provided by the Billy Ireland Cartoon Library & Museum with funding from an Ohio State Energy Partners (OSEP) Award. The staff of amazing women under Jenny Robb's leadership at the Billy Ireland, Kristy Arter, Kay Clopton, Anne Drozd, Emma Halm, Caitlin McGurk, Susan Liberator, Wendy Pflug, and Marilyn Scott, were all involved in some direct or indirect way in supporting the research and conversations that led up to this publication. The atmosphere they create for comics scholarship and teaching at Ohio State is priceless, and their impact on the field at large cannot be understated. Beyond those mentioned above, numerous colleagues at Ohio State and other local institutions offered significant insights and enthusiasm through their dialogue with myself and the volume's contributors. Although I am certainly forgetting someone, I can confidently name Frederick Aldama, Kirby Childress, Isabelle Choquet, Paige Piper, Michal Raizen, Dana Renga, Lucille Toth, Johanna Sellman, Katlin Marisol Sweeney-Romero, and last but very far from least, Jennifer Willging. Julia Billet and Julie Delporte both visited Columbus during the early phases of work toward this project and inspired all present by their grace and generosity. Finally, I must say what a pleasure and privilege it has been to work with all the contributors. Their rigor and care for their work, their care for each other and respect for the challenges of collective labor within the context of a global pandemic that impacted various group members quite differently made this woman's work much easier.

INTRODUCTION

MARGARET C. FLINN

Women in *bande dessinée* have gender trouble, to repurpose the title phrase from Judith Butler's seminal work on gender performativity.[1] Whether that phrase is taken to mean the challenges of working in the publishing industry or if it rather means being a woman character in a *bande dessinée,* being of a nondominant gender in a highly masculine cultural field causes troubles of all kinds. Perhaps no one knows this better than the Châteaugauy-born, (and until recently) Montreal-based artist Sophie Labelle. Labelle's watershed, twice-weekly webcomic, *Assignée garçon* [Assigned Male] started in 2014; she has since also self-published print collections of the webcomic, as well as stand-alone comics and children's books, and launched a graphic novel series, *Ciel,* with a major publisher. By 2017, *Assignée garçon* was reported

---

1. The Met Fifth Avenue exhibition *The New Woman Behind the Camera* (July 2–October 3, 2021), curated by Mia Fineman, included a "Note to the Reader" that states: "The nuances of gender and self-identification are of crucial importance. Women constitute a heterogeneous group whose individual identities are defined by a host of variable factors. Thus the designation 'woman photographer' is imperfect (as is the adjective 'female'), yet it remains a useful framework for analysis." I would offer a similar caveat on the deployment of "women" and "female" throughout this volume.

by the *Montreal Gazette* to get "half-a-million visits per week" (McGillis).[2] In that year, Labelle was not only targeted by right-wing trolls but was also doxed and received serious enough threats to opt for the cancellation of a speaking event at a bookstore in Halifax: within the space of one week, she received over 17,000 hate messages and emails across several platforms (Labelle, "Sophie Labelle"; Labrèche).[3] The escalated harassment garnered press coverage from coast to coast in Canada and strongly resembles other sexist, racist, and homo/transphobic, alt-right driven culture wars, such as Gamergate, that have targeted women and nonbinary professionals active in pop-culture fields with not only online harassment but also threats of sexual and other physical violence.

Sophie Labelle and *Assignée garçon* can be considered emblematic of some of the most current problems for Francophone women and nonbinary comics creators, as well as the kinds of creative solutions afforded to at least some. *Assignée garçon* started as a webcomic (see figure 0.1 below for how the pages appear on Tumblr) and only later became available in self-published print collections. The recent graphic novel series *Ciel*, though, brought Labelle by invitation into a major Québecois publishing house (Éditions Hurtubise), in the process of which she lost the possibility of simultaneous self-translating due to rigidity in contracts and distribution (Falck). *Assignée garçon* (and Labelle's work more broadly) draws criticism for the preternatural theoretical sophistication of its young protagonists' understanding of the world and their place in it yet also resonates with its numerous fans precisely because of what they see as the truth-telling of the clear-eyed youngsters, not to mention, of course, the satisfaction of the sometimes scathing humor: in common parlance, those audiences find Labelle's characters highly "relatable." Labelle's self-taught style is similar to that of Elyon's (another self-published artist with a marginalized identity who has

---

2. The "Assigned Male" entry on *KnowYourMeme.com* assembles the comic's rapid accumulation of likes, followers, and subscribers across various social media/crowd-sourced funding platforms: "On August 31st, 2014, a Facebook page was created for the comic, accumulating upwards of 30,000 likes in the next two years. In early 2015, a Patreon page for the comic was created, reaching over $1,231 in subscriptions per month by the next year. In August, a Twitter account for the comic was created, garnering more than 1,200 followers within seven months."

3. Such hostility has continued as this volume enters production in the winter of 2022–23. The career trajectory of Jul Maroh before and after coming out as transgender and nonbinary would give another instructive case study of how queer, trans, and genderqueer artists are subjected to a compounded, intersectional marginalization with deep roots in sexism.

FIGURE 0.1. Sophie Labelle, *Assignée garçon* #156, Tumblr, 2015. Accessed March 13, 2023.

parlayed crowdfunding and an online fan base into critical recognition)[4]: her characters' features have a distinctive manga influence embedded in a deceptively simple, bubbly, comic line, with flat color planes on bodies and backgrounds (figure 0.1). Micro (and "macro") aggressions feature prominently in the brief vignettes—indeed, Labelle remarks that it's strange how often her comics are called "educational" when so much of the humor comes from her trans, genderqueer, and queer characters simply refusing

---

4. See Michelle Bumatay's chapter in this volume (chapter 6).

to answer "stupid questions" ("Sophie Labelle"). The play between representing young characters in a short-form humor genre comic that explicitly addresses a potentially quite young readership and yet also resonates satisfactorily for much older audiences exemplifies the kinds of crossover publics and tensions between youth and adult markets that has long characterized the comics industry in general, but particularly the place of women in that industry. Such artists are held, by various gatekeeping mechanisms, to the symbolic margins of the industry, in youth-oriented sectors of the market. They are then subsequently considered critically delegitimized as "real artists" because of that very marginalization.

In some ways, Labelle's work reads like an '80s/'90s queer dream-come-true of undoing gender binarisms (in figure 0.1, main character Stéphie says, "I don't dress 'like a girl.' That doesn't mean anything, anyway"),[5] while nonetheless celebrating authentically experienced gender as something every individual should be able to enjoy and asserting there are many valid ways to identify one's self with a commonly used gender category such as "girl." While Labelle publishes in both French and English, she says that the majority of her readership originates in the United States, and indeed, her *bande dessinée* are far easier to procure in their English-language versions than in the original French ("Sophie Labelle"). It seems no accident that a Francophone queer trans comic should emerge in the North American context: individualism, colonial settlerism, and multicultural melting pot mythologies have at least yielded ways of talking productively about difference that are structurally and conceptually disadvantaged by French universalism.[6]

Universalism

In her concise summary of the history of French universalism, Naomi Schor wrote:

> Universalism, and never more so than in its Enlightenment incarnation, was grounded in the belief that human nature, that is rational human nature, was a universal impervious to cultural and historical differences.

---

5. All translations are my own.
6. This is true for both France and most of the French-speaking world, as it contends with the legacies of colonialism and Empire.

Transcultural, transhistorical human nature was posited as identical, beyond particularisms. (46)

Schor points out that one of the very first contestations of universalism came in the form of Olympe de Gouges's *Declaration of the Rights of Woman and the [Female] Citizen* as a response to *The Declaration of the Rights of Man and the Citizen* (47), along with the Black Jacobins of Haiti. Nonetheless Schor's essay is just one piece of an abundant body of scholarship documenting and analyzing the tightness of French universalism's hold on the modern French nation-state, despite the crises that have dogged it from the start.[7]

In the late twentieth- and early twenty-first centuries, one of French feminism's main clashes with universalism has been staged on and through the debates about *parité*. As Schor argues, the main bugaboo for France in debates about political *parité* has not been the United States but rather the stark statistical realities that the other European Union members' data offers about women's representation in electoral politics.[8] While *parité* is discussed legally primarily in relationship to electoral politics, the concept has migrated into discourse around most sectors of employment. Lack of *parité* in various cultural and professional domains has come to serve an immediate and easily (if not completely) visible indicator of persistent structural sexism.

Like the other two major traditions of global graphic narrative (American comics and Japanese manga), *bande dessinée* has a long history of dramatic and sexist marginalization of women creators and characters, as well as a persistent tendency to occlude nonmale readership and to sideline women critics within a highly masculine fan-skewed critical culture. In a nutshell, *bande dessinée* is in no way *paritaire* (numerically equal). Contributions to this volume push back against the ways in which the reduction of women to the margins of *bande dessinée* history have minimized their significant contributions to that history and extend forward to explore the diversity of a flourishing contemporary production. While still far from achieving parity with their male counterparts, female creators are occupying an increasingly significant portion of the French-language comics publishing industry, and creators of all genders are putting forth stories that represent and reflect on the diversity and richness of women's and gender-nonconforming people's experiences. In this introduction, I would like to present (if necessarily

---

7. See, for example, Célestin and DalMolin; Célestin et al.; and Scott.
8. Which is not to say that *parité* is complete or successful in all of Europe. For more on this topic, see Lépinard in Lépinard and Rubio-Marín, as well as other essays in the volume.

briefly) some of the cultural obstacles and specificities of women in the Franco-Belgian tradition of comics, connecting those to trends in *bande dessinée* scholarship. Nuanced explorations of historical materials as well as analyses of the increasingly diverse forms of contemporary *bande dessinée* production by and about women will, in the essays that make up the body of this book, offer a deeper and more detailed understanding of how women have created and been represented throughout the history of *bande dessinée*.

Before advancing further, it may be helpful to include a few brief remarks about the terminology used in this introduction and elsewhere in the volume. Like the Japanese term "manga," *bande dessinée* as used here refers to a particular publishing context and object that is not adequately rendered either by the American English terms "comic book" or "graphic novels." While comics artist/cartoonist or comics/cartoons can be appropriate terms to describe the creators discussed in this book (a decision left to each contributor as a function of their specific corpus), authors in this volume may often prefer *bande dessinée* (or its abbreviation BD), and *bédéiste* in order to respect the cultural and artistic specificity of the Franco-Belgian comics tradition. It is also, however, the umbrella term for "comics" in French, and as such, many *bande dessinée* scholars prefer to use "comics" when writing in English. (This is of course setting aside specific discussions of the professions and practices of caricaturists, colorists, illustrators, letterers, *scénaristes*, etc., which, depending upon the historical moment and individual, may or may not be overlapping categories and identities as that of artist, author, or *bédéiste*.) The "Franco-Belgian tradition" is and of itself complicated: some of this volume's contributors deal with material specifically from or set in France; some carefully excavate the ways that there is a European French-language comics culture that is too French-centered to be truly "Franco-Belgian." Others deal with material that is not European at all but nonetheless negotiates with French-speaking Europe through the history and legacies of European colonialism as it is configured in the fields of education, publishing, and so forth. The primary texts in question throughout this volume are at least published in French or include French as one language of a multilingual publication. I deliberately sought to include chapters on materials that emanate from and represent multiple corners of the perennially problematic realm of "Francophonie," without making the single and driving priority of this volume to be complete and even geographical coverage of "Global French"— a move that likely would have necessarily led to the sacrifice of historical coverage, due to the way that historical "Francophone" publishing outside of France has been a crushingly white and Euro-North American enterprise.

Bad Press, Positive Trajectories

From a feminist perspective, 2016 was something of an *annus horribilus* for the Angoulême International Comics Festival: the Grand Prix competition short list provoked a firestorm when it included only male artists, prompting many of the nominees to withdraw their names from consideration. Franck Bondoux, then the festival executive officer, compounded the scandal by repeatedly making dismissive or historically inaccurate statements, offering specious "justifications" about what qualified an artist for the prize, clearly contradicted by the profiles of various previous Grand Prix winners. If there was an upside to the ugly sexist biases exposed by reactions to the situation from various quarters, it was arguably in the numerous public pronouncements highlighting the quantity and diversity of high-quality female creators engaged in contemporary comics production both within the Franco-Belgian publishing sphere and internationally. It is of course far too soon to conclude that anything has ended well—which we might define as equitable access and eventually numerical equality. However, it is certainly worth noting that the finalists for the Grand Prix in 2022 were Pénélope Bagieu, Julie Doucet, and Catherine Meurisse, with Doucet as the ultimate *lauréate*.[9]

If the mainstream attention to sexism in comics and *bande dessinée* in 2016 was not unwelcome, as per usual, sisters had already "been doin' it for themselves." Since 2008, the Prix Artémisia had been attributed by the Association Artémesia as a means of ensuring that important prizes were not awarded solely to male creators (the Artémesia is only awarded to women artists). Similarly, in 2015, the collective BD Égalité had been formed as a response to the systematic sexism faced by women creators in the Franco-Belgian context. With approximately 250 members to date, the collective published a charter and maintains an explicitly and unapologetically feminist stance, intervening publicly and collectively but also maintaining their website as a means of documenting on-going sexism in the industry. Numbers published by the Association des Critiques et journalistes de Bande Dessinée show that women remain a dramatic minority in the Francophone European industry but also that the twenty-first century has seen a marked rise in their representation in the profession: from 80 of 1,100 (7.2 percent) in 2001 to 182 of 1,419 (12.8 percent) in 2016 (Ratier). If anything, seen from

---

9. Moreover, on 30 November 2022, Catherine Meurisse was officially inaugurated into the French Académie des Beaux-Arts ("Séance").

a qualitative perspective, the critical acclaim consistently earned by *bédéistes* such as Zeina Abirached, Pénélope Bagieu, Aude Picault, Dominique Goblet, Lisa Mandel, Agnès Maupré, Catherine Meurisse, Catel Muller, Vanyda, Tiphaine Rivière, Tanxxx, and the like, or a *scénariste*, such as Marguerite Abouet or Julia Billet, might suggest that Francophone women creators are in a sense critically "outperforming" their male counterparts.

A similarly positive trajectory can be noted in *bande dessinée* scholarship.[10] In 2015, a group of Francophone researchers formed a group named La Brèche with the immediate purpose of networking and supporting a burgeoning, but often disparate, field of research.[11] By 2017, the group went public and opened membership to researchers in any academic field with a serious interest in comics scholarship. It is notable that a significant portion of this group are early career researchers in precarious employment due to the types of institutional constrictions felt across European and North American humanities programs—larger moves toward "adjunctification" and the expansion of "second-tier" (in prestige and pay), teaching-focused faculty positions have amounted to the rebuilding of glass ceilings that are leaving increasing and disproportional numbers of women and BIPOC scholars in less institutionally valued and less monetarily rewarded career tracks. These trends have combined with comics scholarship's less established status to yield paradoxical situations: comics scholarship "publishes well" (due to the real and perceived crossover potential of this work), comics studies course enrollments are consistently high, but the early career scholars who do such labor as trained specialists find themselves with fewer opportunities for stable careers, let alone institutionally prestigious ones. In spring 2020,

---

10. A notable exception to this positive trajectory is in the area of comics theory. In 2014, Leuven University Press published *The French Comics Theory Reader*, edited by Ann Miller and Bart Beaty, an anthology of twenty-five essays (or excerpts) originally appearing from 1969 to the present, not one of which is by a woman author. The editors have not been insensitive to gender issues in their respective, distinguished careers, to say the least. One is thus inclined to conclude that this otherwise fairly uncontroversial selection is conditioned by two things. First, the gender biases present in the in- and out-of-academia field of comics theory and criticism are consistent with those that burden the creative labor of *bande dessinée*. Second, the strength of certain theoretical leanings, such as that of semiotics, and the particular, dominant framings of historiography represented in the book's fourth section, "Reading the French Comics Industry," are not expansive or creative enough for considering how one might tell counter-histories or find documentation for those so often rendered invisible in the historical record.

11. See the website for La Bréche at https://labrechebd.com. The reader who peruses this website may note the significant overlap between this volume's European contributors and La Brèche membership.

a new initiative was born: Les Bréchoises, initially a subgroup of La Brèche, but eventually a larger interdisciplinary team sharing a feminist approach toward *bande dessinée* scholarship ("Les Bréchoises").[12] Members of this group lead the 2021 École Universitaire de Recherche ArTeC project "Créatrices de bandes dessinées: Histoire, mémoire, revendications et representations des femmes dans le neuvième art." This is both an archival project and one that will culminate in an international conference, no doubt yielding significant publications. Meanwhile, *Comicalités*, the only French-language scholarly journal dedicated exclusively to the study of *bandes dessinées* currently has editorial board membership and leadership essentially at *parité*.[13]

Which History? Which Representations?

There is a "straight story" of the history of women in *bande dessinée* that underlines the relative absence of women creators and the poverty of representational possibility in French-language comics through their early and classic phases. While the minority status of women creators remains a fact, there is a kind of vicious circle wherein predominantly male scholars and critics have tended to take such imbalance at face value and have then accepted/determined that further excavation is unnecessary. Especially in

---

12. It's worth pointing out that for La Brèche, Les Bréchoises, and Comicalités, as with most Francophone institutions and organizations, "recherches sur la bande dessinée" is used as the default umbrella term, as "comics scholarship" is in English. Thus these organizations' mandates are to study "bande dessinée" in an international sense, although French language comics are, unsurprisingly, extremely heavily represented, just as American comics are overrepresented in most Anglophone scholarly publications whose explicit scope is "international" comics, with the exception of journals such as *European Comic Art*, whose geographical circumscription necessarily precludes discussion of American comics except as a possible transnational, translation, or comparative case study. Bilingual English-French journals of French and Francophone studies are, like this volume, the place where *bande dessinée* may be used to refer to a specific linguistic and cultural sphere.

13. This numerical shift was already in motion at the time C(h)ris Reyns-Chikuma's essay "Genre, Gender, Sexual, Textual and Visual, and Real Representations in *Bande Dessinée*" went to press—although the website had, in fact, not yet been updated to reflect that change. In this essay, Reyns-Chikuma points out that the journal's "various review committees are also overwhelmingly male" (208). It does remain true that the journal has not yet "dedicated an issue to gender issues" (208), although like La Brèche membership, the current *Comicalités* board is heavily represented among the contributors to this volume. Moreover, the board has recently adopted "écriture inclusive" (gender-inclusive writing) as the publication standard.

condensed forms, this leads critics to make untenable claims such as, "For decades there were no women in *bande dessinée*. Then, basically, in 1963, there was one: the great Claire Bretécher" (Ciment). Even a feminist-minded scholar such as C(h)ris Reyns-Chikuma (one of the coeditors, along with Sophie Milquet, of a significant special issue of *Alternative Francophone* on women in *bande dessinée*, "La bande dessinée au féminin" [Female Comics]) reproduces this kind of gesture, with subtitles such as, "New Beginnings: Forgotten Girls and Women" (197), "The Great Masters: No Girls and No Women Allowed" (198), and "Finally, Some Women" (202) to indicate the significant shift at the moment of Claire Bretécher and *Ah! Nana*. Similarly, when Thierry Groensteen published a two-part essay history of women in *bande dessinée*, he stated, "For a long time, *bande dessinée* was predominantly produced by men for young readers who were themselves also male" ("Femme [1]"), showing the same kind of quick strokes that erase women and girls as readers, leaving them for the most part uncounted.[14]

Consolidated, concentrated histories will, inevitably, tend to accept dominant narratives and viewpoints due to lack of space—which is one reason I deliberately am not attempting to (once again) synthesize that straight story in this introduction. Instead, I seek to contextualize that story and also to indicate the kinds of breaches into which the prismatic nature of the edited volume may refract light. Paradoxically, the history of the marginalized can only be written if, when faced with apparent lacks and absences, scholars dedicate time to looking for and talking about *more* of what is "not there" or focus more attention on that which seems immediately less important because less numerous. Book length studies, whether single-author monographs or edited volumes, of course give authors more leeway to explore such countercurrents. English-language comics studies has been a leader in refocusing attention on gender issues. Seminal scholarship (that has often dipped into non-American corpuses) has tended to gravitate toward autobiography and life-writing (e.g., Hilary Chute's *Graphic Women*, which includes a chapter on Marjane Satrapi) or revisionist histories of superheroes. A more generically heterogenous corpus is assembled by Deborah Elizabeth Whaley for *Black Women in Sequence: Re-Inking Comics, Graphic Novels, and Anime*. Ann Miller's *Reading* Bande Dessinée: *Critical Approaches*

---

14. In contrast, Groensteen gives comprehensive and nuanced, if concise, synthesis of extant data on the contemporary "La féminisation de la profession" in his book *La bande dessinée au tournant*. In the same volume, Groensteen summarizes data showing evidence of persistent male readership. Also see Evans and Gaudet for information about readership, and Jessica Kohn's scholarship for careful and complete consideration of nuances in the publishing industry historically.

to *French-Language Comic Strip* has been pivotal both in the sense of giving more space to gender issues writ large in a book dedicated specifically to *bande dessinée* history and theory and also aligning women's production very strongly with autobiography (there are individual chapters on "Autobiography and Diary Writing" and also "Gender and Autobiography").

Catriona Macleod's recently published book, *Invisible Presence: The Representation of Women in French-Language Comics*, devotes an entire section (one third of the book) to secondary women characters. This type of scholarship asks: what happens when, instead of continuing to focus only on the paucity of female leads, we don't dismiss secondary characters as being irrelevant to the entire system of representation that comics put in place? This is, in essence, the methodological strategy deployed by Jacques Dürrenmatt in his contribution to this volume, revisiting seminal early comics and caricature. In close proximity to our topic, Nelly Chabrol Gagne's sumptuously illustrated *Filles d'albums: Les representations du féminin dans l'album* excavates the complicated and heterogenous representations of girls and women of all ages in the *album* [picture book], an object closely related to the *bande dessinée* both in form and creative/publishing personnel, as well its slippery/ill-defined but marginalized artistic status in the broader hierarchies of cultural productions.

The predominance of such a "straight story" has had important methodological implications for the field of comics and *bande dessinée* studies as a whole in that extant hierarchies between types of comics publications and their audiences, as well as hierarchies in artistic/professional activities, have further erased and minimized the women who were in fact active in the field. Thus, for example, the marginalized status of *illustrés* for girls, particularly in the Catholic press, as an object of study for early twentieth-century print history has meant that the segment of the publishing industry where women were more strongly represented is itself completely occluded from most comics histories. Similarly, the profession of colorist is rarely considered as a focal point for telling comics history, and illustration work is considered of lesser artistic value because of the "compromised" status of the *bédéiste*-working-as-illustrator (insofar as she is not the sole creator at the origin of the story). Historians Jessica Kohn, Sylvain Lesage, and Benoît Crucifix thus use a focus on women in the industry as a means to leverage open larger issues about the hows and whys of *bande dessinée* scholarship, arguing for a more complete and more complex picture of who has contributed, and in which ways, to the production of drawn narratives over time, as well as how *bandes dessinées* are situated in a broader network of artistic activities and objects.

A logical contemporary consideration for this expanded view of comics includes considerations of how creators work not only in standard industrial albums or varied independent graphic novel formats but also how they interact with collective publishing enterprises (which are not new in themselves and certainly have a strongly engaged feminist history), how they work across digital and print, how they engage with fans via digital media, and how structures such as crowd-sourcing have allowed different points of contact between creators and readers, as well as different means by which to navigate the institutional and industrial gatekeeping structures that have created major obstacles for women and creators of color. Thus across this volume's contributions, scholars are attentive to contemporary platforms and funding structures: Jennifer Howell explores how Zainab Fasiki's social media interacts with her print publications; Michelle Bumatay's essay includes a consideration of the engagements of Elyon's with her fan base; and Alexandra Gueydan-Turek's primary text is the product of a multilingual, transnational publishing collective, Samandal, that is highly attuned to the intersectional identities and experiences of its creators and audience. The different strategies leveraged by individual creators through crowd sourcing and publishing collectives (historically associated with engaged feminist artistic practice) also evoke tensions between the *auteure*'s individual promotion and the positioning of creators within a more industrially dispersed workforce (as examined by the historians mentioned above) or within a collective such as Samandal.

The Stakes of Auteure-ism

It is a well-known story in academia that the work of French historians of the Annales school radically influenced the historiography not only of France and the French-speaking world but also humanistic studies more broadly, in many ways paralleling the impact of British Marxist academics on the rise of cultural studies, emerging out of departments of history and penetrating throughout the humanities, as interdisciplinarity became an increasingly explicit value for academic institutions in the late twentieth and early twenty-first centuries.[15] Meanwhile, French-language film and visual

---

15. One can reasonably question how an exciting and productive reconceptualization of intellectual boundaries and labors as necessarily cross-pollinating strikingly has corresponded to the erosion in stability of employment for academic workforces as well as increased demands/expectations for "two for one" (at least) expertise (at equal levels of proficiency and impact) in research institution hiring practices.

culture scholarship as well as English-language scholarship of the French and Francophone world has been strongly influenced by auteurism. These vectors of pressure are evident in what were formerly known as departments of French language and literature, or French literary studies, but also in the fundamentally interdisciplinary disciplines that emerged in no small part from within departments of literature (French, English, Comparative Literature, and others) such as film and comics studies.[16]

Bande dessinée criticism has explicitly dialogued with both literary and cinema studies.[17] As well known as the historiographical shifts evoked above are, waves of influence emit from essays by thinkers such as Roland Barthes (*La mort de l'auteur* in 1967) and Michel Foucault (*Qu'est-ce qu'un auteur?* in 1969), originally written in French and subsequently in translation, on critical theory across French and Francophone studies and literary studies internationally. Along a closely related timeline, we must note the political valorization of the role of the film director as *auteur* that emerged from Cahiers du Cinéma writers in the 1950s and was articulated through dialogue (or dispute) with *Positif* before migrating to the Anglophone world and being popularized as auteur theory thanks to American film critic Andrew Sarris in the early 1960s, ultimately shaping the institutional spread of film studies departments and programs in that sphere. While literary studies was killing off the author in favor of the text, film studies was canonizing the *auteur*, although both disciplines saw the pendulum again swing with the historicist turns of the 1990s. Birthed at the interstices of literary, film, art historical, and historical studies (not to mention creative art practice and training) and typically deprived of the level of structural independence

---

16. I have felt these influences directly and immediately as a scholar of French cinema and popular culture trained by leading feminists in Ivy League literature departments, as well as Paris VII and VIII, during and in the wake of high French theory's heyday. This positional bias may be leading me to overstate the importance of these trends. Yet my experience as a queer woman undergraduate and graduate student trying to make sense of a rapidly evolving institutional landscape embroiled in external culture wars and trending heavily toward economic constriction and austerity feels instructive. My ability to position myself clearly and compellingly in relationship to large and highly contested trends in these fields conditioned my entry into the profession, as the need to make sense of such trends was clearly communicated to be the prerequisite to professional survival—let alone success.

17. The first chapter of Benoît Peeters's *Lire la bande dessinée* (Flammarion, 1998) does one of the most clear and insightful positioning of *bande dessinée*'s artistic specificities in relationship to painting and cinema in print to this day. For thoughtful consideration of intersections of the cultural spheres of *bande dessinée*, literature, and fine arts, Bart Beaty's *Unpopular Culture: Transforming the European Comic Book in the 1990s* (U of Toronto P, 2007) remains invaluable.

achieved by at least some film studies departments due to its "latecomer" status, comics studies as a discipline has always, to my eyes, appeared to make peace rather more cordially with its inherent interdisciplinarity than its more long-lived brethren.

These broad strokes of disciplinary trends have, unsurprisingly, been dominated by male thinkers and overwhelmingly taken as their subject matter male authors, directors, or artists. What then of the *auteure* or *autrice*?[18] As I suggested above, the contribution of women throughout an industry gains significant visibility from nonauteur(e)ist historiography. But individual women creators have also gained stature through their exceptional status, and those names figure prominently in the "straight story" of women in *bande dessinée* as "greats." And as I have evoked in relation to the 2016 Angoulême controversy (and the celebration of the 2022 finalists), if individual artistic merit is recognized through juried festival awards and other publishing prizes, there is a deep problem when women are underrepresented in such awards competitions. It is of course also essential to acknowledge that the type of exceptional *auteure* who is most rapidly and frequently catapulted to exceptional stardom is white. Women of ethnic and racial minorities, often situated outside of hexagonal production, are even more stringently limited in their access to such status. Marjane Satrapi is rather the exceptional exception, then. While the serial publication of *Persepolis* in *Libération* was extremely significant for mainstreaming the autobiographical graphic novel, and Satrapi remains a go-to for Anglophone scholars/educators seeking to vary their research corpus or syllabi by adding international material, that popularity was not without a certain price. Satrapi's position in L'Association can be ambivalently evoked by predominately male scholars, and the taint of mainstream popularity when compared to the house's founders and another early-published woman artist, Julie Doucet, seems indicative of underlying tensions in comics scholarship, theory, and fandom.

The controversy in 2009–11 surrounding the invented *auteure* Judith Forest shows how being a woman creator can serve as a publicity advantage but ultimately exposes how the recourse to exceptionalism can undermine the longer-term project of gender equity, as Marine Gheno has demonstrated. The figure of Judith Forest was invented by a group of male artists/editors, who went so far as to employ an actress to embody Forest for media appearances. Forest's success clearly was not only due to quality art and

---

18. Although both of these feminine versions currently coexist, I give preference to "auteure" here because, however challenging it is to make the "e" in "auteure-ism" audible, the shift in sounds from "ice" to "ism" in "autrice-ism" seems a far worse tongue twister!

engaging storytelling but tied to the more general success of women artists who have inked autobiographical narratives. Ultimately, however, "her" success exposed what Gheno characterizes as the depth of malaise "plaguing the legitimacy of French women authors as well as the media attention given to women's personal narratives in France" (66). Women creators of course gain from the exceptional successes of high-profile artists, but without base-level parity, this remains a kind of trickle-down economics pipe dream of cultural and actual capital that leaves little space and only precarious places for most.

The deceptions and disappointments of a case like Judith Forest show the degree of importance of, and public hunger for, authentic representation of women's experience. In this volume we have not neglected the representations of women by male creators—Jacques Dürrenmatt and Mark McKinney's essays both unpack variations of what Benoît Peeters (speaking of a later period) has called "a misogyny of stereotyped representation" (qtd. in Groensteen, "Femme [1]"). Yet in the section of this book on geographies of identity, the weight is placed upon the role of women creators in representing women's experience of a diversity of identities: from that which is regionally situated, as explored by Armelle Blin-Rolland; to that anchored in the bio-medical experience of pregnancy and abortion, as examined by Catriona MacLeod; to racial and cultural identity in the essay of Michelle Bumatay; and finally to a transnational, multilingual collective explored by Alexandra Gueydan-Turek. In the final section, Isabelle Delorme and Véronique Bragard both explore facets of women's graphic biography. Across these essays, it becomes clear that it does indeed matter that the diversity of women's lived experience gets represented by women.

Volume Overview

The sections of the volume involve substantial overlap in that the issues that characterize each section remain present in essays across the others; however, each constitutes a strong node of questions. Part 1 takes on the question of "Industry, Audience, and Platform." What unites these chapters is how they each engage questions of different industrial figures and how those figures ultimately relate to audiences. Jessica Kohn uses quantitative analysis of women in midcentury French *illustrés* to leverage broader questions about comics history and historiography. Sylvain Lesage considers how large-scale ignoring of the contributions of colorists corresponds to overlooking substantial contributions of women in *bande dessinée* history.

Benoît Crucifix reads the work of Nicole Claveloux across two different sectors of the publishing industry, again, exposing blind spots in how scholarship has privileged some forms of artistic labor over others. Finally, Jennifer Howell considers how contemporary Moroccan artists are leveraging the interaction between social media and traditional publication as a vector for feminist social activism.

Part 2, "Geographies of Identity," considers how gender is mediated by bodily experience and how bodily experience is situated in space and place. Armelle Blin-Rolland explores the relationship between women and nature in Breton regionalist *bande dessinée*. Catriona MacLeod confronts the painful question of abortion and how it is ambivalently explored. Michelle Bumatay considers Black women's bodies through two serial publications by African and Afropean authors, while Alexandra Gueydan-Turek examines the variegated strategies of representing the gender and sexuality of Arab women as undertaken by the Lebanese-based feminist collective, Samandal.

The third and final part, "Representations and History," includes four essays that span from nineteenth-century caricature/early *bande dessinée* to the present day. Jacques Dürrenmatt considers how women are caricatured by Töpffer, Cham, Musset, and Gustave Doré, while Mark McKinney focuses on how the Black women warrior "Amazons" of Dahomey were ambivalently represented over time. Isabelle Delorme considers the hyper-successful artist Catel, who has specialized in the biographical genre, while Véronique Bragard considers Emilie Plateau's *Noire* as a transnational feminist counter-history. Together these essays resist the idea that there is a reductive way to read the representation of women by artists of all genders (and races) but also assert the importance of women's voices in the telling of women's history.

Works Cited

Bréan, Simon, et al. "Faire Genre." *Style(s) de (la) bande dessinée*, edited by Benoît Berthou and Jacques Dürenmatt, Classiques Garnier, 2019, pp. 295–343.

"Les Bréchoises." *La Bréche*, https://labrechebd.com/les-brechoises/.

Butler, Judith. *Gender Trouble: Feminism and the Subversion of Identity*. Routledge, 1990.

Célestin, Roger, and Eliane DalMolin. *France from 1851 to the Present: Universalism in Crisis*. Palgrave MacMillan, 2007.

Célestin, Roger, et al., editors. *Beyond French Feminisms: Debates on Women, Politics, and Culture in France, 1981–2001*. Palgrave MacMillan, 2003.

Chabrol Gagne, Nelly. *Filles d'albums: Les representations du féminin dans l'album*. L'atelier du poisson soluble, 2011.

Chute, Hillary. *Graphic Women: Life Narrative and Contemporary Comics.* Columbia UP, 2010.

Ciment, Gilles. "Femmes dans la bande dessinée: Des pionnières à l'affaire d'Angoulême." *Bulletin des bibliothèques de France,* no. 11, 2017, http://bbf.enssib.fr/matieres-a-penser/femmes-dans-la-bande-dessinee_67374.

"Créatrices de bandes dessinées: Histoire, mémoire, revendications et representations des femmes dans le neuvième art." École Universitaire de Recherche ArTeC, https://eur-artec.fr/projets/creatrices-de-bandes-dessinees/?fbclid=IwAR3vIYZPexrnMzlhuKIozao78jhaDhpejfPClGiuaflyfNadF3TA7rHtXXw.

Evans, Christophe, and Françoise Gaudet. "La lecture de bandes dessinées." *Culture études,* vol. 2, no. 2, 2012, pp. 1–8.

Falck, Alex. "An Interview with Author Sophie Labelle." *Intellectual Freedom Blog,* 17 Dec. 2018, https://www.oif.ala.org/an-interview-with-author-sophie-labelle/.

Gheno, Marine. "'Être auteure, ce n'est pas encore être': La visibilité feminine à travers les BD de Judith Forest." *Alternative Francophone,* vol. 6, no. 1, 2013, pp. 65–79.

Groensteen, Thierry. *La bande dessinée au tournant.* Les Impressions Nouvelles, 2017.

———. "Femme (1): Representation de la femme." *NeuviemeArt2.0,* 2013, http://neuviemeart.citebd.org/spip.php?article677.

———. "Femme (2): La création feminine." *NeuviemeArt2.0,* 2014, http://neuviemeart.citebd.org/spip.php?article727.

Kohn, Jessica. *Dessiner des petits mickeys: Une histoire sociale de la bande dessinée en France et en Belgique (1945–1968).* Les Éditions de la Sorbonne, 2022.

———. "Women Comics Authors in France and Belgium Before the 1970s: Making Them Invisible." *Revue de recherche en civilization Américaine,* no. 6, 2017, https://journals.openedition.org/rrca/725.

Labelle, Sophie. *Assignée garçon.* Tumblr, https://assigneegarcon.tumblr.com/.

———. "Sophie Labelle: Visiting Speaker." *An Evening with Sophie Labelle: Trans Cartoonist and Author,* 21 Jan. 2019, University of Victoria, Victoria, BC, https://www.youtube.com/watch?v=2yuGzmK8k9o. Video recording.

Labrèche, Ariane. "Une bédéiste trans perd ses créations et son logement." *TVA novelles,* 19 May 2017, https://www.tvanouvelles.ca/2017/05/19/une-bedeiste-trans-perd-ses-creations-et-son-logement.

Lépinard, Éléonore. "The French Parity Reform: The Never-Ending Quest for a New Gender Equality Principle." *Transforming Gender Citizenship: The Irresistible Rise of Gender Quotas in Europe,* edited by Éléonore Lépinard and Ruth Rubio-Marín, Cambridge UP, 2018, pp. 62–93.

Lépinard, Éléonore, and Ruth Rubio-Marín, editors. *Transforming Gender Citizenship: The Irresistible Rise of Gender Quotas in Europe.* Cambridge UP, 2018.

Macleod, Catriona. *Invisible Presence: The Representation of Women in French-Language Comics.* Intellect, 2021.

McGillis, Ian. "Quebec Comics Artist Sophie Labelle Draws Attention to Trans Issues." *Montreal Gazette,* 7 Apr. 2017, https://montrealgazette.com/entertainment/books/quebec-comics-artist-sophie-labelle-draws-attention-to-trans-issues/.

Miller, Ann. *Reading* Bande Dessinée: *Critical Approaches to French-Language Comic Strip.* Intellect, 2007.

Milquet, Sophie, and Chris Reyns-Chikuma. "La bande dessinée au féminin: 12,4%: Écouter l'autre voix de la BD." *Alternative Francophone,* vol. 9, no. 1, 2016, pp. 1–4, https://journals.library.ualberta.ca/af/index.php/af/article/view/27188/pdf.

Ratier, Gilles. *Rapport sur la production d'une année de bande dessinée dans l'espace francophone Européen. 2016: L'année de la stabilization.* Association des critiques et journalistes de la bande dessinée, 2016, https://www.acbd.fr/2825/rapports/2016-lannee-de-la-stabilisation.

Reyns-Chikuma, C(h)ris. "Genre, Gender, Sexual, Textual and Visual, and Real Representations in *Bande Dessinée.*" *The Routledge Companion to Gender and Sexuality in Comic Book Studies,* edited by Frederick Luis Aldama, Routledge, 2021, pp. 196–212.

Schor, Naomi. "The Crisis of French Universalism." *Yale French Studies,* no. 100, 2001, pp. 43–64.

Scott, Joan Wallach. *Parité: Sexual Equality and the Crisis of French Universalism.* U of Chicago P, 2005.

"Séance d'installation de Catherine Meurisse." *Académie des Beaux-arts,* 11 Nov. 2022, https://www.academiedesbeauxarts.fr/seance-dinstallation-de-catherine-meurisse, press release.

Whaley, Deborah Elizabeth. *Black Women in Sequence: Re-Inking Comics, Graphic Novels, and Anime.* U Washington P, 2016.

PART 1

INDUSTRY, AUDIENCE, AND PLATFORMS

CHAPTER 1

Women Cartoonists

A New Avenue for Understanding a Little-Known Profession?

JESSICA KOHN

In the course of my doctoral research, I studied 400 cartoonists who worked in France and in Belgium for illustrated magazines between the years of 1945 and 1968. At least 80 percent (320) of them once drew *bandes dessinées*. However, only two or three dozen male comics authors have been recognized in the Franco-Belgian history of comics both by fans and by the first historians of the art form. The work of these famous male authors has strongly shaped the *bande dessinée* canon, especially because they were published in books (as opposed to just serial publications)—the album gave legitimacy to this medium (Lesage, *La bande dessinée*). These male authors also shaped the way the profession has been understood and studied, leading to confusion between the biographies of extraordinary personalities and the histories of professional careers. The latter should be studied as being part of a professional system with specific stakes, as Andrew Abbot has observed.

This very masculine history of the comics world is often held to account for the small proportion of women among comic authors nowadays. Women represent 27 percent of the profession according to an inquiry launched by the États Généraux de la Bande Dessinée in 2016 (3). However, when examining Franco-Belgian illustrated magazines of the 1950s and 1960s, and especially those geared towards girls, I discovered that 7 percent of authors (23 out of 320) who worked in the comics field at the time were women, some of whom had started to work in the field in the 1930s, well before the famous Claire Bretécher and Florence Cestac started to publish their work (Kohn, *Travailler*). While the 7 percent figure may seem small, it is in fact four times higher than expected, since only five of these women are a part of the canonized history of comics nowadays (Liliane Funcken, Suzanne André, Claire Bretécher, Manon Iessel, and Marie-Madeleine Bourdin). Thus, the history of comics has, to date, ignored an entire subsection of authors who, though they were a minority, were nonetheless significantly active in the field. Stories written and drawn by Manon Iessel, Marie-Mad, or Nadine Forster used to be read by young boys and girls every week. I have already provided details of the names and the careers of these postwar women comic authors elsewhere in order to understand the process of "invisibilisation" they underwent, which consisted mainly in restricting these authors to children's illustrations outside of the newspaper world and not publishing their comics in books (Kohn, "Women"). This systematic marginalization made it difficult to promote the emergence of a women's network and reference system in the world of Franco-Belgian comics.

The periodicals I study in the course of this research of women cartoonists are what French and French-speaking Belgians call *illustrés*. Since the end of the nineteenth century, this is the name given to abundantly illustrated serial publications destined for an audience of children and young people. Gradually, from the 1930s and until their decline at the end of the 1960s, *illustrés* became synonymous with any type of publication for young people where one finds mainly comics of Franco-Belgian or foreign origin. *Illustrés* are therefore a privileged place of publication for cartoonists. I break down these periodicals according to an empirically established typology: adult illustrated magazines (such as *Hara-Kiri*); Belgian illustrated magazines (mainly *Tintin* and *Spirou*, which are famous for their social-Catholic stance); French Catholic illustrated magazines; *illustrés*, which are inspired by their American equivalents (and therefore "Americanized," such as *Le journal de Mickey*); and finally the so-called "modern" *illustrés*, which seek to renew the type of comics they publish and, thereby, their audiences (such as *Pilote* or *Vaillant*). As I will explore later, French Catholic magazines such as *Bernadette* were seminal in the careers of female cartoonists, and many of those publications were specifically oriented to a readership of girls.

In this chapter, I examine the subject further, asking to what extent these women's careers were so different from those of their male counterparts. Gender history is an effective method for counteracting an official history of comics that has been constructed around a few male success stories. I first render objective and deconstruct these individual stories, because they are not representative of the professional group that was emerging at the time. Next, I take a comparative look at women's social backgrounds and education, at the type of comics they were asked to produce, and at the way their careers unfolded within the comics world and network. The results show that, generally speaking, women cartoonists followed the same path as many male cartoonists, who, far from being few, were numerous, but worked mainly for French Catholic editors. By studying a small sample of unknown women cartoonists, historians can apprehend an important aspect of the profession after World War II, especially in France. Unfortunately, the legacy of the women working in the comics industry is still too frail. Indeed, my conclusions here open a new avenue for a more robust history of comics: the history of little-known cartoonists and anonymous employees of the Catholic press.

A Scholarly Reading of the Male Cartoonist Success Story: Is "Genius" Male?

When it comes to writing an individual history of comic book authors, or accounting for specific canon formation, biographers tend to rely on a series of stereotypes that are usually used to describe the fantasized lives of male artists and/or male journalists. These stereotypes rely above all on the question of education and talent, and even more so, on what one could refer to as the "myth of the autodidact" (Kohn, *Travailler* 88). Indeed, the personal history of cartoonists' careers—either in their biographies, autobiographies, or in interviews—often follows the same success story pattern. There is a genre of cartoonist biographies: it's a literary exercise that reduces years of training to an early and natural talent for drawing, dislike for school, and lack of artistic training—or if such training has taken place, poor attendance at the lessons that prove useless in the reality of the future profession anyway. According to these stories, comic authors have an innate gift both for drawing and for humor, a gift that justifies their lack of seriousness in school. Hergé is one of the most famous examples of this self-taught paradigm, since he started drawing for *Vingtième Siècle* at the end of secondary school. He did enroll in an applied arts school in Brussels, but he claims: "I went one night to St. Luke's School, but since they made me draw a plaster column and it bored me to death, I never went back" (Goddin 92). A historian like Christian Delporte, in his study on press cartoonists, relays this type of stereotypical comment by explaining that

> few cartoonists, in spite of everything, were brilliant students, as shown by the many anecdotes found in the course of our research. But for all of them, the passion for drawing—and, most of the time, in its artistic form—was revealed from an early age. If their teacher did not always know how to detect the talent that was to manifest itself later on, the future draftsmen practiced caricaturing their classmates and their teachers in class. (100)[1]

As Christian Delporte says, his point is based on many "anecdotes." Yet, the historian's work consists in reading between the lines of such narratives and anecdotes, because they are limited to the posture of the author, defined by Jérôme Meizoz "as the self-presentation of a writer [here an artist], both in the way he manages his discourse and in his public conduct." It is thus this posture that one has to decipher. Indeed, if the discourse of the innate gift returns with such frequency in comics authors' biographies and autobiographies, it is because it is related to the myth of the vocation of the creator-artist, which a certain discourse of legitimization has tried to attach to cartoonists and especially comic book authors, at least since the 1960s and the emergence of bedephilia. Indeed, the first Comics Club was created in France in 1962 (under the name Club des Bandes Dessinées), with an activist standpoint: its goal was to proclaim that comics are art (Demange 218). Nonetheless, in the corpus that I studied, 205 cartoonists, in fact, did have some type of formal training in art, whereas only 103 were self-taught, which is to say, there was a two-to-one ratio of trained individuals to self-taught ones.

The analysis of women's careers helps to deconstruct such a posture, because women are less affected by the "autodidact myth." There are at least three reasons for this. First, the image of the artistic genius is usually depicted as a masculine one, who, at best, uses a female muse as a helper. Severine Sofio's work on female painters deconstructs this myth

> that artistic creation is a man's business. Thus, everyone has a more or less accurate idea of the traditional image of romantic artists: young, white, tortured men who create "against all odds," in poverty and by subverting ancient rules of which the Academy was the guardian.

Second, being a good and serious student is often a quality noticed (but also reproached) in girls, since "prescribed female behavior being in line with the expectations of the institution (obedience, submission, calmness, conformism, attention . . .), they correctly exercise their profession as students."

---

1. Unless otherwise noted, all translations are my own.

However, the positive bias is "limited to behavioral-disciplinary aspects" (Courtinat-Camps and Prêteur 100). As Severine Depoilly states, "Adaptable, serious, and docile female behavior was opposed to unruly, restless male attitudes" (17–18). On the other hand, it is considered a sign of independence for boys when they fail to respect school rules. Thus Marie Duru-Bellat and Anette Jarlégan note, especially concerning mathematics:

> It is as if boys were, more often than not, considered to be pupils with definite potentialities that allow them to work less than girls. Boys are thought of as potential "underachievers": they are intelligent, they have undeniable possibilities but do not always exploit them for lack of sufficient effort. Girls, on the other hand, are able to reach the same level as boys thanks to the attention and efforts they put into their studies. (76–77)

Third, because women were never a part of the history of comics the way it has been written until now, they did not have many opportunities to write about themselves or to be written about and therefore to develop the posture of an author. Consequently, because of these three reasons, it is easier to analyze women's careers in an objective way without having to navigate around socially constructed self-presentation and posture.

If women's careers can give insights to the construction of the profession of comics author, this is especially the case when they are not well known. Indeed, when women happen to be prominent figures in the comics or illustration world, the stories of their lives rely on the same stereotypes as those used in male narratives. This specific point became obvious after Claire Bretécher's recent death (she was the author of the must-read comic strips *Les frustrés* and *Agrippine*). Though she held dual degrees in art and history of art, after a three-year course of study, commentators only mentioned a scant year of studying at Nantes's School of Fine Arts: the shorter the artist's studies, the more deserving her success. This is true of other women in my sample: in the interview I conducted with Nadine Forster, a Belgian cartoonist who worked for many different children's book publishers throughout her life, the author repeatedly maintained that she had never taken a drawing class and had always known how to draw "awesome" things without any training. However, her student record at the Royal Academy of Fine Arts indicates a brilliant educational record of five years punctuated with numerous awards and distinctions until her graduation in 1951 with the first prize of mastery from the city of Brussels (Kohn, *Travailler* 90).

So, it is necessary to deconstruct the posture of a Nadine Forster in the same way one would with a famous male author. Indeed, she had a successful career in the children publishing area: after having drawn for the *illustrés*

Bernadette and *Lisette* and for the comic books editor Dargaud (in the 1950s and 1960s), Forster painted the covers of Walt Disney's long-playing records sold in France by Lucien Adès and also worked for the television producer Christophe Izard and the famous children's book collection, *La bibliothèque rose* (in the 1970s and 1980s). She was also a renowned painter in the 1950s, touring in the United States and in Mexico. Because of her successes in two types of art, she was bound to repeat the type of vocational discourse that has been studied thus far. However, her interview also makes it clear that the self-taught paradigm was not simply a matter of gift. She explained that she considered that the Royal Academy had not "been a drawing school . . . It was for working in oil, in painting, not drawing" (Kohn, *Travailler* 90). This last argument sheds light on the fact that the new generations of cartoonists in the 1950s and 1960s were in fact interested in cartoons, illustrations, comic strips, and advertising. Yet they did not feel they learned these techniques in the course of their formal art school training, which was too academic, as the earlier quote by Hergé shows. In short, by comparing male and female narratives and curricula, one understands that the learning of art techniques has been watered down and rewritten because it did not seem to directly concern the *bédéiste*'s job, and not only because of a "genius posture."

There is a difference of standpoint between a monographic history built around famous authors' lives and the history of a professional group—women's careers play an important role in order to write the latter. First, because they have been less commented upon, women often escape the genre of comic books authors' biographies, and it is therefore easier to get past constructed postures. Second, because women artists are often little known, they make it possible to understand how the profession worked and how careers unfolded for the majority of cartoonists who made a living from their work without ever reaching fame. In other words, thanks to the careers of 41 women cartoonists, of whom 23 drew comics, it is possible to reconstruct a more holistic picture of the profession as it existed before the 1970s: instead of relying on innate talent, one had to build her/his career step by step, working for different media and in different fields in order to make a living, hence favoring the traditional Catholic magazines rather than the modern *Pilote*.

A Nongendered Classic Career

Three items are significant in order to understand an artistic profession through the careers of its protagonists: social background (Is there a specific one for *bédéistes*?), specialized education (How, where, and why did they learn to draw?), and the arc of the career (What type of work were they asked to do? What type of comics did they publish and in what publications? How did they earn a living with it?). In this section, I will consider each of these areas successively, starting with what we know of women's careers in the 1950s and 1960s and then situating them in the profession.

THE LIBERAL UPPER CLASS ENROLLED IN APPLIED ARTS

Among the women that I studied and for whom I was able to retrieve information, almost half belong to an older generation. This generation, which I call the "Elders," is made up of individuals born between 1871 and 1914 and who started their careers before 1943 (see table 1.1). Women comics authors were also overwhelmingly French, as were their male counterparts of the same generation (see tables 1.2 and 1.3). This is less true for what I have labeled the "Classical" (c. 1944–50) and the "Modern" (c. 1951–67) generations. As for women from the "Elder" generation (c. 1900–1943), they generally come from an affluent background, which is indeed a common trait of the Elders in general. The two next generations, which have less of a gender mix, are more representative of the average middle class of both France and Belgium. In that sense, women cartoonists prove to be part of a subgroup: they help us to understand the careers of a specific generation of French cartoonists who started to work before World War II. This shows another historical fact: the "Franco-Belgian" denomination does not in fact make much sense for a number of *bédéistes* at the time, who worked in a national editorial market.

For the older generation then, drawing might therefore be part of a bourgeois education, and even more so for women: the type of education in the artistic activities required for "proper young ladies" to be considered "accomplished"—what in French are called the *arts d'agréments* (Kohn, "Women"). However, it is essential to mention that this generation received important formal artistic training, either in fine arts, decorative arts, or in applied arts schools, and the numbers indicate that this was the case for women as much as men. A difference exists here though: while the older male generation tended to enroll more in fine arts and decorative arts schools, women were not always able to do so because of gender restrictions. Therefore, they enrolled in private courses or applied arts schools, even at the beginning of the twentieth century. This choice of technical training foreshadows a future change in the *bédéiste*'s education. Whereas 45 percent of

TABLE 1.1. Women *bédéiste's* generation according to their date of birth and the start of their drawing work (professional activity)

GENERATION	BIRTH→ ACTIVITY ↓	1871–1900	1901–14	1915–29	1930–36	1937–46	TOTAL
ELDERS	1904–41	5	7	—	—	—	12
CLASSICAL	1944–50	—	1	5	1	—	7
MODERN	1951–63	—	—	2	3	3	8

TABLE 1.2. Geographic origin of *bédéistes* according to their generation

GENERATION	ACTIVITY	FRENCH	BELGIANS	FOREIGN	TOTAL
ELDERS	1900–1943	90	16	13	119
CLASSICAL	1944–50	76	25	13	114
MODERN	1951–67	64	46	11	121

TABLE 1.3. Geographic origin of women *bédéistes* according to their generation

GENERATION	ACTIVITY	FRENCH	BELGIANS	FOREIGN	TOTAL
ELDERS	1904–41	9	1	2	12
CLASSICAL	1944–50	5	0	1	6
MODERN	1951–63	5	2	1	8

the Elders enrolled in fine arts and 23 percent in applied arts, these numbers are reversed at the end of the 1960s, when 45 percent of the Modern cartoonists of the sample enrolled in applied arts schools (see table 1.4).

This shift is due to the excellent reputation of Belgian and French schools throughout the twentieth century, especially in the case of women's schools in France, with the École Duperré leading the way. In this case, women's training helps us to understand the progressive change in cartoonists' education. Women's applied arts schools recruited very widely from all levels of society, both because the decorative arts were considered a necessary part of the education of young women in society and because it was crucial at the time to train qualified workers for industry (Laurent 54). For example, in 1951, when Nicole Constant's mother was asked to find training for her daughter, who was failing high school, she sided with the drawing teacher who proposed the Duperré School. As Nicole Constant explained, "My father died when I was 17, and she thought that I had to work" (Kohn, *Travailler* 719).

TABLE 1.4. Gender of *bédéistes* according to their training

ENROLLMENT	WOMEN	MEN
APPLIED ARTS	7	76
PRIVATE SCHOOL	6	28
FINE ARTS	6	85
DECORATIVE ARTS	1	29
PLAUSIBLY SELF-TAUGHT	3	78
TOTAL	23	296

At the end of the 1950s, the good reputation of the applied arts schools also became an argument for training boys, hence fostering changes in men's education, as Pierre Joubert recalls:

> Already at that time, the word was clear: in applied arts, one works. At the fine arts or the decorative arts, one doesn't do anything. Indeed, I worked a lot in applied arts. For three years, I learned a lot of things: decoration, documentation, art history, geometry and advertising. So, I had some pretty exciting years. The work was very interesting. (11–12)

As time goes on, families seem more inclined to send their children to applied arts schools than to fine arts schools. According to Alain Dubouillon, the latter type of school "had a bad reputation because it was a factory for lazy people, it was not a real profession" (Kohn, *Travailler* 740). Thanks to the example of women's enrollment, it is possible to say that women and men engaged in the comics and illustration field of work after a specific training, that of applied arts. In other words, women are entirely part of the way the profession starts to define itself after World War II, and they foreshadow some of the ensuing changes, especially in terms of education.

The "autodidact myth" has a corollary: the idea that, after a series of "day jobs," the genius author is revealed when his or her first work of quality is published, often thanks to an artistic director. Goscinny, the editor of *Pilote*, played this role for many authors, such as Jean-Claude Mézières, for whom he agreed to publish the science fiction comics *Valérian and Laureline* in 1966. Before that, according to critics, Mézières was not really a *bédéiste*, illustrating encyclopedias for Hachette, working for an advertising agency and for Catholic *illustrés* such as *Fripounet et Marisette* and *Cœurs vaillants*. This classification also applies to a woman such as Claire Bretécher, who worked as an art teacher and published drawings in scouting and Catholic magazines such as *Record* before she was able to work for *Spirou* and, even more importantly, published *Cellulite* in *Pilote*.

In this type of narrative, we can see two hierarchies: first, in the cartoonists' jobs; second, in the publishing media. In both of these hierarchies, women are ranked the lowest, doing the "wrong" jobs in the "wrong" type of publication. It is essential to question these hierarchies if one wants to understand how comics authors' careers most commonly unfolded, beyond the myth.

MAKING A LIVING WITH A PENCIL: "ANCILLARY JOBS"

Let us first have a look at the hierarchy in comics industry jobs: according to the canonical history of *bande dessinée*, any drawing work that does not take place in the publishing or press world, or that is not pure comics, is referred to as a "day job." This term has a negative connotation, and it excludes many individuals working as assistant inkers, colorists, letterers, and whose work remained anonymous. It so happens that many of these anonymous workers were women (Andrieu de Lévis et al. 20–24). Reflecting on women's careers therefore helps us to apprehend the profession as a whole and not only to focus on the final form of the published long story. Because of the reality of the economic market, being a cartoonist meant being polyvalent, a versatile experience for which former students of applied arts had been trained. For example, Claude Soleillant has excellent memories of her first job in an advertising agency, even though her career dream was to become a children's illustrator (Kohn, *Travailler* 796). Many women and men in our corpus indeed started in the advertising business, and women even more than men, because they were often offered illustration work for children's book publishers. Work in the field of posters, graphics, and advertising is therefore closely linked to a career as a cartoonist—far from being incompatible with it.

Thanks especially to the example of women's careers, it thus appears arbitrary to consider the various jobs outside the world of the press and editing as "day jobs" or to presume that assistants were not part of the comics world when the economy of the field was a collaborative one. Even if the profession of cartoonist may be a vocational practice, it is nonetheless exercised for remunerative purposes. The latter therefore partly guide the choices that are made in terms of employment. Even Albert Uderzo, whose career offers an exemplary case study of the male success story, states that "a guy who had talent, who had the gift of drawing, would become an illustrator or go into an advertising studio where he could earn a better living" (Sadoul 36). Rather than talking about "day jobs," then, it would therefore be better to refer to "ancillary jobs," both in regard to the economy and the gender of the profession. The term seems more accurate because it refers, without limiting them to their remunerative aspect, to both the assistant functions that some "little hands" may have had in drawing offices and publishing houses and the feeling expressed by some cartoonists of having a secondary or parallel function to an activity that they would like to have as their main one. These functions are particularly exercised at the beginning of the career, but they do not disappear with the establishment of the cartoonists in the business. Contrarily to the "day job," an "ancillary" one is fully part of the definition of the cartoonists' profession. For women especially, these "ancillary jobs" could take up the major part of their career, which remains nonetheless a career as a *bédéiste*.

WORKING FOR CATHOLIC *ILLUSTRÉS*

The biographic narrative of the male success story entails another type of hierarchy, this time in the publishing area. This is what emerges from the way Jean-Claude Mézières and Claire Bretécher's trajectories are traditionally presented: their work on Catholic illustrated magazines for children has less meaning than their later work for *Pilote*, or, in the case of Claire Bretécher, the even more legitimate *L'écho des savanes* (a publication akin to underground comix magazines) and *Le nouvel obs* (a weekly news magazine for the liberal middle class). Meanwhile, in France, during the two decades after World War II, the Catholic press was one of the most important employers of the time, and it has been seriously overlooked when it should be seen as seminal in the building of *bande dessinée* history. For example, in 1957, *Cœurs vaillants* printed 175,000 copies, when *Spirou* printed roughly 146,000 and *Vaillant* 209,000, these latter being two of the most canonical and reputable illustrated magazines of the time (Lesage, *L'effet codex* 1137). *Cœurs vaillants* used to be the most read Catholic *illustré*, but illustrated magazines of the Catholic press were numerous. They were edited by Fleurus, Montsouris, La Société Parisienne d'Éditions, La Bonne Presse, and Gautier-Languereau. They were created as heirs of the first Catholic magazines for children, which appeared and were successful in France at the beginning of the twentieth century. Until the Vatican II council, there were far more conservative than Belgian *illustrés*, and they did not often feature renowned comic books authors or serialized comics.[2]

As mentioned above, most of the women who I uncovered and who worked after World War II were from the Elder generation. As the results of my research show, the older generation of *bédéistes* published almost half of their work in Catholic illustrated magazines because their economic and professional practices were inherited from the early twentieth century and were very closely related to a readership of children (see table 1.5). This is also due to their social background: cartoonists from the liberal middle class who followed an applied arts program happened to work more in these Catholic magazines, whose outlook was close to that of their education. Consequently, women's careers were generally in line with these criteria because they belonged to the same generation and background. As we can see, the figures dropped slowly with the next two generations. Indeed, until 1962, at least half of the comics in France and in Belgium were published in French Catholic magazines. Even after that turning point, they still represented a third of the publishing opportunities for comic authors, which explains why Claire Bretécher and Jean-Claude Mézières, like many others, started their career in that type of publication. Furthermore, no matter their generation, all the women that I have studied tended to work in Catholic *illustrés* geared specifically toward girls, such as *Bernadette, La semaine de Suzette, Lisette, Annette,* and *Fillette*, which have been even less studied than the Catholic *illustrés* in general. Among the forty-one women who worked as cartoonists, twenty-eight of them started to work in Catholic *illustrés* and twenty-three in those geared toward girls. Furthermore, 28 percent of the work published in girls' Catholic magazines was produced by women, whereas it was only 6 percent of the work published in boys' Catholic magazines. Although male *bédéistes* remained a majority in all children's illustrated magazines, they were less present in those aimed at girls.

Women therefore had a more specialized area of publication than men (see table 1.6) and were also more expected to illustrate children's short stories and books. Nonetheless, this specialization did not mean they would only illustrate stories and would never gain access to the comics form. Their career was as versatile as that of their male counterparts, especially because the periodicals they were published in requested this versality. Indeed, *La semaine de Suzette, Fillette, Lisette,* and *Bernadette* gradually abandoned

---

2. This explains partly why Belgian Catholic *illustrés* are part of the traditional history of comics, whereas French Catholic *illustrés* are not. Furthermore, the former rarely employed women, especially not of the Elder generation, so this is not the place to discuss them.

TABLE 1.5. Type of periodical according to the generation of *bédéiste*

GENERATION	ADULT	BELGIAN	CATHOLIC	AMERICANIZED	MODERN	TOTAL
ELDER	3%	24%	45%	11%	17%	100%
CLASSICAL	5%	27%	43%	8%	16%	100%
MODERN	7%	38%	30%	3%	23%	100%

TABLE 1.6. Type of periodical according to the gender of *bédéiste*

GENDER	ADULT	BELGIAN	CATHOLIC	AMERICANIZED	MODERN	TOTAL
WOMEN	1%	12%	83%	2%	2%	100%
MEN	5%	29%	39%	8%	19%	100%

hagiographical narratives in favor of drawn adventure stories. Because it was economically attractive in terms of revenue, Catholic magazines turned to comics and so did the cartoonists working there. In 1957, in an editorial, *Bernadette* introduced a team of cartoonists and editors composed of three men (Mixi-Bérel, Tiky, and Jacques Remise) and three women (Manon Iessel, Janine Janvier, and Janine Lay), an example of a mixed editorial team presented without hierarchy.

Hence, when studying women's careers and the stories they published, comics historians have access to precious primary sources that have been unfairly ignored, regarding the drawing and editing profession, creative work, and readership. However, the 1950s and the beginning of the 1960s are only a moment in comics history. Especially, as girls' magazines became more singular and made comics a tool of this singularity, they did exclude women. This was the case for the modern magazine *Mireille*, which Marijac created in 1953 without any women on the editorial team. Until the 1950s, novice female cartoonists therefore went to illustrated magazines for Catholic girls to begin their careers; from the end of the 1950s onward, women cartoonists no longer had this outlet and moved into other sectors of publishing. At this point, their careers stop being useful for understanding the careers of comics authors in general. This can be also explained with the shift from an editing atmosphere to a press one in the drawing offices of the time (Kohn, "Les dessinateurs"). While it seems like there were no editorial meetings in Catholic magazines, they existed in other magazines and especially in *Pilote*: this journalistic and all-men atmosphere probably played a role in excluding woman from this area of work. From this point of view,

Suzanne André, Claire Bretécher, Liliane Funcken, and Madeleine Berthélémy are exceptions, since they managed to work in *illustrés* for boys or modern ones.

Remembering the Profession: When Gender Comes to Matter

As I have argued elsewhere,

> Women did find work more easily in children's magazines geared towards girls; and when they did so, their career was often not as long as that of their male counterparts, because it was more easily pursued in the field of children's illustration. But, by emphasizing the difference between male and female comics authors, the history of comics has overlooked an important body of work which was published in magazines read by half of the young population. Women have been forgotten because there were fewer of them, but also and mainly because the field of comics would not acknowledge them. ("Women")

To that conclusion, one might now add that overlooking women's careers has been a mistake when writing the history of comics in France in the 1950s and 1960s because it has meant ignoring the careers of many, as well as ignoring the reading practices of many others. Women's careers as *bédéistes* not only embody the sexual division of labor and the invisibilisation of women in artistic or journalistic professions; examining such careers is also a way to better understand average *bédéiste*'s careers, the organization of the comics world, and the cultural landscape of the time. This is directly related to women's position in the artistic world, as Michael McCall explains, pointing out the absence of any collective identity for women artists to the point that, in a male-dominated artistic world, they ended up occupying a position of "marginal men." Therefore, I would like to conclude by offering some leads to aid the pursuit of a social history of the Franco-Belgian *bande dessinée* and, maybe, of comics in general, as well as to maintain this heritage in a less conservative way.

First, it is now primordial to start working on the anonymous workers of the field, instead of focusing only on comics author superheroes. Much of the work in the comics field has been left unsigned, while the work of assistants remained anonymous because their work was seen as less prestigious. This would give researchers new opportunities to understand the global functioning of the editing process and economy while making women's work more visible, since the assistants were often women and, very often, wives or sisters. Second, it is time to engage in a close study of illegitimate media of *bande dessinée*, as seen in the way Raphaël Oesterlé is analyzing the French Catholic illustrated magazines (Boillat et al.). By studying primary sources that are not part of the canon, historians would be able to better understand the editing world and the press world of the postwar period. They would also be able to put in perspective the unity of Franco-Belgian comics, which does not really exist, at least in professional careers, before the 1970s. Finally, this research should help to improve the way we remember *bande dessinée* and especially its feminine heritage. Even if comics history is no longer written by *bédéphiles*, its patrimony remains very traditional. Though Nicole Claveloux, Bernadette Dupré, and Claire Bretécher have had their own gallery retrospectives, such exhibitions are often temporary, or less impressive than for their male counterparts; there are also fewer interviews, both in specialized and nonspecialized media. Two directions could be taken in efforts to organize the new legacy of *bande dessinée*. First, retrieving the lives and works of talented but forgotten authors, especially women, and thus also discovering new types of artistic influence. Second, promoting research and expertise on the field taken as a whole: instead of always focusing on monographic careers, one could imagine an exhibit on one magazine or one field of editing, which would explore the entire process of publishing.

Works Cited

Abbott, Andrew Delano. *The System of Professions: An Essay on the Division of Expert Labor.* U Chicago P, 1988.

Andrieu de Lévis, Jean-Charles, et al. "Collaborer: Ce que le style doit aux collaborateurs." *Style(s) de (la) bande dessinée,* edited by Benoît Berthou and Jacques Dürrenmatt, Classiques Garnier, 2019, pp. 11–52.

Boillat, Alain, et al. *Case, strip, action! Les feuilletons en bandes desinées dans les magazines pour la jeunesse (1946–1959).* Infolio, 2016.

Courtinat-Camps, Amélie, and Yves Prêteur. "Expérience scolaire à l'adolescence: Quelles différences entre les filles et les garçons?" *Genre et socialisation de l'enfance à l'âge adulte,* edited by Sandrine Croity-Belz, ERES, 2010, pp. 99–113.

Delporte, Christian. *Dessinateurs de presse et dessin politique en France, des années 1920 à la libération.* 1991. Instituts d'études politiques de Paris, PhD dissertation.

Demange, Julie. "Sens et usage de la notion de style par les bédéphiles dans leur entreprise de promotion de la bande dessinée." *Style(s) de (la) bande dessinée,* edited by Benoît Berthou and Jacques Dürrenmatt, Classiques Garnier, 2019, pp. 218–22.

Depoilly, Séverine. "Des filles conformistes? Des garçons déviants? Manières d'être et de faire des élèves de milieux populaires." *Revue française de pédagogie: Recherches en éducation,* no. 179, 2012, pp. 17–28.

Duru-Bellat, Marie, and Annette Jarlégan. "Garçons et filles à l'école primaire et dans le secondaire: La dialectique des rapports hommes-femmes." *La dialectique des rapports hommes-femmes,* edited by Thierry Blöss, 2nd ed., Presses Universitaires de France, 2001, pp. 73–88.

États généraux de la bande dessinée. *Enquête auteurs 2016: Résultats statistiques.* États généraux de la bande dessinée, 2016, http://www.etatsgenerauxbd.org/wp-content/uploads/sites/9/2016/01/EGBD_enquete_auteurs_2016.pdf.

Goddin, Philippe. *Hergé: Lignes de vie.* Moulinsart, 2007.

Joubert, Pierre. *Hop!* No. 108, Association d'étude du mode d'expression graphique de la bande dessinée, 2005.

Kohn, Jessica. "Les dessinateurs dessinés: Les rédactions des illustrés en images (1945–1968)." *Des colonnes et des cases: Presse et bande dessinée, une histoire sans fin,* edited by Alexis Lévrier and Guillaume Pinson, Les Impressions Nouvelles, 2020, pp. 169–89.

———. *"Travailler dans les petits Mickeys": Les dessinateurs-illustrateurs en France et en Belgique de 1945 à 1968.* 2018. Université Sorbonne Paris Cité, PhD dissertation. *HAL Theses,* https://tel.archives-ouvertes.fr/tel-02147283.

———. "Women Comics Authors in France and Belgium Before the 1970s: Making Them Invisible." *Revue de recherche en civilization Américaine,* no. 6, 2017, https://journals.openedition.org/rrca/725.

Laurent, Stéphane. *L'art utile: Les écoles d'arts appliqués sous le Second Empire et la Troisième République.* L'Harmattan, 1998.

Lesage, Sylvain. *La bande dessinée du feuilleton à l'album.* PUFR, 2018.

———. *L'effet codex: Quand la bande dessinée gagne le livre: L'album de bande dessinée en France de 1950 à 1990.* 2014. Université de Versailles-Saint-Quentin-en-Yvelines, PhD dissertation.

McCall, Michael. "The Sociology of Female Artists." *Studies in Symbolic Interaction,* no. 1, 1978, pp. 292–93.

Meizoz, Jérôme. "Ce que l'on fait dire au silence: Posture, ethos, image d'auteur." *Argumentation et analyse du discours,* no. 3, 2009, http://aad.revues.org/667.

Sadoul, Numa. *Astérix & Cie: Entretiens avec Uderzo.* Hachette, 2001.

Sofio, Séverine. "Le genre, un outil d'analyse pour les mondes de l'art." *Labrys: Etudes féministes/estudos feministas,* no. 23, 2013, https://www.labrys.net.br/labrys23/libre/sofio.htm.

CHAPTER 2

Women in Color

Comics Artists and the Ninth Art in France

SYLVAIN LESAGE

In *Les grands espaces* [The Great Outdoors], Catherine Meurisse tells how she became an artist; she recalls the paradise of childhood and analyzes how art and literature make it possible to preserve this paradise. After *La légèreté* [Lightness], which narrated Meurisse's psychological reconstruction after the trauma of the January 2015 Charlie Hebdo attack, *Les grands espaces* met with a very important critical and commercial success in France. Among the responses to Catherine Meurisse's work, one is particularly interesting: a Facebook post on Isabelle Merlet's account, published in January 2020. This post is telling on many levels: it comes from the album's colorist, who was one of the most prominent figures in contemporary *bande dessinée* coloring and one of the rare colorists on the Franco-Belgian comics scene who has made a name for herself. After months of praise of Catherine Meurisse's work in the media, here is how her colorist publicly reacted:

> Since this image is never shown in black and white, here it is . . .
> Do not think that I am trying to get anything from Catherine's more than deserved honors—she is a very dear friend. Absolutely not!

I would like to express my gratitude to Carol Tilley for her support and to Pierre Nocerino for his invaluable help.

> Simply, I have noticed that this color image has been circulating for 2 years online and in the press, without ever mentioning its colorist.
>
> This is part of the job, it will certainly never change, and it's probably not that big of a deal. But on the other hand, what is problematic is that such a badly paid job (in this case without copyright) doesn't give access to social status or healthcare coverage.[1]

This statement is interesting on multiple levels. Isabelle Merlet tries to deconstruct, or render more transparent, the multiple stages in the creation process of comics ("since this image is never shown in black and white, here it is"): Merlet reminds the public of a little-known aspect of the publishing process and showcases the collaborative nature of comics. By offering to her followers a comparison between Catherine Meurisse's published cover and the original art, she exposes that which breathes life into the artwork. The use of color gives legibility and meaning to a drawing that is, after all, only a preliminary stage in a collective industrial process. From the artwork to the bookshelf, publication is a complex process involving many hands (Chartier). As such, Merlet's post is a useful reminder of the collaborative nature of comics (Gray and Wilkins).

More importantly, though, Isabelle Merlet addresses the gap between the visibility given to her own work and Catherine Meurisse's. The latter is an author at the very heart of the ninth art. At the time of this writing, Catherine Meurisse had just been nominated for the Grand Prix at the Angoulême International Comics Festival, alongside Emmanuel Guibert and Chris Ware.[2] Months prior, she became the first *bédéiste* ever to be elected to the Academy of Fine Arts, a respected institution whose origins date from the seventeenth century and the creation of the French Academies by Louis XIV. She was also declared *marraine* [ambassador] of the "2020 Année de la Bande Dessinée" [Year of Comics], a special event launched by the Ministry of Culture to promote comics. In other words, in a country where comics have gained spectacular respectability (Beaty, *Unpopular*; Grove), Catherine Meurisse is one of the most prominent figures of the contemporary scene. In contrast, Isabelle Merlet is one of the most well known of French colorists, but even if her fame is palpable in the *bande dessinée* community, it has limited reach among the general public.

The issue that Isabelle Merlet raises is therefore anything but insignificant. I take this as an invitation to revisit "cultures of comics work" (Brienza

---

1. All translations are my own.
2. The Grand Prix is the main prize awarded by the Angoulême International Comics Festival; it acknowledges an artist's entire career and not a specific book.

and Johnston). Casey Brienza and Paddy Johnston's book is a welcome contribution and incitement to explore further the variety of comics' professions: "pencillers, letterers, flatters, inkers, cover designers, editors, publicists, typesetters, translators, distributors, or retailers" (2). But whereas *Culture of Comics Work* "focuses mainly on *how* such roles have had a significant and pivotal impact on the comics they have helped to create" (2) and chooses "not [to] ask *why* such labors are largely overlooked and obscured" (2), this essay aims to address the why.

Understanding the reasons that led to the canonization of artists and writers over other comics workers sheds light on the gendered distribution of roles in cultural industries in general and comics in particular. Because the profession of colorist has traditionally been feminine, it provides a compelling lens through which to analyze the limits of comics legitimization in France. These deficiencies were notably highlighted during the 2016 edition of the Angoulême International Comics Festival, where the absence of any female author in the final selection raised the question of whether there existed systemic discrimination against women within the institutions of the ninth art and the issue of pervasive masculinity of the comics world (Beaty, *Comics*).

Focusing on colorists, therefore, helps to deepen our understanding of the process of legitimization of comics in France. France holds a particular reverence towards *auteurs* [authors]. If "the idea of the *auteur* is a powerful romantic ideal" (Brienza and Johnson 2), then the French sociology of comics is very singular, and not only because comics were a testing ground for Bourdieu's concept of field of production (Brienza and Johnston; Maigret). The fact that the two founding analyses of how the very notion of the *auteur* was to be deconstructed comes from French intellectuals (notably Roland Barthes and Michel Foucault) is a powerful testimony of the symbolic aura granted to authors within this national tradition of intellectual, artistic, and cultural production.[3] The eighteenth-century "consecration of the writer" (Bénichou) served as a model for the rise in legitimacy of other art forms, with comics following the same pattern as photography and cinema.

In the world of *bande dessinée*, colorists share very little of what Foucault calls the *function auteur* [author function]. I would argue that the field of comics is even more *auteur*-oriented in France than it is elsewhere. In the American production process, even though there is a clear distinction between writers and artists on one hand and other professionals on the

---

3. See Margaret C. Flinn's introduction to this volume for a discussion of *auteurism* and gender in French studies.

other, there is a long tradition of acknowledging the contributions of letterers, pencillers, or colorists—we might reasonably hypothesize that the prominence of a more "industrial" model of comics publishing within the American comics market has rendered those professionals more visible. Despite the fact that these professionals do not share as much of the author function as writers and artists, they still have a clear professional existence. The French *bande dessinée* scene offers a very different situation.[4] Colorists have, it is true, started to receive credit for their work, but they lack access to more symbolic ways of celebrating their work, such as exhibitions or awards for best coloring.[5] This discrepancy between the American and French status of colorists shows how deeply the contribution of ancillary comics labor is rooted in a system of symbolic values. The status of colorists offers a magnifying lens through which to view the construction of professional groups (Abbott) and the limits of legitimization (Lesage, "Une bande dessinée"). The legitimization of comics as the ninth art was therefore built on the fiction of the *auteur*, at the cost of truly acknowledging the variety of other comics workers.

Coloring: A Family Activity?

In the Franco-Belgian comics system, colors were traditionally applied by women, above all, by wives. Undoubtedly the most famous example is Nine Culliford, the wife of Peyo, author of *Les schtroumpfs* [The Smurfs]. Peyo, who first thought of the Smurfs as little forest elves, had imagined them to

---

4. In many regards, the French *bande dessinée* is a Franco-Belgian reality: artists and publishers work for the same market on both sides of the border. However, the expression "Franco-Belgian *bande dessinée*" is problematic and unsatisfactory. It is problematic since the use of "Belgian" to designate French-speaking Wallonia has deep roots in Belgian political and linguistic identities. The expression is also unsatisfactory, as the structuration of *bande dessinée* as an art form is more a French reality than a Belgian one. Despite these reservations, "Franco-Belgian" is commonly used by social actors and, therefore, cannot be dismissed. I reserve my use of "Franco-Belgian" for the history of comics and the general description of the comics scene; for more specific references to institutions of consecration, I usually refer to "French" comics. There is also a consecration of comics in Belgium, but its bases are relatively different. For a seminal analysis of the specificities of the French-speaking Belgian publishing market, see Durand and Winkin.

5. It is worth observing, though, the different categories in the Eisner Awards: the jury rewards best writers and best artists (i.e., individuals); however, the categories for "best lettering" and "best coloring" are defined by the activity. There is a clear difference between the naming of categories rewarding individuals, such as best writer/best artist, and those that acknowledge the work: "best coloring" and "best lettering."

be . . . green. It was Nine Culliford, seldom mentioned in works related to Peyo, who determined the color of the Smurfs, by insisting on the greater clarity provided by the blue bodies in contrast with the background of the forest (Dayez). When Nine Culliford's contribution is mentioned, it is generally limited to this anecdote; but she colored many *Smurfs* albums, even after Peyo's death in 1992. In fact, in the somewhat complicated life of *The Smurfs* after Peyo (five writers and six artists for the main series), Nine Culliford remained the single most stable element, continuing her late husband's legacy. In many ways, one could argue that the artistic integrity of *The Smurfs* is largely due to Nine Culliford's work.

This well-documented case is far from being an exception in the history of Franco-Belgian comics. In fact, in the 1950s and 1960s, the general rule seemed to be the division of labor within the family unit. The artist was the only person contractually bound to the publisher, and he was the one delegating the secondary tasks required for the prompt delivery of his pages.[6] Unprestigious and unpaid, coloring therefore became an extension of women's domestic tasks.[7] This gendered division of labor within the family unit was reinforced by social representations that contributed to designate it a feminine activity. Coloring was (and still is) based on a series of aptitudes traditionally associated with the feminine: patience, meticulousness, and gentleness; the "good" coloring being the one that is transparent, that does not stand in the way of the creative intervention of the man.

This history of designating women as colorists is notably difficult to document, though, precisely because of its familial nature. It has been possible—through meticulous research—to unearth the role of female artists in illustrated magazines, completely reassessing their contribution to the history of French comics (Kohn). Conversely, it doesn't seem possible to conduct such a reevaluation when it comes to colorists. Artists left their names in magazines, and it is therefore possible to retrace women's contributions—provided we go through the painstaking process of systematically searching the pages of these magazines. But colorists very rarely signed anything

---

6. We lack specific works that would enable us to draw parallels with other creative professions: the history of women writers in the twentieth century is more often than not described as that of an emancipation; see, for instance, Marini and Reid. Davis's study of the gendered division of work in the *Annales* offers a fascinating example regarding the production of scholarship from the 1920s through 1930s.

7. Sylvie Schweitzer, in her groundbreaking book *Les femmes ont toujours travaillé* [Women Have Always Worked], showed how our understanding of women at work has long been tampered with by a narrow understanding of what women were actually contributing.

before the 1980s, whether a contract or their own work, making it difficult to unearth traces of their contributions in the archives.

The archives of Franco-Belgian publisher Casterman provide a good example of these challenges. Responsible for publishing Hergé, Pratt, and Tardi among other "great" artists, Casterman deposited its internal archives at the Belgian State Archives in 2009. Unique in its size and its importance, this archive holds hundreds of authors' files (containing contracts and letters) carefully studied by Florian Moine. In the eighty-nine files of this collection directly concerning comics artists, only four mentions of colorists can be found. In other words, colorists up until the 1980s mostly worked as freelance workers, paid more or less under the table, most of the time from the cut of the artist.

The career of Anne Delobel shows the progressive emergence of the colorist as a worker, a skilled professional—rather than just one-time help. Born in 1949, she briefly held the position of editorial secretary of indie magazine *Métal hurlant* before becoming editorial secretary of the feminist comics magazine *Ah! Nana*. However, most of her early career was spent in the shadow of her partner, Jacques Tardi. Indeed, Delobel was responsible for the colors (and the lettering) of Tardi's flagship series, *Adèle Blanc-Sec*, in a muted palette that nourished the Belle Époque atmosphere of the series. Uncredited in the first two volumes published simultaneously in 1976 by Casterman, Anne Delobel appeared as a full-fledged collaborator in the third volume, *Le Savant fou*, published the following year.

Jacques Tardi and Anne Delobel's contracts, kept in Casterman's archives, shed light on the process of her becoming acknowledged.[8] The very first contract for the then-named *Edith Rabatjoie* was only signed between Casterman and Jacques Tardi—a very typical contract in which it was the artist's responsibility to deliver pages by a certain date. In the spring of 1976, Tardi renegotiated his contract with Casterman in order to divide the 800 Francs per page: three-quarters for him as writer/artist and the remaining quarter for the colorist. Their publisher accepted this joint request by Jacques Tardi and his collaborator without problem. What is interesting in the details of the archives is that both workers asked to receive checks made out in their own names despite them only having a joint bank account! Financial practicalities were, therefore, clearly secondary to the symbolic importance of individual recognition. Then, as of July 1979, Anne Delobel's part in the contract was extended to holding copyright, a move then unprecedented within

---

8. All following elements are from Jacques Tardi's file in the Casterman archives deposited in the Belgian State Archives, Tournai.

the comics industry, to my knowledge. This move must have resulted from a negotiation between artist and colorist, as the total royalties disbursed by Casterman remained unchanged. Delobel received 20 percent of Tardi's royalties (i.e., 1.6 percent per copy sold), a fraction that is far from insignificant for a series that was one of Casterman's bestselling comics in the 1970s and 1980s.[9] Delobel's recognition might only be partial, but, symbolically, the evolution seen in this type of renegotiation—remembering that the case of Anne Delobel is but one example—completes the process of making colorists professional collaborators and full-fledged contributors to the albums.

Until the late 1970s, coloring consequently appears as an activity that is mostly amateur, in the sense that it is rarely the object of a specific payment or a contract that could qualify such an activity as a profession. In the American context, it is common to refer to the comics industry. In the Franco-Belgian context, it would be more accurate to refer to it as a proto-industry where work was executed from home. As such, women's labor constituted an important resource for their husbands.

Colors and Authorship: Albums and Divided Jurisdictions

The division of labor within the Franco-Belgian comics proto-industry, as I have explored it thus far, is based on the central role played by the album (Lesage, *L'effet livre*). From the 1950s and 1960s onward, the album gained widespread popularity, first as a by-product of the magazine and then increasingly as the core of comics publishing (Lesage, *Publier*). Gradually, the album became the standard of publication but also a key vector of consecration for artists as *auteurs*. These were four-color albums, and their publication accelerated the move from black-and-white to colored newspapers. Moreover, the books required a more meticulous coloring than magazines, where colors were often applied directly at the printing factory. When René Goscinny and Albert Uderzo started *Astérix* in the pages of *Pilote*, Uderzo's color blindness ("René Goscinny et Albert Uderzo") seemed of little importance, as Uderzo had worked in comics magazines for almost fifteen years by that time. It was only in the 1960s, when the albums started to become immensely popular, that Uderzo had to be replaced for the coloring of the series. In an expensive format such as the album, a mistake such as a green horse (an error that Uderzo actually made) could be potentially disastrous.

---

9. In 1981, 85,000 copies sold, and in 1982, 64,000 copies sold.

But beyond the anecdotal, the Franco-Belgian standard of the forty-eight-page or sixty-two-page color album is deeply rooted in this history of coloring. The well-documented case of Hergé offers a particularly enlightening example of this close connection. Hergé first worked entirely alone, including for the publication of the first *Tintin* books: the editions of *Le petit vingtième* were just a name covering the fact that the business was a self-publication enterprise. After publishing a few albums in black and white, Casterman offered to print Hergé's albums on his brand-new, four-color-offset printing presses. This bold move, executed during World War II, changed Hergé's creation with major consequences on the future of Franco-Belgian comics. The black-and-white albums contained approximately 120 pages, and Casterman realized that it would not be commercially sustainable to sell 120-page color albums. In order to remain competitive, then, Hergé had to reduce the content of his albums to sixty-four pages. He accepted this restriction but was very conscious that he would never be able to carry out this titanic project on his own while publishing new *Tintin* adventures at the same time. Hergé thus decided to recruit assistants, starting with Edgar P. Jacobs (Assouline; Jacobs). These assistants helped him cut and reorganize the layout of the albums but also managed the coloring; this key process of self-remediation by Hergé (and his studio) from 120-page, black-and-white albums into 64-page, four-color albums has been meticulously studied by *Tintin* specialist Philippe Goddin.

Hergé therefore provides a strong case for studying the author function at work in *bande dessinée*. What is crucial in the editorial history of *Tintin* is that the coloring is not only the product of an aesthetic but also the result of an industrial standard: the album. The album is produced collectively, but certain collaborators remain systematically uncredited. Paradoxically, many black-and-white editions of *Tintin* albums did not have Hergé's name on the front cover. Beyond being a printing mistake, such an oversight is easily explained: Hergé's authorship was everywhere inside the book, and it would hardly need to have been reaffirmed. As Hergé employed more people and the process became collective, his authorship required more explicit assertion. The identity of the author is then revealed for what it is: a legal fiction, coupled with a branding strategy based on Hergé's signature.

What makes Hergé's case particularly rich, though, is the way his production sheds light on the professionalization of coloring. The scale of his work and success as early as the late 1940s drove Hergé to create a studio system as yet unheard of in the Franco-Belgian context. In the rare studios producing comics, the distribution of tasks was very unequal and strongly gendered. Unsurprisingly, when women held a creative position, it was limited to coloring. In Hergé's studio, the women were all colorists: Josette

Baujot (head colorist), Monique Laurent, France Ferrari, Nicole Thenen. These women are only known to a handful of fanatic Hergémaniacs. The only famous colorist working for Hergé, Fanny Vlamynck, ironically became notorious through her marital status more than her professional skills.[10] Hergé's other assistants, including Bob de Moor, Jacques Martin, Roger Leloup, and Jo-El Azara, have gained more professional recognition over the course of their careers. For these men, it is not difficult to locate interviews, profiles, fan pages, and sometimes entire biographies (Bourdil and Tordeur; Grossey; Lecigne). For the women, however, one would struggle to find any form of literature.

The paradox is that, in the *ligne claire* [clear line] that defines Hergé's style, color plays a key role.[11] In clear line, readability is paramount; characters, background, and objects are all drawn in an even line; each element forms an individual cell, and therefore each color is separated by a line (Groensteen, "Ligne claire"). To simplify, color is applied homogeneously, in large swathes, and without any light or shadows, even for night scenes. Color contributes to structuring each panel and to guiding the reader's eyes in the story. It is therefore striking to note the discrepancy between the importance Hergé gave to color in his art and the lack of recognition received by his employees. None of the colorists within the Hergé studio were credited. And whereas some of the male assistants have had recognizable and recognized careers as artists, this is not the case with any of the colorists, who remained anonymous second fiddles without a shred of authorship—unless, of course, they married the boss.

Colorists: The Workers Forgotten in the Extension of Authorship

As these examples demonstrate, coloring raises the question of authorship and helps us to understand how authorship in Franco-Belgian comics has been built around a single, masculine authority. The comparison with the American comics industry is striking. As Brenna Clarke Gray and Peter Wilkins show, authorship is dominated by the writer:

---

10. Beginning in 1956 in the studio, Fanny Vlamynck began an affair with the maestro, twenty-seven years her senior, before Hergé divorced his first wife to marry her, twenty years later. Fanny Vlamynck and her second husband, Nick Rodwell, now run Hergé's estate with an iron fist.

11. The concept of clear line was elaborated in the context of a subversive reappropriation in the 1970s. For a discussion of this problematic concept, see Pinho Barros.

> The world of comics . . . celebrates the genius of the writer over the craft of the penciller, colorist and letterer, particularly in the history of the big two comics publishers Marvel and DC, where artists have consistently occupied a lesser position. While images may be the *sine qua non* of comics . . . the writer is still king, a figure of authority and power. (116)

The Franco-Belgian history of comics offers a different pattern, which is that, historically, the artist *is* the author, for a very simple reason: publishers only dealt with one individual. When a writer helped out, he was generally not credited. Yvan Delporte, who contributed to many of *The Smurfs* albums, received no recognition, just as Jacques Van Melkebeke was never credited for his work with Hergé or Jacobs (Mouchart). For many years, being a writer was a side occupation, and writers had other jobs within the comics industry: Jean-Michel Charlier was named in the first *Buck Danny* stories because he also drew the planes (Ratier); Rosy was art director of Dupuis (Rosy and Bocquet); and Yvan Delporte ran *Spirou* (C. Pissavy-Yvernault and B. Pissavy-Yvernault), just to name a few.

From the 1960s onward, writers began to request the status of authorship and to hold copyright, following René Goscinny's claim on Lucky Luke. Morris, who had started the western series on his own in 1946 for *Spirou*, began his collaboration with René Goscinny in 1955: *Des rails sur la prairie* (published in album in 1957). It took seven years and eleven albums before René Goscinny received credit for his work on the script (Ory). The prevailing rule then was that writers were subcontractors working for the artists. It was mostly in the pages of *Pilote*—run by Jean-Michel Charlier and René Goscinny, two prominent authors—that the situation began to change. Beyond *Pilote* and the role played by its two coeditors, the new importance of writers in the Franco-Belgian comics proto-industry was largely due to the rise of the album in the 1960s and 1970s. The weekly magazines were filled with comics constructed around plot twists and turns necessary to entertain their readership. As the forty-eight- and sixty-two-page album became a new publication standard, artists and readers began to feel the need for more structured narratives. Some artists started to specialize in writing stories for others. Such is the case of Maurice Tillieux, a successful comics artist who began a second career as a scriptwriter in the 1960s and played a key role in the standardization of narratives into album format (Lesage, *L'effet livre*). The emergence of writers as a professional category in the field of comics production is therefore a good example of Abbott's divided jurisdictions: as a result of the clearer delineation of new tasks, some of the workers gradually took scriptwriting as a specific responsibility.

However, the transformation of authorship in Franco-Belgian comics is quite perplexing, as writers have quickly become main authors. This profound shift has complex factors, among which bibliographical standards play a major role alongside a deep-rooted tradition of considering that *logos* supersedes image, that writing precedes illustrating. In a collaborative work, the artist is generally treated as the writer's illustrator. As a result, *The Adventures of Lieutenant Blueberry*, by the duo Jean-Michel Charlier and Jean Giraud (the future Moebius), is cataloged by the Bibliothèque Nationale de France [French National Library] as the work of Jean-Michel Charlier (main author) with Jean Giraud being recognized only for illustrating the script written by Charlier.

In short, authorship was dramatically transformed in the French (and Franco-Belgian) comics scene within a couple of decades. But colorists, just like letterers, have very seldom benefited from such a reevaluation. As a result, compared to the American or the Japanese studio systems, authorship is concentrated into the hands of one or two workers. The Franco-Belgian history of comics therefore remains structured around a mythologized ideal of a one-man genius who is able to handle every single aspect of his art. This mythology is not specific to the Franco-Belgian comics worlds, as Bart Beaty has shown (*Unpopular*), among others. But the strength of this romantic myth in the French system of the arts makes it particularly strong, so much so that there is even a specific name to designate these authors: *auteurs complets* [full authors]. Such an expression implies that comics workers who would only manage one dimension of the work would be incomplete authors: this linguistic implication captures the strength of the *auteur* myth in French particularly well.

Colorists started to be more systematically credited from the 1990s onward. At the time, the comics industry entered a period of turbulence, and the escalating overproduction was largely responsible for the growing poverty among authors (Beaty, *Unpopular*). In that context, acknowledging the claim of colorists to a fraction of authorship, via contracts and royalties, has been a fool's errand. For most active colorists, being acknowledged as artists is symbolically enviable, but it means first and foremost that they are no longer paid for a technical service. They are instead paid through the payment of royalties, in an advance on future sales. Crediting colorists as artists thus contributed to making them more economically fragile, especially because these royalties paid to colorists have been drawn from the artists' share and not from an extension of payments allocated by publishers. The symbolic recognition of colorists thus camouflages the general impoverishment of artistic careers.

Coloring and Symbolic Legitimization

As a rarely discussed group, colorists provide a useful lens through which to observe the tensions at work within the process of comics legitimization (Ahmed et al.; Groensteen, *La bande dessinée*). Colorists are unknown authors, who have remained largely on the fringes of the making of the ninth art. The symbolic recognition of colorists to date seems particularly insubstantial, as already underlined in the discussion of Isabelle Merlet's Facebook post. More significant than the reaction of an exasperated colorist is the fact that the Angoulême International Comics Festival has never once had an award specifically for colorists and has so far never held an exhibition on coloring. The 2023 programming includes an exhibition on colors: it thus took the festival fifty years to acknowledge colorists' contributions. When, in 2019, the festival invited colorists to participate in a panel as part of the official program, it was the first time in colorists' memories such a recognition occurred. It comes as no surprise that Isabelle Merlet was one of the panelists, along with Spanish-American colorist José Villarubia, recipient of a Harvey Award in 2011 and notably famous for his work with Richard Corben, who was then president of the Angoulême Festival. But despite the importance of both colorists in their respective fields, they were only *entrées* to the *pièce de résistance*: Jean-Marc Rochette, author of *Le transperceneige* [Snowpiercer], whose Netflix adaptation had just been announced (Joo). *Le transperceneige* was an iconic and popular black-and-white, long-format series that through its publication in *(À suivre)* played a central role in defining the French graphic novel. Rochette came to the 2019 Angoulême Festival to promote the colorization of the new spin-off of the series. During the panel, Rochette directly attributed the shift to color to a strategy aimed at getting a foothold in the American market and targeting an audience who would discover the movie and the series on Netflix (Merlet et al.). Bluntly put, the panel was not so much an opportunity to celebrate the importance of colorists as it was about promoting an ambitious transmedia franchise (colorized by Villarrubia) while also celebrating his more intimate and elegiac graphic novel on his coming-of-age love for the mountains (colorized by Merlet).[12]

The absence of recognition of colorists goes further than Angoulême: it is challenging to find examples of festivals that pay tribute to the role of colorists. Significantly, the only French festival that attributed an award to a

---

12. *Le transperceneige* is even more complex when it comes to authorships: written by legendary writer Jacques Lob, it was initially drawn by Alexis (penname of Dominique Vallet), who died after completing only a few pages. After the death of Jacques Lob in 1990, Rochette worked with several writers.

colorist operates from the margins of the French comics scene, as it is located on Réunion Island. However, far from recognizing an avant-garde artist, the Cyclone BD festival chose to celebrate Claude Guth, a colorist whose career has been conducted in the fantasy series *Lanfeust de Troy*. A problematically sexist series where scantily clad, big-breasted female protagonists gallivant around, *Lanfeust de Troy* is probably the epitome of the stereotypes plaguing the genre (Reyns-Chikuma). The limited critical response to the series puts it rather at odds with such a rare honor for a colorist. In other words, it is an irony of the French symbolic hierarchy that authorship is more easily perceptible in the standardized, mainstream production rather than in the avant-garde subfield. It remains to be seen if this type of recognition helps further the cause of colorists.

Colorists, then, help us nuance the structuration of the field of comics defined by the axes of economic and cultural capital (Boltanski). Beyond this case and a small number of isolated examples, colorists are rarely invited to festivals where the main attractions are the exhibition and the book signing, a gift/counter-gift (Mauss) in which colorists find it hard to partake. Thus the collaborative nature of the colorists' job undermines the mystique of the *auteur* that predominates in French and Belgian festivals. Colorists therefore help us understand the differences between the field of comics in North America and its counterpart in France and Belgium. In many regards, the professional structure of the comics industry in the United States is organized in a similar fashion to the film industry (albeit on a smaller scale). There certainly exists a strong hierarchy between stars and more technical roles, but the profession's festivals and awards demonstrate a willingness to take into account all the roles in the production chain. However, in France, the consecration of the BD *auteur* has resulted in a difficulty when thinking about the role played by other comics workers, such as letterers, colorists, graphic designers, and so on. Situated at the very end of the creative chain and at the start of the printing process, colorists find themselves at the intersection between art and technique: they are supposed to translate an artist's vision into a language that the printing presses will understand. Coloring is never just about colors and atmospheres: it is also about the density of inks, the absorbance of a paper, the brightness of a glaze; it requires understanding the specificities of a printing plant. This technicality of the trade certainly does not help us to think of colorists as artists.

But there is certainly more to it. To understand why coloring is still very seldom acknowledged, and even less studied by comics scholars, we have to come to terms with the fact that the history of comics was written in the singular masculine form, in the way that Geneviève Sellier described the French New Wave. Just as the history of cinema has long been written from the male perspective of directors, comics legitimization as a ninth art has been built from the idea that art was that which was made by exceptional, individual males.

For *bande dessinée*'s initial fan culture, it was unthinkable to take into account collaborations. On the contrary, early fans chose to highlight the creative genius of artists, reproducing the tropes of romantic art history. That partly explains why black and white played such a big role in the first exhibitions and reprints. Against the standards of mainstream publishing, showing black-and-white original art gave the impression of accessing the artist's most intimate creation, stripped from the compromises that go with industrial reproduction. This is, of course, forgetting the fact that a page is only one intermediary step in a mass production.

The celebration of comics in France, which reached a peak with 2020's "Année de la Bande Dessinée," is still very much rooted in this romantic myth of the artist, perpetuating long-gone understandings of art history as the linear succession of individual geniuses (see, for instance, Svetlanta Alpers for a revisionist approach to art history). In this symbolic construction of comics as high art, it was necessary to separate the creative gesture from everything that could be linked to technique. In the 1970s and 1980s, indie publishers like Futuropolis adopted the idea of black and white as the purest artistic expression (Cestac; Lesage, *Publier*), a position soon embraced by Casterman and its magazine *(À suivre)*, which brought to the mainstream long, black-and-white graphic narratives. The strength of the commercial/artistic polarization, which structures the field of comics, has only been reinforced by the next generations of indie creators (Dony et al.) and the editorial success of graphic memoirs that revived the ideal of the "complete author."

Colorists blur the boundaries of comic art. Understanding their contribution and analyzing their work helps us rethink the consecration of the *auteur*, largely thought of as a singular, masculine figure. Observing the role of colorists, then, is not only a measure of academic justice toward a long-ignored profession. These workers present a compelling case of multilayered authorships and a unique vantage point from which to probe the fault lines that crisscross the field of comics. A revisionist scholarship embracing the contributions of women enables us to deconstruct the mechanisms of comics legitimization.

Works Cited

Abbott, Andrew. *The System of Professions: An Essay on the Division of Labor*. U of Chicago P, 1988.

Ahmed, Maaheen, et al. *Le statut culturel de la bande dessinée: Ambiguïtés et évolutions.* Academia-L'Harmattan, 2017.

Alpers, Svetlana. *Rembrandt's Enterprise: The Studio and the Market.* U of Chicago P, 1990.

Assouline, Pierre. *Hergé: Biographie.* Plon, 1996.

Beaty, Bart. *Comics Versus Art.* U of Toronto P, 2012.

———. *Unpopular Culture: Transforming the European Comic Book in the 1990s.* U of Toronto P, 2007.

Bénichou, Paul. *Le sacre de l'écrivain: 1750–1830.* Librairie José Corti, 1973.

Boltanski, Luc. "La constitution du champ de la bande dessinée." *Actes de la recherche en sciences sociales,* vol. 1, no. 1, 1975, pp. 37–59, https://doi.org/10.3406/arss.1975.2448.

Bourdil, Pierre-Yves, and Bernard Tordeur. *Bob de Moor: 40 ans de bande dessinée, 35 ans aux côtés d'Hergé.* Le Lombard, 1986.

Brienza, Casey, and Paddy Johnston. *Cultures of Comics Work.* Palgrave Macmillan, 2016.

Cestac, Florence. *La véritable histoire de Futuropolis.* Dargaud, 2007.

Chartier, Roger. *La main de l'auteur et l'esprit de l'imprimeur: XVIe–XVIIIe siècle.* Gallimard, 2015.

Davis, Natalie Zemon. "Women and the World of the Annales." *History Workshop Journal,* vol. 1, no. 33, 1992, pp. 121–37, https://doi.org/10.1093/hwj/33.1.121.

Dayez, Hugues. *Peyo l'enchanteur.* Niffle, 2003.

Dony, Christophe, et al. *La bande dessinée en dissidence: Alternative, indépendance, auto-édition.* Presses Universitaires de Liège, 2014.

Durand, Pascal, and Yves Winkin. "Des éditeurs sans édition: Genèse et structure de l'espace éditorial en Belgique francophone." *Actes de la recherche en sciences sociales,* vol. 1, no. 130, 1999, pp. 48–65, https://doi.org/10.3406/arss.1999.3311.

Foucault, Michel. "Qu'est-ce qu'un auteur?" *Dits et écrits I.* Gallimard, 1994, pp. 789–821. Originally published in *Bulletin de la Société Française de Philosophie,* vol. 3, no. 63, July–September 1969, pp. 73–104.

Goddin, Philippe. *Hergé: Chronologie d'une œuvre: Tome 4, 1939–1943.* Moulinsart, 2003.

Gray, Brenna Clarke, and Peter Wilkins. "The Case of the Missing Author: Toward an Anatomy of Collaboration in Comics." *Cultures of Comics Work,* edited by Casey Brienza and Paddy Johnston, Palgrave Macmillan, 2016, pp. 115–29, https://doi.org/10.1057/978-1-137-55090-3_8.

Groensteen, Thierry. *La bande dessinée au tournant.* Les Impressions Nouvelles, 2017.

———. "Ligne claire." *NeuviemeArt2.0,* 2013, http://neuviemeart.citebd.org/spip.php?article690.

Grossey, Ronald. *Bob de Moor.* Uitgeverij Vrijdag, 2013.

Grove, Laurence. *Comics in French: The European Bande Dessinée in Context.* Berghahn Books, 2010.

Jacobs, Edgar P. *Un opéra de papier: Les mémoires de Blake et Mortimer.* Gallimard, 1981.

Joo, Suk Hee. "Du transperceneige de Jacques Lob et Jean-Marc Rochette à Snowpiercer de Bong Joon-Ho: Une inspiration mutuelle entre arts visuels dans le domaine de la science-fiction." *ReS Futurae. Revue d'études sur la science-fiction,* no. 9, 2017, https://doi.org/10.4000/resf.1014.

Kohn, Jessica. *"Travailler dans les petits Mickeys": Les dessinateurs-illustrateurs en France et en Belgique de 1945 à 1968*. 2018. Université Sorbonne Paris Cité, PhD dissertation. HAL Theses, https://tel.archives-ouvertes.fr/tel-02147283.

Lecigne, Bruno. *Les héritiers d'Hergé*. Magic Strip, 1983.

Lesage, Sylvain. "Une bande dessinée adulte? Usages et mésusages de la légitimation." *Belphégor: Littérature populaire et culture médiatique*, vol. 1, no. 17, 2019, https://doi.org/10.4000/belphegor.1607.

———. *L'effet livre: Métamorphoses de la bande dessinée*. Presses universitaires François Rabelais, 2019.

———. *Publier la bande dessinée: Les éditeurs Franco-Belges et l'album, 1950–1990*. Presses de l'ENSSIB, 2018.

Maigret, Éric. "Bande dessinée et postlégitimité." *La bande dessinée: Une médiaculture*, edited by Éric Maigret and Matteo Stefanelli, Armand Colin/INA, 2012, pp. 130–48.

Marini, Marcelle. "La place des femmes dans la production culturelle: L'exemple de la France." *Histoire des femmes, Vol. 5: Le XXe siècle*, edited by Françoise Thébaud, Plon, 1992, pp. 275–96.

Mauss, Marcel. *The Gift: Forms and Functions of Exchange in Archaic Societies*. Cohen and West, 1954, http://archive.org/details/giftformsfunctiooomaus.

Merlet, Isabelle, Jean-Marc Rochette, and José Villarrubia, panelists. "Couleur et bande dessinée." Angoulême International Comics Festival, 24 Jan. 2019, Conservatory auditorium, Musée de la Bande Dessinée, Angoulême, France.

Meurisse, Catherine. *Les grands espaces*. Dargaud, 2018.

———. *La légèreté*. Dargaud, 2016.

Mouchart, Benoît. *À l'ombre de la ligne claire: Jacques Van Melkebeke, entre Hergé et Jacob*. Les Impressions Nouvelles, 2014.

Ory, Pascal. *Goscinny, 1926–1977: La liberté d'en rire*. Perrin, 2007.

Pinho Barros, David. *The Clear Line in Comics and Cinema: A Transmedial Approach*. Leuven UP, 2022.

Pissavy-Yvernault, Christelle, and Bertrand Pissavy-Yvernault. *Yvan Delporte: Réacteur en chef*. Dupuis, 2009.

Ratier, Gilles. *Jean-Michel Charlier vous raconte*. Le Castor Astral, 2013.

Reid, Martine. *Des femmes en littérature*. Belin, 2010.

"René Goscinny et Albert Uderzo à propos des adaptations cinématographiques d'Astérix et Obélix." Interview conducted by Roger Kahane and François Chatel. *L'invité du dimanche*, 1966, http://www.ina.fr/contenus-editoriaux/articles-editoriaux/1966-uderzo-daltonien-j-ai-une-fois-dessine-un-cheval-vert/.

Reyns-Chikuma, Chris. "De Bécassine à Yoko Tsuno: Entre stéréotypes, oublis et renaissance. Réflexions sur les personnages féminins et leurs auteur(e)s en bande dessinée." *Alternative Francophone*, vol. 9, no. 1, 2016, pp. 155–70, https://doi.org/10.29173/af27279.

Rosy, Maurice, and José-Louis Bocquet. *Rosy, c'est la vie!* Dupuis, 2014.

Schweitzer, Sylvie. *Les femmes ont toujours travaillé: Une histoire de leurs métiers, XIXe et XXe siècle*. Editions Odile Jacob, 2002.

Sellier, Geneviève. *Masculine Singular: French New Wave Cinema*. Duke UP, 2008.

CHAPTER 3

Between *Ah! Nana* and *Okapi*
Nicole Claveloux at the Crossroads

BENOÎT CRUCIFIX

A Belated Recognition

In January 2020, the Hôtel Saint-Simon in Angoulême held a retrospective exhibition on Nicole Claveloux, spotlighting the breadth of graphic work made by the French *dessinatrice* since the late 1960s.[1] Walls were filled from floor to ceiling with paintings, illustrations, and original comics pages. At the award ceremony, a seventy-nine-year-old Nicole Claveloux, bright red hair pinned into a chignon and comfortably leaning on a gnarled wooden cane, walked onto the stage to receive the Fauve d'honneur—a recognition for her entire career—in front of a standing ovation. The same evening, *La main verte* [The Green Hand], a recent reprint edition of her work beautifully assembled by the publisher Cornélius, garnered the Fauve Patrimoine. The award ceremony at the international festival of Angoulême was, for a surprising

---

1. For access to primary sources, I have relied on the collections of the Royal Library of Belgium, the Fonds Michel Defourny (Centre de littérature de jeunesse et de littérature graphique, Liège), and the Billy Ireland Cartoon Library. This chapter is an outcome of the COMICS project funded by the European Research Council (ERC) under the European Union's Horizon 2020 research and innovation program (grant agreement no. 758502).

change, in tune with the feminist comics organization Artémisia that had, three weeks before, selected *La main verte* for its Prix du Matrimoine.

By contrast, the Angoulême International Comics Festival had, a few years prior, been at the heart of contentious and vivid debates around the place of women in comics, after they had released the long list of nominees for its 2016 Grand Prix without including one single female creator.[2] The immediate public backlash forced the festival director and press representatives into formulating some kind of explanation or excuse. Their line of defense rested on a hackneyed argument, holding that "the Festival cannot revise the history of comics" and that there were fewer "great" women cartoonists with a long career whom they might recognize.[3] The festival thus repeated old arguments, with pitfalls that had already been pinpointed by the art historian Linda Nochlin in her seminal 1971 essay "Why Have There Been No Great Women Artists?" Nochlin's answer indeed lies less in the search for individual achievement than in the many hurdles that have made it "institutionally impossible for women to achieve excellence or success on the same footing as men, no matter what their talent, or genius" (508). The ideology of individual achievement and of the author as singular genius—taken over from other fields by the comics world (Beaty)—has also obstructed the recognition of women creators, who often are not so much absent as unrecognized and marginalized in the comics world.

As in other domains of popular visual culture,[4] female actors and makers have been disregarded in *bande dessinée* because of the ways its history has been written and conceptualized, biased by preferences for certain genres, formats, and models of authorship that have undermined the value of female roles and experiences. Looking at women's cartooning careers in the immediate postwar period, Jessica Kohn has described how "their lives and careers have been forgotten, they have been restricted to their status of wives and mothers, and their work has not had the chance to be published" (6). Women cartoonists before the 1970s primarily found work in the illustrated children's magazines, often targeted toward girl readers—a corpus delegitimized by fan historians. As Kohn's and Sylvain Lesage's respective chapters in this book further show, by inquiring into different types

---

2. For a broader context on these debates, see Marys Renné Hertiman's article on the mobilization of women creators for the valorization of their work in comics.

3. All translations, unless otherwise indicated, are mine. The press release is today only accessible through the Internet Archive (Festival international de la bande dessinée).

4. Cheryl Buckley's essay on women and design, for instance, would yield an interesting comparison with the comics world because of the proximity between these two fields of visual culture.

of careers and unexamined professions, detailed attention to the gendered economies of comics can be a prism through which to reveal blind spots in our historiographic methods.[5]

If she stands as one of the few women whose name has been recorded in comics histories (albeit discreetly),[6] Nicole Claveloux has remained a comparatively overlooked figure in the field of *bande dessinée,* in striking contrast to her reputation in the world of children's literature and picture books. It is telling that Claveloux, whose career in comics kicked off in the year prior to the first festival in Angoulême in 1974 and whose work appeared in the award-winning magazines, would only see her cartooning work celebrated decades later, reframed as an important piece of *patrimoine,* or rather *matrimoine.* The symbolic recognition of Claveloux's work in the world of *bande dessinée* runs a quarter century behind her reputation in children's publishing, where she has been a celebrated illustrator, spotlighted in benchmark professional publications (Houillot; "Entretien") and exhibited in 1995 at the Salon du livre de jeunesse in Montreuil (which is to picture books what Angoulême is to comics) before traveling to other venues.[7] This uneven chronology is telling of a cultural rift between comics and picture books, which, despite their formal proximities and the number of creators working across both fields, have "developed under very different pulling forces and with distinct cultural considerations" (Trabado 11). This break also follows gendered conceptions of media, which have influenced what, how, and for whom women have been expected to draw (Bréan et al. 299).

Looking at the comics of Nicole Claveloux between 1970 and 1981, this chapter reexamines the gendered intersections between comics and children's literature. By the mid-1980s, Claveloux had more or less abandoned the field of comics while continuing to work for picture book publishers. In the previous decade, she had been, as a young and multifaceted *dessinatrice,* involved at the crossroads of different developments both in picture books and in comics—all of this against the larger background of post–May 1968 social movements. The early 1970s were a crucial moment in Second Wave feminism, marked by the Mouvement de libération des femmes (MLF); but the decade also witnessed the emergence of *bande dessinée adulte* and the

---

5. For a parallel approach in the Anglophone context, see for instance Galvan and Misemer's special issue of *Inks* on the "counterpublics" of comics or Grennan et al.'s work on Marie Duval (see in particular Sabin's chapter on Duval as "women's cartoonist").

6. Claveloux is mentioned twice in Groensteen's *La bande dessinée: Son histoire et ses maîtres* and only in the chronology that runs at the bottom of its pages.

7. On that occasion her publisher Christian Bruel edited a lavish catalogue, including biographical and thematic essays about her work (Bruel and Claveloux).

blossoming of avant-garde players in children book's publishing. My focus on Nicole Claveloux's work in the 1970s, between Les Humanoïdes Associés' and Harlin Quist's *Ah! Nana* and *Okapi,* allows me to explore the intermedial connections and exchanges between comics for adults and for kids, graphic novels and picture books, at a moment when comics were increasingly turning away from children's audiences in their quest for legitimacy. Instead of following a chronological order, I begin by situating Claveloux's comics in the context of the feminist collective *Ah! Nana* between 1976 and 1978 and then consider earlier interactions between picture books and comics that cut through her graphic work, against the background of contemporary debates around children's culture.

Comics by Women and for Adults

Claveloux's name is often listed alongside those of Chantal Montellier and Florence Cestac—peers from the short-lived feminist comics magazine *Ah! Nana*—or Claire Brétécher and Annie Goetzinger, all names that are regularly cited to pin the 1970s as a turning point for the emergence of women in the comics world.[8] When considering Claveloux's work within the history of women's cartooning in France, the link to *Ah! Nana* is inevitable because of the emphatic role played by the magazine in advocating for female voices in the comics world. Published from 1976 to 1978, *Ah! Nana* was one of the first initiatives in France to claim visibility for women creators in comics and to tackle feminist themes. It was modeled after other magazines made by and for women: the French small press produced by various activist groups linked to the MLF (titles like *Le torchon brûle, Les pétroleuses,* or *Sorcières*) and from North American underground feminist comics anthologies such as *It Ain't Me Babe* and *Wimmen's Comix.* Trina Robbins, Sharry Flenniken, and other North American artists would see their work appear in *Ah! Nana,* which, as Leah Misemer argues in her article "Hands across the Ocean," mobilized the cosmopolitanism of the underground *bande dessinée* circles to construct a transatlantic network of feminist creators.

The magazine, however, ran for only a short course, and if *Ah! Nana* offered unprecedented visibility and a creative freedom to female cartoonists while inscribing their work within a collective movement, the network traced by the magazine did not ultimately succeed in establishing a solid

---

8. See for instance Thierry Groensteen's "Femmes (2)" entry in the "aesthetic and thematic dictionary" *Le bouquin de la bande dessinée.*

space for feminine production. As Blanche Delaborde has shown in her historical inquiry into the magazine, *Ah! Nana* indeed struggled with internal and external tensions related to its publisher Les Humanoïdes Associés and to the residual effects of the July 1949 law on publications for youth. Launched in 1975, *Métal hurlant* was the product of charismatic editor and science fiction aficionado Jean-Pierre Dionnet, together with a handful of like-minded cartoonists. The magazine was born out of a growing movement to produce comics for adults in the late 1960s and directly inspired by the *Pilote*-mutineers who founded *L'écho des savanes* in 1972. The 1970s continued the trends of the previous decade, with a large countercultural movement in *bandes dessinées* accumulating momentum through several magazines that explored new themes and new styles in a radical transgression of previous traditions.[9] Those years would be understood as key to the emergence of a *bande dessinée adulte*, decidedly not meant for children.

Ah! Nana both benefited from this transgressive undercurrent, with its liberation of creative expression and its new publishing opportunities, while offering a reaction to the often sexist and misogynist masculine fantasies that got free play in comics magazines like *Métal hurlant* and others. Indeed, the same year that *Ah! Nana* was launched, *Métal hurlant* was admonished by the commission in charge of the law of July 16, 1949, because of its objectifying depictions of women (Delaborde 41). Yet, as much as it was made "by and for women," *Ah! Nana* did not generate a collaborative dynamic in its editorial functioning: as demonstrated in Blanche Delaborde's study, cartoonists were little involved in editorial meetings and most decisions were made by the editor in chief, Janic Guillerez, also the wife of her *Métal hurlant* counterpart Jean-Pierre Dionnet. Her two editorial associates, Anne Delobel and Keleck, eventually abandoned ship and were replaced, under female pseudonyms, by male *Métal hurlant* collaborators. Conversely, the editorial role played by women—Janic Guillerez, but also Claudine Conin, Marjorie Alessandrini, and Isabelle Morin—in *Métal hurlant* was overshadowed by Jean-Pierre Dionnet and Philippe Manœuvre but was crucial to the life of the magazine. While the editorial discourse of *Ah! Nana* frequently emphasized its autonomy, it thus remained a kind of sister magazine to *Métal hurlant*. Bound to Les Humanoïdes Associés at several levels of the magazine (in terms of networks, production, distribution, advertising, layout), *Ah! Nana* nevertheless tried to carve out a space where women could reclaim their position more vocally.

---

9. For an in-depth stylistic, thematic, and political analysis of this period, see Andrieu de Lévis and also Michallat.

Over its two years of publication, *Ah! Nana* thus attempted to form a "counter-public" at a moment when comics audiences were shifting, with comics periodicals aiming at teenagers and adults, pushing against the legal and political definition of comics as a children's medium and struggling against the masculinist fantasies of adult comics.[10] The cover of the first issue by Keleck is famous for its programmatic tone: it portrays a man stripteasing in front of three women in a playful reversal of the male gaze; in the foreground, one of the women knowingly winks at the readers. Each issue presented comics and texts around a single theme, regularly exploring taboo issues of sexuality and the body, usually advertised by a provocative cover: little girls and sex, sadomasochism, and homosexuality were but some examples of themed issues that attracted the attention of the commission in charge of the law of July 16, 1949—despite the fact that the commission had already relaxed its pressure on *bande dessinée* with its gradual legitimization in the 1960s (Méon 49). Right after its issue on homosexuality (at the time still criminalized in France), *Ah! Nana* was banned from distribution to minors for reasons that have remained unclear. Because of the ban, the magazine had to be shelved next to pornographic and other "adults only" publications; in practice, it disappeared from newsstands and was thus barred from a significant chunk of its revenues (Delaborde 38–45). With overall sales too low to keep the magazine going, *Ah! Nana* published its last issue to date.

Dreamy, Freaky, and Queer Stories?

All along its short publication history, *Ah! Nana* retained Nicole Claveloux as a staple cartoonist: she drew the covers for the fashion issue and contributed short stories to every single issue of the magazine. Contrasting with the spunky political tone of Chantal Montellier, who had started her drawing career by publishing cartoons in the leftist press, Claveloux's stories adopted a less evidently feminist position, instead embedding her politics into fantastical stories and visual metaphors. Claveloux was coming to adult comics with an already established reputation as an illustrator for children's books; her first stories in *Ah! Nana* accordingly offer parodies of fairy tales, amalgamating their tropes into grotesque stories. She frequently engages with gender expectations and bodily standards, themes that appear throughout

---

10. In doing so, it joins a magazine like *Wimmen's Comix*, which tried to assemble a counter-public to the dominant underground comics (see Galvan and Misemer).

her contributions to the magazines. Her short story, tellingly titled "The Little Vegetable Who Dreamed He Was a Panther," is an allegorical take on gender standards imposed on women and their internalization of such standards, as it displays a thick beetroot dreaming of turning into a panther, portraying external pressure and internal conundrums alike. The panther embodies a hypersexualized image of liberated womanhood set in contrast with the relatively ungendered and asexual form of the beet. The story plays up the confrontation between desired images, social pressure, the vegetable's "grand ambitions," and varying ways of relating to one's appearance. This has the effect of unsettling gender as a given and lays the emphasis on becoming and transformation as a process that balances individual desires and social expectations, unfolding at different paces: in a dash of confidence, the vegetable might turn into a panther and leap over obstacles; other times it patiently leans against a brick wall until it breaks through the wall's joints.

Claveloux's most explicitly feminist take in the magazine is perhaps located in her contribution on masturbation and menstruation, *Une gamine dans la lune*. The short narrative starts with a little girl humping an armchair and dreaming of a fantasy world of giant pea pods and tiny flying naked beings. The page stages a gradual metamorphosis of the setting: the title crosses over panels to figure a moon, the armchair turns into an unrecognizable beast, the parquet grows into a field of green peas. The short story repeats this visual transformation of a familial environment into a curious dreamscape: when later pressured to eat her tapioca (which she says she does not like), the same girl fantasizes her stuffed dog turns into a terrifying beast that ravages the table companions and licks her plate. In a familiar Slumberland awakening, the girl's dreams always end up interrupted by an adult's moral reproach. In its grotesque depiction of sexual fantasies, dark private thoughts, and menstrual torrents, Claveloux's story highlights the social taboos around children's bodies and undercuts the dominant twentieth-century narrative that considers children as "innocent of sexual desires and intentions" while repeatedly depicting their affective lives within the scripts of adult heteronormativity (Bruhm and Hurley ix).

In *Ah! Nana*, Claveloux worked through personal themes in short fantastical narratives, without ever making their autobiographical tone explicit, as she describes it: "I most of all wanted to draw fantastic-dreamy-freaky stories that were also personal" (Schwartz 100). In this, her work contrasts with the life-writing mode that has been instrumental in tackling feminist issues in underground comics, which is more likely to be read, studied, and analyzed in this perspective (Chute). It can be argued that her "fantastic-dreamy-freaky stories" are less an exploration of *écriture féminine*—a widespread concept in the 1970s—than a way of queering comics, in the broad sense of the word.[11] Her graphic stories regularly display forms of relationships, love, and friendships that are outside heteronormative narratives, while her mixed use of anthropomorphized animal characters (i.e., speaking vegetables and objects) alongside human characters tacitly blurs binary gender lines. Breaking boundaries between human and nonhuman, adult and child, Claveloux puzzles her readers with babies that talk like adults, children with curious pleasures, odd interspecies fairy-tale couples, and other bizarreries. Eschewing any militantly feminist tone, Claveloux's fantastical stories in *Ah! Nana* nevertheless participated in unsettling traditional conceptions of gender, exploring a queer way of drawing comics more than actually claiming a space for women in comics.

From Picture Books to Comics and Back

The bizarreness of Claveloux's stories is matched by a graphic style that she developed and adapted to particular publication venues. It is after all her professional reputation as a *dessinatrice*, both for children's books and commercial venues, that drew the eye of Jean-Pierre Dionnet, who invited her to contribute to both *Ah! Nana* and *Métal hurlant* in 1976. In the editorial preceding her first publications, Dionnet introduces Claveloux to readers as "the best illustrator for children there is" (3). The declaration might seem a little puzzling given that the same editorial precisely presses against kids' comics and the weight of the July 1949 law on the French comics market: "The crux of the matter, which you are of course already familiar with if you are aware of press matters, is that we depend on a law from 1949, modified in 1961 and which makes of all comics a comic for kids" (3). Such a stance appears less paradoxical when we consider that Claveloux made her reputation by drawing for the avant-garde New York–based publisher Harlin Quist who, in collaboration with François Ruy-Vidal, published a series of innovative children's books across both parts of the Atlantic in the late 1960s and who was struggling in France against the conservative inertia in children's publishing. In the countercultural spirit of May 1968, new comics and children's books publishers were sharing a struggle—although with different objectives in mind—against the French protectionist legislation that had

---

11. For a clear panorama of different conceptions of women's and queer writing in the French-language graphic novel, see Jan Baetens's analysis of Dominique Goblet's work (163–67).

constrained the postwar field to adopt self-censorship strategies and avoid any sensitive issues.

The credo of the editor Ruy-Vidal opposed the overprotection of children readers and railed against children-targeted productions that, in his eyes, only offered a reassuring and comforting view of the world around them (Nières-Chevrel 254–55). Instead, Ruy-Vidal wanted to offer picture books that did not shy away from difficult realities. In reaction to the increasing everyday presence of visual media produced for child consumers, Ruy-Vidal further wanted to offer children new contemporary visual styles, contrasting with the more conservative illustration styles that were dominating the field of French picture books—which brought him to hire younger artists like Nicole Claveloux. She had already published fantastical drawings in Planète as well as Heinz Edelmann–inspired illustrations for the women's magazine Marie-Claire. Granted with a great liberty toward the text they work with, the main reference for the Harlin Quist illustrators was the psychedelic pop style of late 1960s graphic design, as represented by the Czech-German designer Edelmann (famous for his art direction on Yellow Submarine) or the New York–based Push Pin Studios, with such known figures as Seymour Chwast or Milton Glaser. Claveloux's early albums for Harlin Quist, such as Alala: Les télémorphoses written by Guy Monréal and published in 1970, particularly bear the mark of that surreal psychedelic style, which celebrates imaginative disorientation against the repetition of well-worn tropes (Heywood, "Power").

The countercultural charge and the call for liberating children's imaginations in the Harlin Quist books was at times met with skepticism and caution by librarians (Nières-Chevrel 256). This skepticism would break out into a wider polemic when the famous child psychologist Françoise Dolto consigned a severe criticism in a 1972 interview for the popular magazine L'express, accusing Ruy-Vidal's project of perverting and confounding youth. In an implicit strand of iconophobia, the psychologist pinpoints, without explicitly naming her, the graphic style of Nicole Claveloux—by referring to her illustrations for Richard Hughes's Gertrude et la sirène (1971)—and disparages the confusion between reality and dreams, the mixing of animal and mineral registers, as problematic for child readers: "Nothing is as harmful for a child as this confusion of kingdoms. It is important that men look like men, and trees like trees" (89). If Claveloux moved away from the 1960s pop psychedelic style of her Harlin Quist books, her work remained suffused by this same principle of instability and mutability, by the blurring of boundaries between opposites: human and nonhuman, animate and inanimate, child and adult.

When taken on board Les Humanoïdes Associés' project to publish comics for adults, Claveloux's comics implicitly build on these debates around childhood and visuality. As already touched on before, her short stories in *Ah! Nana* engage with children's inner imaginations, private worlds, and sensual pleasures, celebrated as a capacity to affirm choices in the margins of or against adult authority. Shortly after *Ah! Nana*, in 1978, she contributed to the French-Italian feminist children's book enterprise Editions des femmes and illustrated two fairy tales by Hans Christian Andersen whose endings had been rewritten by the editor Adera Turin to assert female independence and liberty. In *Poucette*, for instance, Thumbelina declines the prince's proposal to continue her life of travel with her friend the swallow. While again avoiding a militant position, Claveloux's illustrations were nevertheless understood by editors as corresponding to the intersection of feminist aspirations with new pedagogical projects and ideas in children's book publishing (Heywood, "Fighting"). When Claveloux was interviewed in 1981 for a special issue of the feminist magazine *Sorcières* on childhood (Perdu et al.), her work in adult comics and children's books was discussed in the same breath.

Claveloux's graphic narratives in the 1970s are an excellent example of intermedial crossovers between picture books and comics, precisely because her graphic style adapts equally well to the specificities of each media while frequently mingling their main properties. In her picture books, Claveloux benefits from a large autonomy from the text and can make use of large double pages for devising the kind of sprawling images, crowded with small details, that are a common trait of her work. But this dissociation of text and image is also an opportunity to introduce narrative elements in her drawings, for which she sometimes relies on "comicitous" forms, visual properties used in other media but noticeably associated with comics (Beineke). In her illustrations for Lewis Carroll's *Les aventures d'Alice au pays des merveilles* (1975), one of her most celebrated works, she integrates a regular grid layout and uses speech bubbles in her wordless illustrations. These formal techniques, however, are not used in their conventional ways. The grid is not used to break down a sequential movement in a linear reading, but rather to favor a disorienting tabular reading that matches the maze in which the characters seem entrapped: the recurring characters are shown in different movements or contrasting sizes, without being organized in chronological order.

In another illustration (figure 3.1), Claveloux uses speech bubbles to figure a dialogue scene in Carroll's text. While dialogue in comics had rested on all sorts of techniques (Glaude), the speech bubble had by then become

FIGURE 3.1. Nicole Claveloux, *Les aventures d'Alice au pays des merveilles*, 1974, n.p. Fonds Michel Defourny.

the dominant format in the field and in the pop years had become virtually synonymous with *bande dessinée*: in 1968, the French late surrealist Robert Benayoun devoted to it a book-length essay, titled *Vroom tchac zowie* after the popular fashion of the day. Here, however, Claveloux does not use the speech bubble in a pop aesthetic, based on the visualization of words or their onomatopoeic effects. Rather, the speech bubble is used to figure the reported storytelling and its constant interruption by other characters, creating a cacophony of voices and an intertwining of stories told and storytelling characters that confuses the reader not only about who is saying what but also about what is what and who is who in a free play of absurdist humor.

An Insufferable Little Girl

This kind of diversion of the speech bubble was not unfamiliar to Claveloux, who had already used it in February 1973 to introduce her characters in the pages of the children's magazine *Okapi*. A completely wordless page, the comic stages a tiny little girl in a polka-dotted dress and a cartoony lion engaged in a competition of imaginative bubbles, as the gag builds up into a crescendo (figure 3.2). In this opening page of "L'insupportable Grabote et le lion Léonidas," Claveloux plays with the speech bubble by avoiding its main verbal function in favor of its graphic and aural features. The bubble becomes an object nearly tangible in its materiality, which can also fall apart like a failed *soufflé*. The whole gag is a beautiful and innovative example of wordless comics that visually maximizes the lack of words.

This opening page shows that Claveloux's work was not limited to avant-garde scenes: Grabote would become her most popular creation, well remembered by a generation who grew up reading *Okapi* and who "loved to hate" the little character (Boulaire). Published by Bayard, a seasoned press group in the Catholic tradition who had been producing children's periodicals since the late nineteenth century, *Okapi* was a magazine full of contradictions: released in the aftermath of May 1968, it introduced progressive ideas—especially about new educational reforms—and radical aesthetic choices, without completely shaking off more reactionary standpoints in a curious blend of progressivism and conservatism (Boulaire). Running from 1973 to 1981, Claveloux's *Grabote* is a good example of these tensions.[12]

The insufferable character not only tortured her fellow character Léonidas but has also displeased some readers of the magazine—a small fire whose flames the editors seemed keen to gently fan in order to inflate the (un)popularity of the newly introduced character. In a reader's letter dated May 1973, Pascal writes: "Mom and I don't like the insufferable Grabote. Let this story end soon!" (*Okapi* no. 36). Two issues later, another reader delivers an even more general suggestion to the editor: "I don't like crazy drawings with weird colors. I like clean and well-drawn drawings" (*Okapi* no. 38). Of

---

12. *Grabote*'s episodes in *Okapi* can be found on an online portal: http://www.resaclic.net/grabote/.

FIGURE 3.2. Nicole Claveloux, "L'insupportable Grabote et le lion Léonidas," *Okapi*, no. 30, 1973, p. 1. Cité internationale de la bande dessinée et de l'image, Angoulême.

course, what exactly a "well-drawn drawing" is remains a question of social and cultural conventions. While other comics in the magazine were drawn in more familiar styles, the vivid colors and changing layouts of Claveloux's series was visibly out-of-tone with a segment of the audience. The letters column was not a sheer flurry of objections against Grabote, however, some readers also relayed enthusiasm: eventually the character would become a veritable mascot for the magazine, as suggested by her recurring appearances on the title page and as decorative add-on for other editorial contents.

While the character was never in danger of coming to a short end, Claveloux implicitly played with these readers' letters by integrating the magazine editor—in the form of its title animal—into her gag strip. Grabote becomes so insufferable that her starring role is put under threat, as the strip literally sends her to the margin (figure 3.3). The gridlines become a wall that separates Grabote from the rest of the characters: from the margin, and during several episodes, she makes all sorts of commentaries on the events occurring inside the panels in a comical self-reflexivity. While Leonidas is looking for other possible candidates for his strip, the arrival of the extravagant duck "big canou" distorts the conventional grid into a theatrical stage with a decorative layout, until the lion finally kicks him out into the margin. In *Okapi*, Claveloux uses the very structures of comics—frames, margins, speech bubbles, layout—to maximize a self-reflexive humor within the economy of the gag page.

This sort of theatrical play with margins and frames, using the comics panels as a stage for characters' appearances and disappearances, has a long history in serial comics that are accustomed to the repetitive and temporal constraints of periodicals and newspaper culture. To cite just one of the most famous examples, Krazy Kat and Ignatz Mouse were quietly promoted from the bottom strip of *The Family Upstairs* to the Sunday pages, in part due to the enthusiasm of readers. In periodical publications, margins have often been a space of experimentation to test out readers' appetites or to comment on a title's main content. While *Grabote* started out immediately as a gag strip, it is the only one-page comic of the magazine, and its location in the pages of the magazine changed various times, moving back and forth between the first to last pages. Claveloux knew well enough that the character could also be sent back to the margins very quickly, especially drawing for the adult-controlled public of children readers. In a later episode, she further stages Grabote and Léonidas spotting a conspiracy of black-hooded figures throwing a bunch of *Okapi* issues into a bonfire, dismissing it as a "heretical and satanical magazine," condemning it for talking about the human body (*Okapi* no. 62).

FIGURE 3.3. Nicole Claveloux, "L'insupportable Grabote et le lion Léonidas," *Okapi*, no. 42, 1973, p. 7. Author's collection.

FIGURE 3.4. Nicole Claveloux, *Go, Go, Go, Grabote!*, 1973, n.p. Billy Ireland Cartoon Library & Museum, The Ohio State University.

The debates around children's publications and what constitute "fitting" images for them were still resounding echoes. In 1973 Claveloux published with Harlin Quist *Go, Go, Go, Grabote!*, an album that reworks a few gags from *Okapi* into a mise en abyme of Grabote, jumping from Claveloux's eye pupil and taking up ink and brush to draw a world of her own. Moving through all sorts of fantastically drawn worlds, the character strips her clothes, only to get a phone call that indicted her behavior for corrupting youth (figure 3.4). The dialogue mocks the chain of actions taken in the circuit of children's book publishing and the pressure put on by commercial interests and integrated censorship.

Unacceptable, insufferable, intolerant: Grabote has nevertheless never really been censored. After her brief stay in the margins of her own comic, Grabote would become a steadfast part of the magazine. When editor in chief Denys Prache—who had spotted Nicole Claveloux in the Harlin Quist stable of illustrators—left *Okapi* in 1978, *Grabote* would survive for a few more years until its unexpected and final exit from the magazine in 1981. Claveloux would keep on contributing to *Okapi* with another title and another insufferable character, *Louise XIV*, published from 1980 to 1982 in the pages of the magazine. The capricious queen's first appearance, however, was in a one-page contribution to *Métal hurlant*, demonstrating again the porosity of boundaries between drawing for kids and drawing for adults in Claveloux's work.

Shape-Shifting Lines

It was in *Métal hurlant* that Nicole Claveloux published her most famous comics, with the collaboration of scriptwriter Edith Zha: serialized as separate episodes in the magazine in 1977 and 1978, *La main verte* and *Morte saison* were quickly collected into hardcover albums published, respectively, in 1978 and 1979 by Les Humanoïdes Associés. *La main verte* remains the most celebrated of her work, also because of its formal conception in direct colors. Rather than moving coloring to a later, separate stage, the cartoonist first applies a mixed technique of gouache, inks, and airbrushing to the original pages—scaled at the same size as the printing format—and only thereafter lays out the black outlines (Gauthey 14). It was also *La main verte* that was chosen as the main title for the first book-format publication of her work into English, *The Green Hand and Other Stories* by the American publisher New York Review Comics which, by translating and reprinting her work in 2017, preempted the French rediscovery of Claveloux.

The cartoonist, however, had already been introduced to the US in *Heavy Metal*, the North American version of *Métal hurlant*, during its earlier years and preceding the greater autonomy that the US magazine would adopt as of the 1980s. As Nicolas Labarre points out in his history of the periodical, Claveloux and Zha's longer narratives *La main verte* and *Morte saison* have been among the most talked about, prompting dubious reactions or vivid celebrations; in this, "they are witness to the US magazine's commitment to publishing more experimental narratives from *Métal hurlant* rather than sticking to easier stories or more immediately recognizable forms" (98). Labarre further suggests that Claveloux ranks in among the "established authors that readers of *Heavy Metal* expect to find in the magazine" (165). The attractiveness of Claveloux's work is undoubtedly found in her graphic style: details excerpted from her comics are frequently used to illustrate editorial items of the magazine such as the contents section or subscription ads; her drawing is thus given a prominent place in defining the visual and thematic identity of the magazine.

Claveloux's surprising popularity in *Heavy Metal*, at that moment, suggests interesting proximities with Moebius, who has always fascinated American readers, in terms of their respective graphic styles, both marked by mutability and a specific use of hatching and thin lines. Claveloux even paid homage to Moebius in her story "Journée à la campagne," merging human bodies and futuristic ecologies in a graphic and haptic treatment that is characteristic of his *Arzach* series.[13] In her own comics, Claveloux demonstrates a masterful command of drawing, alternating various techniques and graphic styles, equally at ease with black and white as with color. While extremely mutable, her narrative drawing style in comics usually privileges the rapidograph—favoring thinner lines of consistent density—and works with different types of hatching and cross-hatching that produce a contrasted balance between thickly hatched areas and clear thin lines. She proposes a degree of graphic density that arrests the reader's eye and draws it in, inviting them to inspect more closely the composition and the numerous background details or simply to revel in the image itself rather than to speed up the storytelling. The graphic style corresponds to stories that are imaginative and fantastical, sometimes absurd and hard to decipher, often playing with puns, loops, or metaleptic turns.

Claveloux, however, ultimately did not build up the kind of recognition that Moebius garnered. While women remained largely absent from the spotlights of the festival and comics culture of the time, Claveloux's presence in comics magazines dimmed in the early 1980s amidst a return of reactionary ideologies and economic neoliberalism. With a decline in magazine sales across the board, the adult comics periodicals launched in the late 1960s and 1970s either folded or were bought by larger publishing houses. This restructuring of the comics publishing field left few opportunities to publish the kind of work that Claveloux had been doing in titles such as *Ah! Nana* and *Métal hurlant*.[14] Claveloux confided in a 1981 interview that the

---

13. See Marion (97–102) for a close analysis of Moebius's style in *Métal hurlant* in haptic terms.

14. For a study of the economic restructuring of the publishing sector in the 1980s, see chapters 8 and 9 in Lesage's *Publier la bande dessinée*.

freedom she once experienced by moving into adult comics had ultimately left her with an impression of greater constraint: "We often have the feeling we work for a group of maniacs, each with their own habits, waiting for the same stories, the same images, the same adventures" (Perdu et al. 124). On the opening day of the twelfth salon in Angoulême, on January 25, 1985, the same year as François Mitterand's visit in its alleyways, the four young women cartoonists Nicole Claveloux, Florence Cestac, Chantal Montellier, and Jeanne Puchol cosigned a "manifesto" in *Le monde* addressing the unembarrassed masculinism in the (comics) magazines of the time: "This so-called new press crippled with the oldest and crassest macho fantasies is repellant" (Claveloux et al. 11).[15] By the mid-1980s, comics' claim upon an adult readership had drawn a thick line between "adult comics" and "kid comics": the rift became clear in 1986 when the Syndicat national de l'édition (the French publishers' union) added to its market research analysis a distinction between "adult" and "youth" comics (Lesage, *L'effet livre* 264). With the general marginalization of women creators and the implicit delegitimization of children's comics, Claveloux's comics would be quasi-forgotten for another thirty years; although she successfully kept on drawing for children's books.

Claveloux's work thus invites us to cast a different light on the history of *bande dessinée* in the 1970s, often seen as the turning point of "adult comics" with its implicit narrative of maturation and natural development.[16] As Lara Saguisag suggests for the US context, underground comix were caught in an ambivalent position of "subvert[ing] dominant conceptualizations of childhood" in their narratives while at the same time having to act as "gatekeepers themselves" in presenting their comix as "adults only" (72). Similar tensions were cutting through the 1970s *bande dessinée* in its confrontations with the July 1949 law on publications for the youth. At the same time, as the case of Claveloux suggests, this short period allowed for rich and productive crossovers between comics and picture books, blurring boundaries that quickly became rigid in the 1980s. Claveloux was at the forefront of the new impulses in both comics and children's books, while also contributing to popular magazines, such as *Okapi*, which remain completely overlooked in comics histories.

---

15. All translations, unless otherwise indicated, are mine.
16. There is here a likeness with what Christopher Pizzino has described as the *Bildungsroman* narrative of the graphic novel.

Works Cited

Andrieu de Lévis, Jean-Charles. *De la ligne claire à la ligne "pas claire": Émancipations esthétiques de la bande dessinée en France et aux États-Unis à l'orée des années 70*. Université de la Sorbonne, 2019.

Baetens, Jan. "Dominique Goblet: Écrire au féminin?" *Interférences littéraires/Literaire interferenties*, no. 14, 2014, pp. 163–77.

Beaty, Bart. *Comics versus Art*. U of Toronto P, 2012.

Beineke, Colin. "On Comicity." *Inks: The Journal of the Comics Studies Society*, vol. 1, no. 2, 2017, pp. 226–53.

Benayoun, Robert. *Vroom tchac zowie: Le ballon dans la bande dessinée*. André Balland, 1968.

Boltanski, Luc. "The Constitution of the Comics Field." *The French Comics Theory Reader*, edited by Ann Miller and Bart Beaty, Leuven UP, 2014, pp. 281–301.

Boulaire, Cécile. "Okapi, a 'Fantastinouï' Magazine for Pre-Teens in the Spirit of May '68," translated by Elaine Briggs, *Strenae*, no. 13, May 2018, https://doi.org/10.4000/strenae.1901.

Bréan, Simon, et al. "Faire Genre." *Style(s) de (la) bande dessinée*, edited by Benoît Berthou and Jacques Dürrenmatt, Garnier, 2019, pp. 295–343.

Bruel, Christian, and Nicole Claveloux, editors. *Nicole Claveloux & Cie*. Le Sourire qui Mord, 1995.

Bruhm, Steven, and Natasha Hurley. "Curiouser: On the Queerness of Children." *Curiouser: On the Queerness of Children*. U of Minnesota P, 2004, pp. ix–xxxxviii.

Buckley, Cheryl. "Made in Patriarchy: Toward a Feminist Analysis of Women and Design." *Design Issues*, vol. 3, no. 2, 1986, pp. 3–14.

Carroll, Lewis, and Nicole Claveloux. *Les aventures d'Alice au pays des merveilles*. Translated by Henri Parisot, Grasset-Jeunesse, 1974.

Chute, Hillary L. *Graphic Women: Life Narrative and Contemporary Comics*. Columbia UP, 2010.

Claveloux, Nicole. *Une gamine dans la lune et autres récits*. Cornélius, 2021.

———. *Go, Go, Go, Grabote!* Harlin Quist, 1973.

———. *The Green Hand and Other Stories*. Translated by Dan Nicholson-Smith and Dustin Harbin, New York Review Comics, 2017.

———. *Okapi*, no. 30, Bayard Press, 1973.

———. *Okapi*, no. 36, Bayard Press, 1973.

———. *Okapi*, no. 38, Bayard Press, 1973.

———. *Okapi*, no. 42, Bayard Press, 1973.

———. *Okapi*, no. 62, Bayard Press, 1974.

Claveloux, Nicole, and Édith Zha. *La main verte*. Les Humanoïdes Associés, 1978.

———. *La main verte et autres récits*. Cornélius, 2019.

———. *Morte saison*. Les Humanoïdes Associés, 1979.

———. *Morte saison et autres récits*. Cornélius, 2020.

Claveloux, Nicole, et al. "Navrant." *Le Monde*, 27 Jan. 1985, p. 11.

Delaborde, Blanche. *Le magazine Ah! Nana (1976–1978)*. 2005. Université Marc Bloch–Strasbourg II, MA thesis.

Dionnet, Jean-Pierre. "Editorial 1." *Métal hurlant*, no. 9, 1976, p. 3.

Dolto, François. "Littérature enfantine: Attention danger." *L'express*, no. 1118, Dec. 1972, pp. 89–90.

"Entretien avec Nicole Claveloux." *La revue des livres pour enfants*, no. 242, 2008, pp. 81–90.

Galvan, Margaret, and Leah Misemer. "Introduction: The Counterpublics of Underground Comics." *Inks: The Journal of the Comics Studies Society*, vol. 3, no. 1, 2019, pp. 1–5.

Gauthey, Jean-Louis. "Introduction." *La main verte et autres récits*, by Nicole Claveloux and Édith Zha, Cornélius, 2019, pp. 7–14.

Glaude, Benoît. *La bande dialoguée: Une histoire des dialogues de bande dessinée (1830–1960)*. Presses Universitaires François-Rabelais, 2019.

Groensteen, Thierry. *La bande dessinée: Son histoire et ses maîtres*. Skira Flammarion; Cité internationale de la bande dessinée et de l'image, 2009.

———. "Femmes (2): La création au féminin." *Le bouquin de la bande dessinée: Dictionnaire esthétique et thématique*, edited by Thierry Groensteen, Robert Laffont, 2020, pp. 303–11.

Hertiman, Marys Renné. "La valorisation du travail des femmes dans la bande dessinée: Entre médiation, remédiation et mobilisation." *RELIEF*, vol. 14, no. 2, 2020, pp. 60–72.

Heywood, Sophie. "Fighting 'on the Side of Little Girls': Feminist Children's Book Publishing in France after 1968." *Nottingham French Studies*, vol. 59, no. 2, 2020, pp. 206–20.

———. "Power to Children's Imaginations. May '68 and Counter Culture for Children in France." *Strenae*, no. 13, May 2018, https://doi.org/10.4000/strenae.1838.

Houillot, Michelle. "Nicole Claveloux, graphiste: Le hors-champ de la représentation." *La revue des livres pour enfants*, nos. 163–64, 1995, pp. 73–80.

Kohn, Jessica. "Women Comics Authors in France and Belgium Before the 1970s: Making Them Invisible." *Revue de recherche en civilisation Américaine*, no. 6, 2016, pp. 1–18.

Labarre, Nicolas. *Heavy Metal, l'autre Métal hurlant*. Presses Universitaires de Bordeaux, 2017.

Lesage, Sylvain. *L'effet livre: Métamorphoses de la bande dessinée*. Presses Universitaires François-Rabelais, 2019.

———. *Publier la bande dessinée: Les éditeurs franco-belges et l'album, 1950–1990*. Presses de l'Enssib, 2018.

Marion, Philippe. "Nomadisme et identité graphique: Moebius, une poétique de l'errance." *MEI*, no. 26, 2007, pp. 89–108.

Méon, Jean-Matthieu. "L'illégitimité de la bande dessinée et son institutionnalisation: Le rôle de la loi du 16 juillet 1949." *Hermès*, no. 54, 2009, pp. 45–50.

Michallat, Wendy. *French Cartoon Art in the 1960s and 1970s: Pilote Hebdomadaire and the Teenager Bande Dessinée*. Leuven UP, 2018.

Misemer, Leah. "Hands across the Ocean: A 1970s Network of French and American Women Cartoonists." *Comics Studies Here and Now*, edited by Frederick Luis Aldama, Routledge, 2018, pp. 191–210.

Monréal, Guy, and Nicole Claveloux. *Alala: Les télémorphoses*. Harlin Quist, 1970.

Nières-Chevrel, Isabelle. "François Ruy-Vidal et la révolution de l'album pour enfants dans les années 1970." *L'image pour enfants: Pratiques, normes, discours. France et pays francophones, XVIe-XXe siècles,* edited by Annie Renonciat, Presses Universitaires de Rennes, 2007, pp. 251–63.

Nochlin, Linda. "Why Have There Been No Great Women Artists?" *Woman in Sexist Society: Studies in Power and Powerlessness,* edited by Vivian Gornick and Barbara K. Moran, Basic Books, 1971, pp. 480–510.

Perdu, Lou, et al. "Les faiseuses d'images." *Sorcières,* no. 23, 1981, pp. 122–28.

Pizzino, Christopher. *Arresting Development: Comics at the Boundaries of Literature.* U of Texas P, 2016.

Racine, Bruno. *L'auteur et l'acte de création.* Ministère de la culture, 2020.

Sabin, Roger. "A Women's Cartoonist?" *Marie Duval: Maverick Victorian Cartoonist,* by Simon Grennan et al., Manchester UP, 2020, pp. 216–37.

Saguisag, Lara. "X-Rated: Childhood and the 'Adults Only' World of Underground Comix." *Inks: The Journal of the Comics Studies Society,* vol. 3, no. 1, 2019, pp. 70–91.

Schwartz, Madeleine. "An Interview with Nicole Claveloux and Edith Zha." *The Green Hand and Other Stories,* by Nicole Claveloux, New York Review Comics, 2017, pp. 97–100.

Trabado, José Manuel. "Ecosistemas gráfico-narrativos: La novela gráfica y el álbum ilustrado." *Encrucijadas gráfico-narrativas: Novela gráfica y álbum ilustrado,* edited by José Manuel Trabado, Ediciones Trea, 2020, pp. 11–33.

CHAPTER 4

Gender Equality? *Hshouma!*
Women, Sexuality, and Comics Activism in Morocco

JENNIFER HOWELL

One summer afternoon in 2010 while I was studying at the Arabic Language Institute in Fes, a young man followed me and a female friend on our way to the institute's student center in the medina. As we waited for the concierge to open the door, the young man—who could not have been more than fifteen years old—tried to kiss me. Remembering the advice given to us by our Moroccan host family, my American classmate quickly began shouting *hshouma*, which means "shame" in Moroccan Arabic or Darija. Her reaction was surprisingly effective: within seconds, the concierge appeared and chased the perpetrator away. After much reflection, I have come to realize that the fact that *hshouma* was one of the first words we had learned in Darija was not coincidental. Moroccan children understand this important cultural signifier early on: "*Hshouma* is a concept that has been instilled in us since childhood. To be well-behaved, to be a good citizen, also means to have shame" (Slimani and Coryn 13).[1] Less than one year after my experience, the Arab Spring would lead to the unprecedented raising of international awareness of gender-based violence and of the ways in which various political and cultural forces in the Middle East and North Africa (MENA) have

---

1. Unless otherwise indicated, all translations are my own.

used violence against women to preserve and maintain the order and founding principles of patriarchal society (Skalli 245).

Based on their "shared desire to expose and thus hopefully change ingrained cultural patterns of patriarchal oppression" (Lund 46), the comics studied here constitute clear examples of a feminist comics activism that denounces gender-based violence and promotes gender equality in Morocco.[2] This chapter will therefore examine the ways in which female artists have challenged *hshouma*, the byproduct of patriarchal oppression and hypocrisy within Moroccan society, through comic art. Of particular interest are two Moroccan comics, Zainab Fasiki's *Hshouma: Corps et sexualité au Maroc* [Hshouma: The Body and Sexuality in Morocco] and Leïla Slimani and Laetitia Coryn's *Paroles d'honneur* [Words of Honor]. Rather than provide close readings of these works, this chapter will explore the artists' use of comics as a vector for social activism, one that embodies emerging expressions of Moroccan feminism, seeks to create a new Moroccan vernacular for the twenty-first century, and actively participates in the vibrant youth culture of today's Middle East and North Africa.

Reading *Hshouma* and *Paroles d'honneur* in Context

Among MENA nations, Morocco is often considered to be one of the most progressive. In 2004, the Moroccan parliament reformed the Personal Status Code or Moudawana so that it promoted gender complementarity in the domestic sphere. The code raised the minimum age of marriage from fifteen to eighteen years for both sexes, eliminated legal guardianship as a condition for women to marry, prohibited repudiation, made divorce accessible by mutual spousal agreement, and criminalized sexual harassment (Chafai 827; CPI). Later in 2011, King Mohammed VI announced a series of changes in response to the February 20 Movement (also known as the Moroccan spring), which would constitutionalize gender equality and parity (Sadiqi, "Assessment" 59). Nevertheless, these measures have done little to change Moroccan cultural norms and have had scant effect on the penal code. To

---

2. Fasiki and Slimani are not alone in this endeavor. According to its Facebook page, "Masaktach," which means "I will not be silenced" in Darija, "is a collective/community of men and women who condemn violences [sic] and abuse against women and the legitimization of Rape culture in Morocco." While this collective does not rely solely on a virtual comics activism, its profile cover—which depicts the diversity of Moroccan women—reveals the interconnectedness of artistic practices and social movements. For more on #Masaktach, visit the group's Facebook page. See also Ollivier.

cite just one example, in 2017 a group of teenaged boys was arrested for sexually assaulting a twenty-four-year-old disabled woman on a bus in Casablanca only after a video of the assault went viral. What is more, neither the driver nor any of the other passengers were determined to have intervened ("Casablanca"). What can be gleaned from this is that enforcement and implementation of the law fail to follow pace with legislative changes.

Instead of disempowering women activists, Olivia Lewis argues that "the weaknesses of the law and the conservatism of the institutions have motivated feminists to find creative ways to fight back." Zainab Fasiki is one such feminist.[3] Although her web comics, which frequently depict nude women, have sparked controversy on social media, they have also served as an inspiration for other female artists. The Moroccan pop singer Manal, for example, has projected Fasiki's images at some of her concerts (zainab_fasiki, "Always happy"). On the one hand, Fasiki's work is personal and stems from her own experiences of sexual harassment and gender discrimination in Morocco; on the other, her comics are also collective and designed to empower women. Just after the Casablanca bus incident went viral, Fasiki shared a drawing on Instagram depicting a woman whose clothes had been partially torn off. The image, still available on social media, reads: "Buses are made to transport people not to rape girls" (zainab_fasiki, "An illustration"). One could argue that the woman's silhouette resembles that of a pin-up girl with her hourglass figure and sex appeal. Sara Shaker contends that even the well-intentioned visualization of the female body by some women comic artists in Egypt "end up . . . reproducing gender stereotypes rather than subverting them" (206). In Fasiki's image, the pastels (predominately pink and light blue) partially reinforce stereotypical femininity. However, the character's partial nudity, which certainly grabs the viewer's attention, does not inspire voyeurism. Instead, the pink side panels of the bus bleed into the crimson red of the floor, evoking the violence of the situation depicted. The character's distraught face, with her red lips and flushed cheeks, allows her to blend in with the background, as if she were not really there. Her reddened cheeks also evoke the concept of shame: the victim is ashamed of what has happened and perhaps of how it will affect her family's honor. Moreover, her positioning in front of rows of empty seats, criticizes the passivity of the other passengers. Fasiki's drawing implies that the bus might as well have been empty during the assault.

---

3. For an excellent overview of Fasiki's work, including *Feyrouz versus the World* (2018) and the first version of *Hshouma* (2018), see Garratón Mateu.

FIGURE 4.1. Girl on a bus. Zainab Fasiki, *Hshouma: Corps et sexualité au Maroc*, 2019, p. 54. Used with permission from the author and Massot Éditions. Billy Ireland Cartoon Library & Museum, The Ohio State University.

A related image appears in *Hshouma* (see figure 4.1). Here the reader sees a veiled woman dressed modestly—only her face and hands are visible—riding a bus. Unlike the aforementioned image, this one is entirely in black and white, which establishes an interesting visual contrast between the woman, who is wearing a black tunic, and the two amorphous, ghost-like figures in white standing on either side of her. On their faces is the same predatory smile, revealing their intent to victimize the woman before them. Furthermore, the bus is reduced to a series of vertical poles that appear to imprison the woman as she waits for her stop. Studied together, these bus scenes emphasize Fasiki's perception of Moroccan society where, according to her, rape, sexual harassment, and honor crimes are regrettably commonplace. Due to the normalization of such acts, Fasiki's pin-up and hijabi figures are equally likely to become the victims of gender-based violence.

Fasiki is not the only artist who has used comics to explore female sexuality and body politics in Morocco. Shortly after the publication of her first novel, *Dans le jardin de l'ogre* [Adèle] in 2014, the Moroccan French writer Leïla Slimani went on tour in Morocco. Described by the French weekly *L'express* as "a slut's story" (Liger), the novel's candid exploration of female sexuality inspired many Moroccan women to share their own stories with the author at promotional events (Slimani, *Sexe* 12–13). Their narratives would become the focus of Slimani's nonfictional *Sexe et mensonges* [Sex and Lies], as well as its graphic novel adaptation, *Paroles d'honneur*, published the same year with illustrator Laetitia Coryn and colorist Sandra Desmazières. *Paroles d'honneur* aims to liberate women's voices by sharing not only personal accounts but also commentaries from prominent Moroccan figures, including Islamic feminist Asma Lamrabet; filmmaker Nabil Ayouch, whose controversial film about prostitution in Marrakesh, *Much Loved* (2015), was banned in the kingdom; and Slimani herself, whom French president Emmanuel Macron appointed as his Minister of Francophone Affairs in November 2018 (Edemariam). All of these individuals denounce the moral hypocrisy that plagues a society in which as little as 100 Moroccan dirhams (approximately $10) can make the police turn a blind eye to sexually deviant acts. When a teenaged couple is found kissing in their car, for instance, they give the officer money in exchange for his silence. For Slimani, 100 dirhams is "the price of shame" (Slimani and Coryn 14). As a result, many of the women represented in Slimani's narrative have requested to remain anonymous to avoid dishonor and, in some instances, persecution. Her sources admit to sexual transgressions such as prostitution, premarital sex, abortion, adultery, and homosexuality—all of which constitute crimes punishable by law under Articles 449, 454, 455, and 489 through 491 of the Moroccan penal code.

Narrative Form and Content

Before moving to a more concerted analysis, first a word on how Fasiki and Slimani and Coryn structure narrative. Slimani and Coryn's *Paroles d'honneur* is a more traditional example of *bande dessinée* with its characteristic division into panels separated by horizontal and vertical gutters, use of speech balloons and captions, and inclusion of an introductory splash page that situates narrative in time (May 2015) and space (Rabat) (9). Even though Coryn traveled with Slimani to create a visual record of their encounters, her drawings render speakers anonymous through fictionalized names and faces. Characters remain realistic enough to allow for reader identification and for the author to give a clear face and voice to Moroccan women. With respect to content, *Paroles d'honneur* is divided into three chapters and an epilogue. The first chapter recreates witness testimony from Slimani's book tour; the second provides commentary on various events that caused an uproar in Morocco in 2015, including the release of Nabil Ayouch's film *Much Loved*, a Jennifer Lopez concert, and the public appearance of two topless FEMEN activists in Rabat; the third delves more deeply into Ayouch's film and prostitution in general and includes additional information about homosexuality and LGBTQIA rights; finally, the epilogue comments on the symbolic capital of the Moroccan woman in contemporary society.

Paroles d'honneur and *Hshouma: Corps et sexualité au Maroc* have several narrative traits in common. For example, both associate the lack of open dialogue about sexuality with the concept of *hshouma*. And both point to the seemingly ubiquitous practice of sexual transgressions like homosexuality, premarital sex, prostitution, and the consumption of pornography. Nabil Ayouch, for instance, tells Slimani that Morocco is the fifth largest consumer of internet pornography in the world (Slimani and Coryn 71). Fasiki represents this reality visually with the drawing of a man whose gaze is transfixed on his computer screen, his pupils spiraling as if hypnotized. The caption reads: "We must also be careful about addiction: sexual intercourse, masturbation, compulsive relationships, cybersex, consumption of pornographic films . . . we mustn't be obsessed with satisfying our sexual desires!" (73; ellipsis in original). Fasiki and Slimani highlight other dark realities of Moroccan society like hymenoplasty, the abandonment of unwanted children in the streets, the cold detachment with which educators teach reproduction in school, and the problematic tethering of the female body to sexuality. Fasiki considers this last aspect to be of singular importance. For this reason, her book, *Hshouma*, is organized into two separate chapters: "the body" and "sexuality."

Despite the above similarities, *Paroles d'honneur* and *Hshouma* differ significantly with respect to form. On hshouma.com, Fasiki refers to *Hshouma* as a comic book or *bande dessinée*. In contrast to *Paroles d'honneur*, *Hshouma* does not conform to the medium's conventional division of narrative space into panels or framing of text in speech balloons. Furthermore, Fasiki's drawings illustrate text more than create narrative dissonance between word and image. Less concerned with form than content, her objective is to provide a manual for sexual education and to create a neutral, inoffensive language of sex and sexuality in Darija. Yet the limited use of Moroccan Arabic throughout *Hshouma* arguably serves as an innovative source of narrative tension. While hinted at, the tension in Fasiki's work remains largely imperceptible to non-Moroccan readers. However, to Moroccans, the predominance of French over Arabic, and specifically the Moroccan vernacular, emphasizes the fact that *hshouma*, as a cultural signifier, severely limits the development of an unbiased lexicon to describe key aspects of both the female body and sexuality. It is therefore the absence of one language in particular that provides the pretext, context, and subtext of Fasiki's publication. Her exasperation with the social construct of *hshouma* reveals itself in other ways; for example, the color scheme used throughout *Hshouma* is restricted to black, white, and red. The artist often uses red to indicate violence (e.g., as blood spilling from a slain women's throat), but it can also underscore biological characteristics of the female body like menstruation or the tearing of the hymen during intercourse. Elsewhere, black pages that are completely devoid of images contrast sharply with text printed in white capital letters. Readers also find the inverse (i.e., white pages with black text). As the reader turns each page, the combination of Fasiki's bold typography, limited color palette, and large images (where they appear) effectively communicates the urgency of her message, as well as her frustration with the patriarchal heteronormativity of Moroccan society. Indeed, at times her text appears to scream at the reader by way of font style and size, as well as via the recurrent use of exclamation points.

If *Hshouma*'s global distribution has contributed to Fasiki's growing popularity among feminists and other likeminded individuals, her social activism predates the comic book's publication in September 2019. To raise public awareness about street harassment and gender inequality before working on *Hshouma*, Fasiki invited aspiring female Moroccan artists to collaborate on a comic book whose purpose was to help women safely navigate Moroccan public space. Known as the Women Power Collective, this initiative has become a recurring event (Eddo-Lodge et al. 102; Lewis). Since then, Fasiki has accepted invitations to speak and lead similar workshops throughout the kingdom and around the world. One year before *Hshouma*'s publication, Amnesty International recognized Fasiki on its International Day of Women Human Rights Defenders. These honors attest to her growing influence. The artist's larger *hshouma* project (i.e., the published comic book *Hshouma*, together with its online component and numerous gallery prints) embodies this same collaborative spirit as Women Power by encouraging Moroccan women to share their experiences of harassment and discrimination on the web. It follows that Fasiki's work transcends the comic book page and engages in cyber activism. Melissa Y. Lerner has convincingly argued that internet use in MENA has redefined how social movements take root and germinate in even the most restrictive of societies (558). However, Lerner also states that virtual activism rarely supplants more traditional forms of protest; social movements are more successful when activism in the virtual world complements activism in the real world (557). To promote change, Fasiki's online presence must therefore "inspire sympathetic individuals to palpable political action. Without demonstrable political activities, social movements risk losing their followers to the disconnected anonymity [of the internet]" (557). Still in its infancy, Fasiki's *Hshouma* project has yet to result in the political activity that Lerner describes. To date, what it has successfully accomplished is the creation of a new space for community dialogue, tolerance, and peace.

Moroccan Feminisms[4]

During a live forum hosted on Alianza Francesa De Cartagena's Instagram account on April 21, 2020, Fasiki was asked to define her feminist activism. After followers mentioned FEMEN—an international feminist movement that uses "sextremism" to combat patriarchy (FEMEN)—Fasiki acknowledged the movement while carefully distancing herself from it. She wants to normalize the female body in art practices and disentangle female nudity from eroticism and sexuality. She finds value in and demonstrates respect for other feminisms, including Islamic ones, but she ultimately identifies with intersectional feminism because it validates personal experiences framed within institutions and their associated hierarchies of power (Urcaregui 46). Intersectionality, a term first coined by Kimberlé Crenshaw in 1991, deconstructs the notion of a "universal woman" by demonstrating that gender equality and its effect on women are contextually determined. Intersectional feminists focus on "eradicating the three-fold oppression of race, gender and class" (Deliu and Ilea 14). Another characteristic of intersectional feminists is the active role they play in the production of knowledge; they favor "freedom to" over "freedom from." The former "means to

---

4. Fatima Sadiqi argues in favor of the plural due to the "diverse, polyvocal and complex voices" of Moroccan feminists even within secular and Islamic organizations ("Assessment" 51). Khadija Hamouchi concurs stating that "feminism has now, more than ever, become a plural concept, embodying the opinions, perspectives, and voices on a wide spectrum."

authentically and legitimately express a woman's experience and creativity, the freedom to feel at home in the world" (Deliu and Ilea 19). Fasiki's concluding section of *Hshouma* reiterates her desire for the freedom to perform and embrace difference. Quite fittingly, the penultimate image appears to be of a trans man endowed with the third eye: the esoteric symbol of higher consciousness. Inscribed in his three pupils are the words حرية ("freedom"), سلام ("peace"), and حب ("love") (106).

Intersectionality falls under the aegis of Third Wave feminism. Fatima Sadiqi situates the emergence of this movement in Morocco at the dawn of the new millennium and at the intersection of four major cultural elements: "identity, Islamism, globalization and new technology, and the uprisings in the region" ("Assessment" 58). The development and availability of new technologies are of particular interest because they have allowed for the near-immediate and largely unregulated sharing of information related to identity, religion, and revolt. The February 20 Movement has been partially credited to virtual activism on Facebook and other social media sites, as well as to young, cyber-sensitive, and technologically savvy feminist voices (Sadiqi, "Assessment" 60–61). Moreover, the expansion of the internet throughout MENA, particularly in the wake of the Arab Spring, has allowed millennials like Fasiki to disseminate their socially engaged artwork to a broad fanbase. Her active presence on social media mirrors current trends in virtual comics activism observed in the region and "the commitment of the artists to bring the medium directly to the public sphere during significant historical moments so as to participate directly in public and political events" (Di Ricco 194).

Notwithstanding the undeniable impact of her activism online, Fasiki's collaborative efforts attest to her interest in and ability to mobilize other female artists and members of her community on the ground. The purpose of her mentorship program, Women Power, is "to prepare . . . female artists each month to navigate exploitation in Morocco's art industry, which she encountered at the beginning of her career" (Hincks 102). Similarly, hshouma.com purports to initiate a collective, constructive dialogue about gender, sexual education, the body, and gender-based violence and discrimination in Moroccan society. Visitors to her website are encouraged to take an active role in this dialogue through web content and live events. More than just a comic book, Fasiki envisions *Hshouma* as a free educational platform that will supplement sex education in schools. In a 2015 study, Zohair Gassim found that textbooks used throughout Morocco focused exclusively on the biological aspects of sex and sexuality rather than on their social and psycho-affective importance for sexual orientation and gender identity

(106). Given the insufficiency of sexual education in Moroccan schools in addition to the nonnegligible influence of religion on society, new vectors of knowledge are needed to break cultural taboos and deconstruct "imbalanced gender identity" (Chafai 830). Furthermore, Fasiki's activism is necessary because the internet has allowed Moroccan youth to have greater access to unmediated sexual content than was previously possible. Her site provides a mediated introduction to sex education, but it also attempts to provide one that is comprehensive and that may prevent future incidents of sexual harassment such as the one on public transportation described earlier. Some critics have attributed the crime to the boys' lack of sex education (Bermime). A male university student writing for *Morocco World News* states that "Morocco's only chance at getting ahead of the sex-related social problems that are growing every year is to implement a comprehensive sexuality education program" (Bermime). While positive reactions to her work can be seen via her followers' comments and reactions online, Fasiki explained during the aforementioned live Instagram event that mothers have come to book signings with their children to thank her for providing a more inclusive presentation of sexuality and identity. Her work has facilitated difficult discussions about sex and sexuality at home.

Despite the conservatism with which certain families address such topics in the domestic sphere, many Moroccan children's first uncensored experience of the female body is in the hammam. Here women undress in front of each other and their children, including prepubescent boys whose definitive exclusion from this female space usually happens upon circumcision. Given the importance of the hammam in Moroccan culture, this space figures prominently in Moroccan literature.[5] Rather than evoke an Orientalist sensuality, the hammam provides inspiration for Fasiki's realistic portrayal of the female body in *Hshouma* and related images. Rather than sexualize the body, she uses unconventional beauty—as it exists in the hammam—as a source of empowerment. The artist draws fully nude bodies as a manifestation of female agency, one that seeks to decouple the body and sex, albeit not à la FEMEN. In *Hshouma,* nude women are portrayed unshaven and in the raw. They exhibit a diverse array of body types and gender identities. Some are young, others old; some are thin, others stout. In this way, Fasiki creates new narratives of femininity and womanhood that some of her social media followers applaud. Her recalibration of beauty standards for cis- and transgender men and women empowers individuals whose

---

5. See, for example, Fatima Mernissi's *Dreams of Trespass* and Tahar Ben Jelloun's *Harrouda.*

nonnormative expressions of gender identity and sexuality have resulted in their marginalization and victimization in Moroccan society. Fasiki's images have, of course, generated negative criticism online from more conservative members of the virtual community who find such images "degrading" (Eddo-Lodge et al. 102). The body that she has drawn the most, however, is her own.

Despite her critics, she continues to draw her naked body in Moroccan public space. In one image, she towers over the Casablanca Twin Center, which further accentuates her own self-identified role as protector. Rather than insert a masked male superhero into the Moroccan cityscape, Fasiki unapologetically usurps this role. In an interview for *Time* magazine, she explains: "This is me trying to protect the city. I'm here, and I can change some things" (Eddo-Lodge et al. 102). Jacob Høigilt argues that adult comics in the contemporary Arab world, unlike American mainstream comics, have not had to contend with a long tradition of male-dominated superheroes. This has made artists "freer to mould their own comics culture from scratch" (90). Women's involvement in the Arab uprisings, as well as the importance of gender issues for those involved, have allowed female artists and their heroines—like Fasiki's Super Khadija (zainab_fasiki, "The exhibition")—to "challenge the state politically, ignoring dominant patriarchal values that equated women's bodies with the national honour" more openly in popular culture (Høigilt 90). It is therefore not surprising that, in various drawings and even photographs, Fasiki is made to look like a superhero herself (see, for example, zainab_fasiki, "Thank you"). In one such image, Fasiki's stance and the red lining of her jacket evoke Clark Kent, ripping off his civilian clothes to become superman (zainab_fasiki, "I dream Hard"). Fasiki's self-portrait mirrors strategies of youth activism among MENA millennials: "The millennial leaders also created a sympathetic image for themselves as crusaders for an end to torture, corruption, and police repression, an image with which other, initially less engaged youth could identify" (Cole 287).

Fasiki's work reflects another important trend specific to North Africa. Fatima Sadiqi ascertains that Morocco's secularist feminist movements have benefited from the emergence of youth culture and the valorization of Berber/Amazigh culture and language. She describes Amazigh as "a centuries-old women-related language" ("Assessment" 62). Among the various constitutional reforms that were enacted after the February 20 Movement was the adoption of Amazigh as one of the kingdom's official languages alongside Arabic. In recognition of this national, pre-Islamic heritage, Fasiki opens *Hshouma* with the assertion that female oppression began with the Arab conquest of North Africa. Before the arrival of Islam and under the leadership of the warrior queen Kahina, the indigenous Berber tribes celebrated women. The artist draws several women, beginning with the one on the book's cover, with the facial tattoos commonly associated with Amazigh women. Carolyn McCabe writes that traditional female body art, once revered in Morocco and, more generally, across North Africa, has since become "a source of shame." Stated differently, Amazigh tattoos have become *hshouma*.

Because it contradicts the national narrative, Fasiki reportedly failed to find a Moroccan publisher who would allow her to keep this introductory, historical section of *Hshouma*.[6] As a result, she turned to a French publisher, Éditions Massot, who distributes their titles in Morocco and other MENA countries (Snaije). Despite tendencies to discredit Berber identity and history, Fatima Sadiqi acknowledges Kahina's importance with respect to North African history as only she alone could unite the region's heterogeneous tribes against the invading Arabs. Kahina surfaces as the ultimate female crusader: "Kahina's boldness has been and is being used by the youth (male and female) in modern times to defend personal liberty and self-determination, carve out space to act in spite of patriarchal constraints, or to become free and in control of one's destiny" (*Moroccan* 60). The scholar calls Kahina "the most powerful woman military leader in modern Berber history" (59), one that is frequently overlooked in children's literature and history textbooks (61).[7] Fasiki's continued insistence on Kahina's resistance and exercise of female agency is thus representative of new cultural attitudes among Moroccan youth. As recently as May 1, 2020, she shared her "New Order" collection, which positively depicts Amazigh women, on Instagram (zainab_fasiki, "New Order").

A New Moroccan Vernacular

In addition to their recognition of minority cultures, Jacob Høigilt has convincingly argued that contemporary Arab comics—especially those produced during or after the Arab Spring—are culturally innovative in that they

---

6. Fasiki's *Hshouma: Corps et sexualité au Maroc* does, however, subscribe to the national narrative regarding the Western Sahara. The map of Morocco in North Africa that appears on the third page of her book includes the contested region as an integral part of the kingdom.

7. Interestingly, Yomad Éditions, a Moroccan publisher who specializes in children's and young-adult literature, included Laurence Le Guen's *Kahina reine des Berbères* in its 2011 catalog. This title belongs to the series "Raconte-moi l'histoire" [Tell Me the Story/History]. Unlike Fasiki, Le Guen is a French writer and scholar.

have increasingly started to incorporate colloquial Arabics, of which Darija is but one example. There are various practical reasons for this, including concerns about reader accessibility and linguistic competency (Høigilt 162). While Høigilt's interest lies in "the social and political function of the informal literacy practices we see in comics" (161), Fasiki and Slimani—each in her own way—underscore the limitations of Moroccan Arabic when it comes to sexuality. The perceived paucity of Darija is bound to the concept of *hshouma*, which Soumaya Naamane-Guessous defines as follows: "Sometimes it is shame, shame for having committed a particular act; sometimes it's modesty and hchouma forbids certain behaviors. But hchouma is in fact none of those: more than shame, more than modesty, it is constantly present in every place, in every circumstance" (5–6; trans. by Hassa 299).

In their work, Fasiki and Slimani explore *hshouma* as a cultural signifier that controls the female body and sexuality in Moroccan society. Fasiki's *Hshouma* project purports not only to raise awareness about sexual harassment and gender discrimination but also to develop an acceptable vocabulary for sex and sexuality in Darija. According to the artist, "There is a problem with vocabulary. There are no words for breasts or vagina, for example. The ones used are 'dirty,' or *hshouma*" (Snaije). When asked about *Hshouma*'s language of publication during a live Instagram forum, Fasiki commented that she had originally wanted to write in Darija. But because she felt blocked by her native language, she chose French instead. Postcolonial scholars frequently analyze an author's decision to write in a colonial language rather than in an indigenous or local one. However, Massimo Di Ricco contends that "pragmatic linguistic choices in the area [MENA] are often the result of individual decisions by the artists rather than being influenced by a colonial history as such" (199). Although French remains a vehicular language in Morocco as a result of colonialism, Fasiki views French as a unifying or bridge language with positive consequences; French unites communities who would otherwise be incapable of communicating with each other.

Darija's lexical deficit has allowed for the continued repression of sexuality and gender identity, as well as for the disempowerment of Moroccan women who, to quote Fasiki, "can't even describe [their] own bodies" (Snaije). Samira Hassa concurs, stating that "in Moroccan Arabic, obscene and insulting words often involve genitals and sexual terms pertaining to the mother" (305). Fasiki plays with this idea in several images from *Hshouma* and elsewhere in which asterisks replace anatomical words (in the way vulgar language is often represented in the United States) and text boxes with the word *hshouma* prevent the viewer from seeing women's

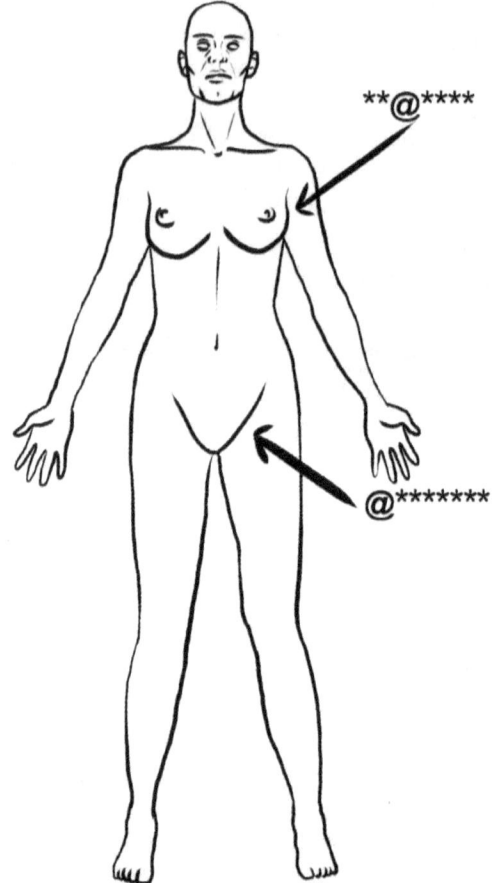

FIGURE 4.2. The female body shown in anatomical position. Zainab Fasiki, *Hshouma: Corps et sexualité au Maroc,* 2019, p. 7. Used with permission from the author and Massot Éditions. Billy Ireland Cartoon Library & Museum, The Ohio State University.

breasts and genitals. Unable to properly label an anatomical map of the female body, the artist instead inserts "**@****" in lieu of the Darija equivalent of "breasts" and "@*******" in lieu of "pubis" (see figure 4.2). Moreover, the female depicted appears asexual: she has no body hair (including on her head), and her pubis is reduced to a curved triangular shape. The absence of external genital organs further denies the woman her sexuality and sexual identity. In another image available on Instagram (zainab_fasiki, "All artworks"), Fasiki's placement of text boxes not only censors female nudity but also demonstrates the frequency with which the word—and perhaps even the concept of—*hshouma* stands in for more biologically appropriate terminology. In contrast to these reductive notations, Fasiki clearly labels in Arabic other objects (a stool and a bucket) that appear in the same image.

An unfortunate consequence of this language deficiency is that doctors sometimes delay discussing sexual health with their patients (Hassa 305). Malika, one of the women whose story appears in *Paroles d'honneur*, is a doctor who works in a remote area of the kingdom. Reunited with a friend, she expresses her professional malaise with respect to certain patients and colleagues: "I was unaware of the importance of virginity before becoming a doctor" (Slimani and Coryn 26). In one instance, a woman asks Malika if a young bride lost her virginity recently (i.e., on her wedding night) or before (i.e., during premarital sex). In another, Malika recounts the heated exchange between her and one of her male colleagues who wanted to denounce, not treat, a single woman diagnosed with an ectopic pregnancy. Habiba Chafai has further argued that "language is the primary tool through which social control is constructed, reproduced and maintained" (834). From this perspective, Fasiki's efforts to collectively establish a useful vocabulary to discuss the body, reproduction, and sex, more generally, can be read as a new Moroccan feminist praxis intended to disentangle the female body from notions of honor and shame, to eradicate gender-based violence, and to ensure greater access to sex education.

While Fasiki appears confident in her ability to speak openly about sexuality, the women depicted in Slimani and Coryn's graphic novel reveal the extent to which this "uncensored language" (3) remains an obstacle to the majority of Moroccan women. The first chapter of their graphic novel is thus titled "To Free Speech" (5). Throughout this chapter, Slimani appears alongside Moroccan women whom she met during her 2015 book tour. Surprised that a woman of Maghrebi heritage would publish a novel about sex addiction, Slimani's French critics seemed concerned with her lack of propriety. Subsequent conversations with her Moroccan readership nevertheless reveal the extent to which such assumptions of modesty are often based on carefully engineered subterfuges. Carla Makhlouf Obermeyer contends, for example, that "in some ways . . . social taboos and silences relating to sexual behavior provide a space of negotiability and make it possible to accommodate norms to the untidy reality of relationships between the sexes" (249). It is therefore not surprising that some of Slimani's interviewees identify to a certain degree with the novel's central protagonist. In confidential conversations, they explain that it is not uncommon, for example, for women to engage in premarital sodomy instead of vaginal intercourse as a way to preserve their virginity and, for those who have already engaged in the latter, undergoing surgery to restore their hymen (Slimani and Coryn 42).

Although many of the women represented in *Paroles d'honneur* engage in what is perceived as culturally unacceptable behavior, the underlying message is this: in order to live one's sexuality freely and openly, women and men must first be granted the freedom to talk about it and to do away with doublespeak (for example, when single young women maintain a veneer of purity for their families all the while secretly exploring their sexuality). In one vignette, a young hijabi with two faces appears with one face addressing her family and the other, her friends. To her family, she states, "I'm a virgin," and to her friends, "I have sex" (Slimani and Coryn 24). What makes this particular image so striking is that only the duplicity of language is shown, not that of outward appearance. The woman's two faces mirror each other completely. In the following panels, Slimani and Coryn demonstrate that veiling does not necessarily preclude sexuality. Some young college women don the veil the morning after a night out partying. When will Moroccan society be more accepting of this social reality and recognize the fluidity of spaces that individuals occupy within that society? Near the end of Slimani's encounter with Nour (one of her Moroccan readers), the author expresses her unfettered optimism for the liberation of the sexes in the new millennium: "The Arab revolutions, the emergence of the middle classes, and the advent of social networks have, to some extent, allowed tongues to wag. I find that very positive and encouraging for the future!" (Slimani and Coryn 51). Contrary to Fasiki, whose comics (*Hshouma* but also those published on social media) tend to be multilingual (French, English, Arabic, and Darija), Slimani's narrative is limited to French. There are, of course, important reasons for this: first and foremost is that she published her graphic novel with a French press. Nevertheless, Samira Hassa has demonstrated in her study of the French-language magazine, *Femmes du Maroc* [Women of Morocco], that "French, despite not being the native or official language of Morocco ... becomes a linguistic outlet that allows Moroccans to read and talk about sexuality more freely" (315). As indicated above, Fasiki's decision to write the majority of *Hshouma* in French—after not finding the words in Darija—confirms Hassa's assertion.

Conclusion

By way of conclusion, I should add that I discovered *Hshouma* and *Paroles d'honneur* somewhat fortuitously while researching educational comics that human rights organizations publish and distribute for free in Moroccan public schools. Topics vary greatly from road safety to the abolition of the death penalty. The chairperson of the Regional Human Rights Commission of Souss-Massa, Mohamed Charef, stated in a personal conversation in March 2019 that activists in Morocco have learned that because children take these comics home to share with their parents, these publications have resulted in small but noticeable changes. In many ways, the works discussed here belong to this emergent, educational, and engaged comics culture in Morocco. That Moroccan women are attending public book signings to speak to Zainab Fasiki and Leïla Slimani about their personal experiences of sex and sexuality attests to the generally positive reception of their comics activism, as well as to the meaningful ways in which these intersectional feminists encourage readers to deconstruct one of the central tenets of Moroccan culture: *hshouma*. The hope is that comics activism—particularly one whose playfulness speaks to Moroccan youth in the way *Hshouma* and *Paroles d'honneur* do—will one day translate into real-world political action and social change.

Works Cited

Ben Jelloun, Tahar. *Harrouda*. Denoël, 1973.

Bermime, Youness. "Morocco Needs an Alternative to 'Halal Sex Education.'" *Morocco World News*, 29 Sept. 2019, https://www.moroccoworldnews.com/2019/09/283633/morocco-needs-an-alternative-to-halal-sex-education-that-works/.

Bouknight, Sebastian. "Illustrator Zainab Fasiki Takes on Taboos and Patriarchy with Art." *Inside Arabia*, 22 Sept. 2018, http://insidearabia.com/illustrator-zainab-fasiki-patriarchy-with-art/.

"Casablanca Bus Sexual Assault: Six Teenagers Arrested." *Morocco World News*, 21 Aug. 2017, https://www.moroccoworldnews.com/2017/08/226671/casablanca-bus-sexual-assault-six-teenagers-arrested/.

Centre for Public Impact (CPI). "Reforming Moroccan Family Law: The Moudawana." 2 May 2016, https://www.centreforpublicimpact.org/case-study/moroccan-moudawana-reform/.

Chafai, Habiba. "Contextualising Street Sexual Harassment in Morocco: A Discriminatory Sociocultural Representation of Women." *The Journal of North African Studies*, vol. 22, no. 5, 2017, pp. 821–40. EBSCOhost, https://doi.org/10.1080/13629387.2017.1364633.

Cole, Juan. *The New Arabs: How the Millennial Generation Is Changing the Middle East*. Simon and Schuster Paperbacks, 2015.

Crenshaw, Kimberlé. "Mapping the Margins: Intersectionality, Identity Politics, and Violence against Women of Color." *Stanford Law Review*, vol. 43, no. 6, 1991, pp. 1241–99. JSTOR, https://www.jstor.org/stable/1229039.

Deliu, Ana-Maria, and Laura T. Ilea. "Combined and Uneven Feminism: Intersectional and Post-Constructivist Tendencies." *Metacritic Journal for Comparative Studies and Theory*, vol. 4, no. 1, 2018, pp. 5–21, https://doi.org/10.24193/mjcst.2018.5.01.

Di Ricco, Massimo. "Drawing for a New Public: Middle Eastern 9th Art and the Emergence of a Transnational Graphic Movement." *Postcolonial Comics: Texts, Events, Identities*, edited by Binita Mehta and Pia Mukherji, Routledge, 2015, pp. 187–203.

Eddo-Lodge, Reni, et al. "Next Generation Leaders." *TIME Magazine*, vol. 194, nos. 16–17, 21–28 Oct. 2019, pp. 92–105.

Edemariam, Aida. "*Sex and Lies* by Leïla Slimani: Review—Exploring Secret Lives." *The Guardian*, 12 Feb. 2020, https://www.theguardian.com/books/2020/feb/12/sex-and-lies-leila-slimani-review.

Fasiki, Zainab. *Feyrouz versus the World*. Tosh Fesh, 2018.

———. *Hshouma*. Matadero/AECID, 2018.

———. *Hshouma: Corps et sexualité au Maroc*. Massot Éditions, 2019.

———. *Hshouma*, https://www.hshouma.com.

FEMEN. *FEMEN Official Blog*, 15 Apr. 2020, https://femen.org/.

Garratón Mateu, Carmen. "El proyecto *Hshouma*, el arte como motor de cambio social." *Al-Andalus Magreb*, vol. 26, no. 9, 2019, pp. 1–24, https://revistas.uca.es/index.php/aam/article/view/5789/6022.

Gassim, Zouhair. "Genre et éducation sexuelle dans le système éducatif marocain." *Kohl: A Journal for Body and Gender Research*, vol. 1, no. 2, 2015, pp. 98–107.

Hamouchi, Khadija. "New Arab Feminism: Consciousness, Art and Action." *The New Arab*, 30 Oct. 2018, http://www.alaraby.co.uk/english/indepth/2018/10/30/New-Arab-feminism-Consciousness-art-and-action.

Hassa, Samira. "The French Language, Gender, and the Discursive Construction of Sexuality in Morocco." *Journal of Language and Sexuality*, vol. 6, no. 2, 2017, pp. 292–319. EBSCOhost, https://doi.org/10.1075/jls.6.2.04has.

Hincks, Joseph. "Zainab Fasiki: Comics Crusader." *Time*, 10 Oct. 2019, pp. 102–3.

Høigilt, Jacob. *Comics in Contemporary Arab Culture: Politics, Language and Resistance*. I. B. Tauris, 2019.

Le Guen, Laurence. *Kahina reine des Berbères*. Yomad Éditions, 2011.

Lerner, Melissa Y. "Connecting the Actual with the Virtual: The Internet and Social Movement Theory in the Muslim World—The Cases of Iran and Egypt." *Journal of Muslim Minority Affairs*, vol. 30, no. 4, 2010, pp. 557–74. EBSCOhost, https://doi.org/10.1080/13602004.2010.533453.

Lewis, Olivia. "'Hey, sexy': Long Road Ahead to Combat Sexual Harassment in Morocco." *Middle East Eye*, 7 Aug. 2018, https://www.middleeasteye.net/features/hey-sexy-long-road-ahead-combat-sexual-harassment-morocco.

Liger, Baptiste. "Dans le jardin de l'ogre: L'histoire d'une 'salope' par Leïla Slimani." *L'Express*, 9 Oct. 2014, https://www.lexpress.fr/culture/livre/dans-le-jardin-de-l-ogre_1575872.html.

Lund, Martin. "Comics Activism, a (Partial) Introduction." *Scandinavian Journal of Comic Art*, vol. 3, no. 2, 2018, pp. 39–54.

Masaktach. About. *Facebook*, 15 Oct. 2018, https://www.facebook.com/pg/Masaktach1/about/?ref=page_internal. Accessed 6 May 2020.

McCabe, Carolina. "The Disappearing Tradition of Amazigh Facial and Body Tattoos." *Morocco World News*, 7 Apr. 2019, https://www.moroccoworldnews.com/2019/04/269903/tradition-amazigh-facial-tattoos/.

Mernissi, Fatima. *Dreams of Trespass: Tales of a Moroccan Girlhood*. Perseus Books, 1995.

Naamane-Guessous, Soumaya. *Au-delà de toute pudeur: La sexualité feminine au Maroc.* Eddif, 1992.

Obermeyer, Carla Makhlouf. "Sexuality in Morocco: Changing Context and Contested Domain." *Culture, Health and Sexuality,* vol. 2, no. 3, 2000, pp. 239–54.

Ollivier, Théa. "Au Maroc, la parole des femmes victimes de violences sexuelles commence à se libérer." *Le monde,* 23 Feb. 2020, https://www.lemonde.fr/afrique/article/2020/02/23/au-maroc-la-parole-des-femmes-victimes-de-violences-sexuelles-commence-a-se-liberer_6030524_3212.html.

Sadiqi, Fatima. "An Assessment of Today's Moroccan Feminist Movements (1946–2014)." *Moroccan Feminisms: New Perspectives,* edited by Moha Ennaji, Fatima Sadiqi, and Karen Vintges. African World Press, 2016, pp. 51–75.

———. *Moroccan Feminist Discourse.* Palgrave Macmillan, 2014.

Shaker, Sara. "Gender Binaries and Sexual Violence in Adult Comics during Post-Revolutionary Egypt." *Kohl: A Journal for Body and Gender Research,* vol. 3, no. 2, 2017, pp. 205–15.

Skalli, Loubna Hanna. "Young Women and Social Media against Sexual Harassment in North Africa." *The Journal of North African Studies,* vol. 19, no. 2, 2014, pp. 244–58. EBSCOhost, https://doi.org/10.1080/13629387.2013.858034.

Slimani, Leïla. *Dans le jardin de l'ogre.* Gallimard, 2014.

———. *Sexe et mensonges: La vie sexuelle au Maroc.* Éditions des Arènes, 2017.

Slimani, Leïla, and Laetitia Coryn. *Paroles d'honneur.* Éditions des Arènes, 2017.

Snaije, Olivia. "Zainab Fasiki, Fighting 'Hshouma.'" *ArabLit,* 16–18 Dec. 2019, https://arablit.org/2019/12/18/zainab-fasiki-fighting-hshouma/.

Urcaregui, Maite. "Intersectional Feminism in *Bitch Planet*: Moving Comics, Fandom, and Activism Beyond the Page." *Gender and the Superhero Narrative,* edited by Michael Goodrum, Tara Prescott, and Philip Smith. UP of Mississippi, 2018, pp. 45–73.

Yachoulti, Mohammed. "The Women of 20-February Movement in Morocco: A New Feminist Consciousness." *Moroccan Feminisms: New Perspectives,* edited by Moha Ennaji, Fatima Sadiqi, and Karen Vintges. African World Press, 2016, pp. 163–83.

zainab_fasiki. "All artworks of the @hshouma exhibition . . ." *Instagram,* 2 January 2019, https://www.instagram.com/p/BsJQG8hgqoP/.

———. "Always happy when the talented @manalbenchlikha . . ." *Instagram,* 30 July 2019, https://www.instagram.com/p/BojfrjcB-8f/.

———. "The exhibition is for 2 weeks!" *Instagram,* 6 Mar. 2018, https://www.instagram.com/p/Bf_fvobgQC2/.

———. "I dream Hard . . ." *Instagram,* 28 October 2019, https://www.instagram.com/p/B4LLgjVB2BS/.

———. "An illustration I made . . ." *Instagram,* 21 August 2017, https://www.instagram.com/p/BYEuxGrAKbn/.

———. "New Order." *Instagram (Stories),* 1 May 2020, https://www.instagram.com/stories/highlights/18027760513267474/?hl=en.

———. "Thank you @parismatchbe from Belgium! . . ." *Instagram,* 15 May 2019, https://instagram.com/p/Bxf6bTwBj4i/.

PART 2

GEOGRAPHIES OF IDENTITY

CHAPTER 5

Graphic Entanglements
Images of Women, Nature, and Brittany in Contemporary Comics

ARMELLE BLIN-ROLLAND

The study of entanglements of gender and the environment is a productive strand of feminism, from ecofeminism's understanding of the domination of women and of nature as "intimately connected and mutually reinforcing" (King 18) to material feminism's radical rethinking of "the agency, semiotic force, and dynamics of bodies and natures" (Alaimo and Hekman 6). This chapter aims to contribute to this line of work through a medium- and place-specific approach, with a dual focus on comics and Brittany that brings different perspectives to the (de-)construction and (re-)imagining of associations and interactions between women and nature. The rich and flexible form of comics as a medium of hybridity and relationality means that graphic works can explore, materialize, and reconfigure these dynamic links not only textually but also through images, colors, frames, and linear and nonlinear relations. The locus of Brittany enriches the analysis due to its situated sociopolitical dimensions as a stateless culture shaped by a history of unequal power relations with France and one whose imageries and imaginaries have drawn on and redrawn women and nature in shifting ways. This chapter is also a contribution toward and a call for an "ecographics": a field that explores how graphic narratives can throw open new perspectives on environmental humanities locally and globally, as developed for instance in relation to posthumanism and human-technological-nonhuman relations in Latin America (King and Page), animal comics (Herman), or space and landscape in Spain (Fraser).[1] Within French and Francophone studies, this means giving *bande dessinée* the "significant place" that it does not yet have, as Margaret C. Flinn points out in one of the few studies of comics and nature in France (16), in the developing field of "écocritique" (Posthumus).

The guiding notion developed throughout this chapter is that of graphic entanglements. It is indebted to and puts into dialogue feminist, environmental, and comics theorizations of relationality, as I explain in the first section, after sketching out contemporary representations and realities of women in Breton culture and society. I then explore graphic entanglements of gender and nature and the human and the nonhuman in three recent women-authored or coauthored comics that center on different environments (woodland and rivers, the coast, and the land) and female figures: first, *Brigande!* [Bandit!], by Laëtitia Rouxel and Roland Michon, a biography of eighteenth-century bandit Marion du Faouët; second, *Plogoff*, by Delphine Le Lay and Alexis Horellou, a chronicle of the sustained mobilization between 1974 and 1981, most prominently by women, against the French State's plan to build a nuclear power plant in the Plogoff area; and finally, Christelle Le Guen's *Anjela*, a bilingual adaptation of selected letters and poems by twentieth-century Brittophone peasant-poet Anjela Duval.

Entanglements

Rouxel, Le Lay, and Le Guen are among a small but increasing number of female comics artists and writers in contemporary Breton comics, which, as I have explored elsewhere, is a predominantly Francophone, rather than Brittophone field, and, significantly for this chapter, is a privileged cased study for an ecographics in *bande dessinée* ("Breton").[2] *Brigande!*, *Plogoff*, and *Anjela* do not only bring gender diversity to a field that has long been dominated by male authors and artists. They also contribute to diversifying images of Breton women in how they flesh out or go beyond the recurrent tropes of costume-clad women or female figures from the Celtic imaginary that populate the land, islands, coasts, and forests of *armor* ("the land of the sea") and

---

1. For a discussion of ecographics through the concept of "ecological storylines" and taking French-language comic art as a case study, see Blin-Rolland ("Ecographics").

2. Other women *bédéistes* who are of Breton origins and/or publish in Brittany, and whose work engages with aspects of Brittany's culture and history, include Fanny Montgermont, Gwénola Morizur, Annaïg, and Mandragore.

argoat ("the land of the woods") in comics representations of Brittany.[3] Any discussion of women and Brittany in *bande dessinée* must, of course, start with Bécassine, who is also important for my analysis of comics that offer reconfigurations of intertwined images of femininity, rurality, and Bretonness. Bécassine emerged in the early twentieth century as a pastiche of the nineteenth-century cliché of the young peasant girl as an embodiment of Brittany, crystallized in Breton Francophone poet Auguste Brizeux's 1830 creation *Marie* (Williams). Posited as "all of Brittany" (Caumery and Pinchon 9),[4] Bécassine is a stupid, loyal, and often literally mouthless character, her backward rural environment functioning as an exoticized space against which the center can project its own modernity (Forsdick). The character was subverted and reappropriated during Brittany's "reinvention" in the 1960s and 1970s, turning from a negative symbol into a vocal and combative figure in left-wing political iconography and in Paol Keineg's 1972 play on the 1675 peasant rebellion, *Nevez-amzer ar bonedoù ruz / Le printemps des bonnets rouges* [The Spring of the Red Caps]. Through this period, Bécassine was a frequent parodic presence in the then-emergent field of Breton comics.

Yet while female figures have been overinvested as symbols of Brittany—carriers of its traditions, guardians of its environment, figureheads of its rebellions—Breton women have been underrepresented as cultural producers and political agents (Blanchard and Thomas). The crucial role they played in the transformation and modernization of Brittany was largely made invisible, and the tenacious notion of a "Breton matriarchy," whereby women rule in the private sphere, has across the twentieth century served to "thwart the idea of the inferiorization of women and/or neutralize any debate on the subject" while glorifying "an image of maternity and conjugality" (Gautier and Guichard-Claudic 18–19). Feminism, and the issue of gender equality, have gradually taken hold in local and regional politics since the 1980s. However, the *Emsav* (Breton cultural and political movement) still seems to be lagging behind in this regard, according to a 2019 article by Mélanie Jouitteau published in *Le peuple breton / Pobl Vreizh* [The Breton People], the magazine of the left-wing, autonomist, and environmentalist party Union Démocratique Bretonne (UDB). In counterpoint to the *Emsav*'s

---

3. See, for instance, Bruno Le Floch's 2004 *Trois éclats blancs* [Three White Flashes]; Bertrand Galic and Marc Lizano's 2015 *Le cheval d'orgueil* [The Horse of Pride]; Didier Quella-Guyot and Sébastien Morice's 2015 *Facteur pour femmes* [Postman for Women]; or Soleil Celtic albums such as Thierry Jigourel and Nicolas Jarry's 2007 *Les fées* [The Fairies] and Jean-Luc Istin, Thierry Jigourel, and Jacques Lamontagne's *Les druides* [The Druids] (since 2005).

4. Unless otherwise noted, all translations are my own.

progressive vision for Brittany, Jouitteau depicts a movement that has long been reluctant to see women's perspectives and feminist articulations as part of the Breton project and has dismissed gender issues and confined women to their "natural" roles as mothers and wives of male militants (10–12). This has however started to be countered by initiatives such as the feminist and bilingual collective *Gast!* [Bitch! or Bloody Heck!], which was active between 2013 and 2018.

Jouitteau, revealingly, uses *bande dessinée* characters to illustrate her point: Bécassine, of course, and *Astérix*'s Falbala and Bonemine all demonstrate the limited and limiting roles available to women in the Breton left. *Bande dessinée* has, to be sure, contributed to consolidating stereotypes of Breton women, but comics can clearly do a lot more than form, draw on, and disseminate clichéd images. Hillary Chute, for instance, has explored the rich possibilities that the medium offers to challenge, expand, and invent visualizations of female subjects (*Graphic Women*). My argument is that comics offer rich possibilities, too, for visualizations of complex, bodily, and discursive entanglements of women and nature. This image of entanglements has been key in the urgent task of developing renewed understandings of the more-than-human world. My use of the term is indebted in particular to the work of feminist and ecocritical scholars such as Donna Haraway, Karen Barad, Stacy Alaimo, and Serenella Iovino and Serpil Oppermann, who have radically rethought relations between nature and culture by positing matter as neither mute nor inert but agentic. Such scholars have explored ways to account for the profound significance of social and cultural construction *and* "the agency, 'thought,' and dynamics of bodies and natures" (Alaimo, "Feminisms" 242).[5] Graphic entanglements, as I explore in this chapter through the lens of Breton comics, are words, images, and frames emerging with interweaving discourses of femininity, nature, and identity, as well as relations and interactions of lines and textures forming more-than-human perspectives, landscapes, and narratives.

The notion of entanglement, and the textile/textual images it conjures up of "knottings, threadings and weavings" (Sharp et al. 24), offers comics

---

5. I should note that the connotations of entanglements that I draw on in this chapter are much broader than Barad's notion of (quantum) entanglement, whereby to be entangled is "to lack an independent, self-contained existence. . . . Individuals do not preexist their interactions; rather, individuals emerge through and as part of their entangled intra-relating" (ix). My use of the term is also specifically graphic, and in this sense it echoes the approaches taken in King and Page's edited volume *Posthumanism and the Graphic Novel in Latin America*, which explores the potential that the medium holds for investigations of "dynamics of relationality and emergence" in "human-technological-animal entanglements" (11, 4).

studies a way to think ecologically about relationality, whose dynamics have long been part and parcel of theorizations of the medium.[6] Graphic entanglements form when knots of "natureculture" (Haraway, *Companion Species*; *When Species Meet*) become palpable in and across a comic, emerging between panels and pages, words, images and frames, intertextual relations and colour (*Brigande!*), *tressage* effects (*Plogoff*), or linework (*Anjela*). Regarding *tressage*, it is important to note that the idea of graphic entanglements both takes inspiration and departs from Groensteen's seminal concept. *Tressage* (weaving or braiding) occurs when spatially distant images in the comic, as a network, form a series that is "inscribed like an addition that the text secretes beyond its surface," a supplementary relation that enriches but is "never indispensable to the conduct of the story" (*System* 146–47). Graphic entanglements are not a matter of seeing *tressage* effects everywhere but of taking a feminist and ecological approach to the arthrological notion that in a comic every panel "exists, potentially if not actually, in relation with each of the others" (146). The case studies to which I now turn will, I hope, give a sense of some of the multiple ways in which comics can redraw and reconfigure entangled images of Breton women and natures.

Brigande!: Colorful and Embodied Transgressions of "Women's Nature"

Brigande! is comics artist Laëtitia Rouxel and filmmaker Roland Michon's second collaboration as part of a project that, as Rouxel explains, aims to "rebalance" dominant representations of gender in *bande dessinée*. As a way of redressing in particular the sexualization of female characters and the prominence of male-authored histories of male heroes, Michon and Rouxel "highlight female figures that take charge of their own destiny" (Le Doujet). Their focus is, again in Rouxel's words, on "strong women from Brittany" (Le Doujet), such as Brest-born *communarde* Nathalie Lemel in their first album *Des graines sous la neige* [Seeds under the Snow] (2017). Eighteenth-century bandit leader Marion du Faouët, the subject of their second *bande dessinée*, is a well-known figure in Brittany and one whose representation in collective memory has shifted and transformed across time. First remembered in oral tradition as a sinner and a witch, she was reinvented in the late nineteenth century by historian Julien Trévédy as a "Breton Robin Hood"

---

6. For instance, see Pierre Fresnault-Deruelle's linear and tabular readings, Groensteen's arthrology (*Système*), Laurence Grove's text/image mosaics, and Charles Hatfield's art of tensions.

figure who stole from the rich and gave to the poor, before being reclaimed in the 1960s as a symbol of a modern and progressive Brittany (Evain). This contemporary resonance is referenced in the comic with an opening sequence set in 1969, when Marion du Faouët is evoked by a young feminist, and a closing one in 2017, when her name is graffitied on the walls of her native town by the far-left group Dispac'h (which means "revolution" in Breton). I am interested in the ways in which the *bande dessinée* reconfigures entanglements of women and nature in its reimagining of the life and afterlife of a rural woman turned bandit turned counter-symbol and nineteenth- and twentieth-century Marie- and Bécassine-type images of femininity, rurality, and Bretonness.[7] *Brigande!* is, clearly, a *bande dessinée* that is firmly focused on its human subject. Yet the environment, and specifically the woodland and rivers of inland Brittany, are not drawn as a mere background to her story but a potent visual presence given vibrancy and density by Rouxel's line and color work. This becomes palpable early in the *bande dessinée*, on a double page (12–13) where intertextual associations of the female body and the nonhuman are transformed into images of immersion and interaction (figure 5.1).

The scene is set by the wooded banks of the Ellé River, where Marion du Faouët meets with her childhood friend Olivier Guilherm, who unlike her is well born and educated (and who will later act as the gang's bookkeeper). She has by this stage left her position as a servant in a city household and returned to a rurality that she finds plagued by economic exploitation and famine, whereas he is off to Nantes to read law. From the first glance, the double page presents a contrast between a text-dominated page showing two human figures in conversation and one on which vegetal greens swell as the focus turns to Marion du Faouët's interaction with her surroundings after Olivier Guilherm has left. Their conversation establishes Marion du Faouët as a woman who does not accept social inequalities, which will lead her to formulate the idea of a "tax on poverty" a few pages later (21). As part of the rural poor living "among apples and peasants," as she puts it, she is bound to nature by her class. She is also associated with it by her gender, as becomes apparent when the conversation veers from politics to poetry. The page ends with a reference not to Brizeux's creation, Marie, who would not appear until 1830, but to another poetic trope of the provincial girl. This is Pierre de Ronsard's poem "Marie, vous avez la joue aussi vermeille . . ."

---

7. This feminist reappropriation of Marion du Faouët as a counter-symbol of dominant images of the Breton woman is seen perhaps most evocatively in Colette Hélard-Cosnier's 1975 play *Marion du Faouët: La catin aux cheveux rouges* [The Red-Haired Strumpet], which is still regularly staged today.

[Marie, your cheek is the crimson . . .] (1555), the beginning of which is read out loud by Marion du Faouët and the end recited by Olivier Guilherm. Ronsard's poem employs natural imagery to represent the eroticized body of the poet's muse, an Angevin country girl. The most erotic verses are between the panels, the comic both making a cut into the poem and inscribing this gap in the "rich empty space" (Chute 8) of the gutter. In gendering nature and naturalizing woman, this poem turns both into surfaces upon which the male seeing eye inscribes cultural signification. The poetic fusion of "woman" and "nature" echoes with the feminization of landscape as analyzed in feminist geography (Rose), whereby the dualities of nature/culture and female/male are woven together into the metaphor of the body-landscape as text (Wylie 84). This scene in *Brigande!* weaves a third duality into this knot, as the body of the provincial country girl—whose name, of course, echoes Marion's—is a text that is written in French (established by their conversation as a language of culture and books) rather than in Marion du Faouët's native Breton, which is highlighted by Olivier Guilherm complimenting her progress in reading the language.

This intertext points toward entanglements of women and nature that stem from a masculine "cultured knowledgeable look" mapping the surface of the female body (Rose 97). Significantly, this is juxtaposed with a page on which nature is viewed from a perspective that is female as well as immersive, as Marion du Faouët, now alone, feels the sun on her face, walks along the bank among plants and trees, and looks out to the river, taking visual and haptic pleasure in her surroundings. This page not only follows the strip in which the poem is read but also echoes it. The sun recalls the Aurora/dawn line, Marion du Faouët too has crimson cheeks, and there is a reference to an animal: Marie has the heart of a lioness, Marion sings the (anachronistic) song "Je mène les loups" [I Lead the Wolves].[8] The poem that is woven into the comic is absorbed and transformed into another text (Kristeva 146) in which the relation between the female body and nature is colorfully reconfigured in terms of interaction.

Color is, as Jan Baetens argues, not an "isolated" but an "intertwined" parameter of comics (116), and what makes vegetal colors surge across the double page is also the movements of text receding, frames elongating, and strokes becoming denser. Whereas on the first page framing quickly cuts out the characters' surroundings to focus on their conversation, as the reader follows Marion du Faouët's bodily immersion in nature, panels grow

---

8. "Je mène les loups" was written in the 1990s by Yvon Guilcher, who adapted traditional melodies that were first collected in the nineteenth century. This is also a reference to a *gwerz* [ballad] on Marion du Faouët in which she is called a she-wolf.

FIGURE 5.1. On this double page, set by the wooded banks of the Ellé River, graphic entanglements of women and nature emerge and are subverted across text, image, and color, as intertextual associations of the female body and the nonhuman are transformed into images of immersion and interaction. Roland Michon and Laëtitia Rouxel, *Brigande! Marion du Faouët: Vie, amours et mort*, 2019, pp. 12–13. Billy Ireland Cartoon Library & Museum, The Ohio State University.

spacious, stretching with greenery. Her human figure is a key presence but not the dominant one: in a corner of the second panel and in the center of the third and fourth panels, but immersed in vegetal greens growing thicker with dense pencil strokes. The page closes with a panel (positioned next to, though not aligned with, the strip on which she reads Ronsard's poem) where the reader shares the character's gaze upon the river. The female body-landscape intertext transforms into a "landscape panel" (Groensteen, "Paysage"), or what I would call a panoramic view of nature in a strip-panel, of a tangled bank, viewed through a gaze that is embedded and embodied, with textured trees, foliage, an insect in front of flowing waters, dense woodland in the background—and, above, a sky turned green.

This double page is an evocative representation of the environment shifting from background to foreground and of the female body's graphic (textual and visual) entanglements with nature. *Brigande!* is, to be clear, a *bande dessinée* that is green without being "about" nature, but from this chromatic moment it continues to thread color, shade, and texture through the woman-nature knot. On the next green-blue double page, the Ellé River becomes the setting for an erotic scene in which Marion du Faouët meets her partner Henry Pezron, who joins her after seeing her bathing naked (14–15). His irruption seems to revert to portraying a female body-centered association with nature through a masculine and voyeuristic gaze, but this shifts into a scene that shows her sexual agency and identifies both characters with nature: Ronsard's poem wrote of Marie as a "May rose," and Pezron tells her that they are "two white swans, petals of May." Further on, the image of Marion du Faouët immersed in light and color singing a song about leading wolves morphs into her figure as a bandit in the night, leading her men dressed in animal skins (23, 25). Further still, on two echoing bleed pages, the vegetal (trees, grass, flowers) act as living frames for green scenes of her bandit life. The first (27) shows the outlaws setting camp in the forest, taking refuge, like Robin Hood, "outside the bounds of normal society" (Stephens and McCallum 183), but forming a notably feminized counterpoint to his band of merry men. The second features a stagecoach attack on a woodland road, captioned with *récitatifs* (in her male associate Robien's voice) comparing her to first-century Celtic queen and twentieth-century symbol of Breton resistance Boudica (43).[9] Finally, the image of Marion du Faouët sitting by a riverbank is repeated with a difference, this time by the Scorff River, where she attempts to heal after the society against which she rebelled branded her flesh with the "v" of thieves, in a scene that invokes the mystical power of

---

9. See Paol Keineg's 1980 *Boudica: Taliesin et autres poèmes*.

a feminine nature ("Mother Nature") to heal the beaten body of a transgressive woman (54–55).

The environment, redrawn as a space not idyllic—nor, by the end, even safe—but with scope, depth, and width, provides Marion du Faouët with a place in which to take shelter and attack. Its visual expanse also forms a counterpoint to the restrictions imposed upon her by a Rousseauian "nature" that made all men equal and women inferior. As she puts it in a late scene in the comic, "Woman is restrained in the choice of her qualities; is it nature that wants it so?" (58). The *bande dessinée* ends with Marion du Faouët by a riverbank again (now with a barrel full of coins), after she sees the posthumous resonance of her name. Back during her conversation with Olivier Guilherm, she asked him to teach her the French words "liberté, équité, justice" [liberty, equity, justice], and she is now conjured up as a symbol of revolution as a Breton word ("dispac'h") by a group whose independentist, feminist, anti-capitalist, and environmentalist vision for Brittany turns against itself the image of a backward, conservative, and feminized rural province constructed in the nineteenth century. The *bande dessinée* closes with a landscape panel whose width across the double page gives space to the dark blues, browns, and greens of the turbulent flow of water, textured rocks, and trees. Marion du Faouët sits by the bank, a woman in nature, woven into twenty-first-century Brittany's cultural imaginary *and* revolutionary and feminist genealogy.

Plogoff: Frames, Landscapes, and Performing Gendered Environmental Activism

Our next *bande dessinée* takes us from the woodland and rivers of inland Brittany to the Penn-ar-Bed/Finistère [World's End] coast, redrawn in grayscale as the site and stake of an antinuclear struggle that was spearheaded by women and mobilized the inhabitants of Plogoff from 1974 to 1981, when the project to build a nuclear power plant in the area was abandoned by the newly elected socialist president François Mitterrand.[10] The aesthetics and politics of Le Lay and Horellou's *Plogoff* clearly echo with Etienne Davodeau's oeuvre as a pioneer of "la BD du réel": *Un homme est mort* [A Man is Dead] (2006) for the Breton setting; *Rural!* (2001) for its representation of "the countryside not as a place of tranquility but of combat" (Miller 123);

---

10. For a discussion of Plogoff in Breton comics and cartoons, see Blin-Rolland ("Tu te décolonises" and "Breton").

and *Les mauvaises gens* [The Bad People] (2005) as a narrative of politicization (both albums notably recreate the countdown to Mitterrand's victory). Plogoff is a struggle that contributed to the emergence and consolidation of political environmentalism in Brittany and that also powerfully reactivated Bretonness (Simon 342), the mobilization used as a symbol of standing up to the centralized French State as an apparatus of repression. This is rendered in *Plogoff* for instance on a page whose *gaufrier* [grid] layout gives a sense of both the diametrical opposition and asymmetrical warfare between, on the left, militants throwing stones and, on the right, mobile guards firing rifles (121). This French-language comic also includes images of slogans in Breton on demonstration placards, a sequence that shows a Breton-language Catholic hymn repurposed as an antinuclear protest song (90), and a mobile guard shamed for speaking Breton, turning against itself the Republic's practice, well into the twentieth century, of instilling shame for speaking the language (81).

That Plogoff—a key reference in Brittany to the entanglement of the environmental, the social, the political, and the cultural—is a struggle in which women held a prominent and mediatic place makes it a fruitful case study for what Vincent Porhel, in his study of the conflict, characterizes as "the ambiguities of gendered readings of the environment." Women's involvement in the Plogoff affair is hardly surprising given that, as one interviewee in *Femmes de Plogoff* puts it, "here, there is a majority of women; apart from a few old ones, the men aren't here" (Conan and Laurent 63). Most of these women were housewives, and many were sailors' wives, and therefore women with frequently absent husbands, a state of affairs which had already led them to cross conventional gender boundaries in their daily life. If the women of Plogoff's marital status provides a pragmatic explanation for their involvement in the conflict, their gendered identity as mothers and homemakers was key to the framing of their environmental militantism as stemming from "a concern that is indeed feminine" for their children's future, in the words of socialist councilor Jacqueline Desouches (qtd. in Simon 303). As Gilles Simon notes, the portrayal of Plogoff as a feminine struggle was evidently strategic (302) and indeed contributed to the wide media coverage of the affair.

The Plogoff affair therefore raises the question of women's, and more specifically mothers', "natural connection" to the environment, which has been the subject of continuing feminist and ecofeminist debates around the ethics and politics of (earth)care (MacGregor). Two echoing scenes in the *bande dessinée* form a *tressage* effect that productively entangles the issue of strategic essentialism—that which underlies the eco-maternal connotations of Plogoff—with the notion of gender performativity theorized by Judith Butler as "the processes of being acted on and the conditions and possibilities for acting" (63).[11] These scenes show Marie and Yvette, the two characters through whom the reader follows the mobilization, putting pressure on mobile guards. In the first, Marie remains soft-spoken as she attempts to manipulate the young guard's emotions as a mother herself, making him feel visibly uncomfortable (109). The second maternal performance is different in the sense that it is aggressive, mocking, and belittling (120). Yvette, whom the reader knows does not have children, expresses shame at the thought of having a son like one of the young mobile guards.[12] The repetition with a difference of female militants acting as mothers makes palpable the possibility of reading the women's own mode of protest in terms of a performance that strategically draws on "gender-assigning strategies" (Butler 64). Marie and Yvette perform variations of motherhood, weaponizing the construction of a "natural" gender identity as part of an ongoing war—echoing the images of men throwing stones on the page adjacent to Yvette's scene, in a similarly gendered role as warriors. Strategic essentialism is drawn into the performativity of protest in performances that do not, in themselves, disrupt the norms of gender, but weaponize the political potential of eco-maternal connotations—and as such, the political potential of "playing mother" and, in Alaimo's words, "playing nature" (*Undomesticated* 136).[13]

Three echoing scenes of Breton women being interviewed enable us to explore further how the *bande dessinée* redraws and reframes the women of Plogoff. The first interview (46–47) is in relation not to Plogoff (at this stage, the authorities seem to have abandoned the project) but the 1978 Amoco Cadiz oil spill, the fourth on Breton coasts in ten years (figure 5.2). Two women who are taking part in a demonstration voice their anger at the French State's treatment of Brittany, which is cast as an environmental issue: "Brittany is France's bin. What future do we have in Brittany?" This televised interview is being watched by Plogoff inhabitants, whose conversation, panel after panel, breaks down the impossibility of disentangling

---

11. As Alaimo argues, strategic essentialism and performative identities are two continuing debates to which ecofeminism brings fruitful perspectives, which shows that it is a strand of feminism that should not be dismissed as a monolithically essentialist field (*Undomesticated* 9).

12. Insulting and verbally harassing the mobile guards was a commonly used strategy, as the women were taking advantage of the fact that they were less likely to be arrested than men (Porhel).

13. At a later stage of the mobilization, women are seen at barricades again outside the courthouse where some militants are on trial, this time holding slingshots and therefore symbolically taking up arms (Le Lay and Horellou 156).

FIGURE 5.2. A televised interview of Breton women about the 1978 Amoco Cadiz oil spill is watched by inhabitants of Plogoff on a double page that breaks down the impossibility of separating society from nature and whose images of frames within a frame entangle with later scenes to deconstruct the binaries at play in framings of women's environmental activism. Delphine Le Lay and Alexis Horellou, *Plogoff*, 2013, pp. 46–47. Billy Ireland Cartoon Library & Museum, The Ohio State University.

society from nature: oil spills are due to economic concerns for profitability, authorities care neither about dead fish and birds nor the fisherman that "are going to die" due to the repercussions on their trade, and the double page ends on the slogan "covered in oil today, radioactive tomorrow," which refuses to distinguish between human and nonhuman toxic bodies. The double page features two panels that "bring" the reader directly to the demonstration as well as panels that include the TV frame and reactions to the interview.

This image of a frame within a frame productively entangles with another scene of women (Yvette and Annie Carval, who was the president of the Plogoff committee) being interviewed, this time about Plogoff, almost one hundred pages later (140–41). The interviewer questions their technical knowledge and understanding of nuclear energy and asks them whether they are against nuclear energy only in Plogoff or in general. Literal and conceptual frames entangle in a *tressage* effect that gestures toward the ways in which women's environmental activism is, precisely, framed through a gendered binary of reason and emotion (women's fear of technology and science) and by casting women's concern for the future of Brittany and antinuclear stance as a (maternal) defense of *their*—rather than *the*—environment. A third interview, sixteen pages later, further reframes women's activism beyond gendered dualisms (157). It takes place outside the courthouse in which militants are on trial, and this time a man and a woman (Marie) are interviewed. It is the man who expresses an emotional response to the Plogoff affair (it "terrifies" him), while Marie denounces the hypocrisy of a system of institutional violence condemning the violence of resistance. This series of images of female militants being interviewed shows women's activism being portrayed as "feminine" (emotional, maternal, selfish) and reconfigures it in terms of women acting as environmental citizens, which implies questioning, marching, and resisting against the "underlying structural (political, economic, and social) causes of environmental problems" (Barry 23).

The *bande dessinée* not only materializes and reconfigures the ideological entanglements of women and nature at play in Plogoff, but also refuses to portray their antinuclear mobilization as a human-centered environmentalism, which is implicit in views of women defending the environment *of their children*. The comic recasts this apparent human-centeredness within its first twenty pages as a concern for the more-than-human, as Marie tells Yvette after their first information meeting that "nuclear power is crud for us, for the sea, for the land . . . We can't allow it to happen" (19; ellipsis in original). These words resonate across the comic, echoing in particular with coastal landscape panels that are far from the traditional function of panoramic views of nature as, according to Groensteen, "descriptive pauses between two action sequences" ("Paysage"). The *bande dessinée* often combines images "on the ground" with the militants and distanced views that show them as little more than dots as part of the more-than-human environment for which they are fighting. The beauty of the landscape is arguably toned down by the album's grayscale palette, giving a sense that this struggle is about something more and something other than preserving idealized or romanticized nature and a rural way of life.

One *tressage* effect is a powerful materialization of asymmetrical understandings of the environment. Early in the comic, panoramic views of the coast are combined with the state's words, in *récitatifs* and quotation marks, extolling the benefits of the nuclear power plant that is to be built, describing it as a "modern cathedral" and an "authentic work of art" that will be in harmony with the "current coastal landscape" (25). To borrow Alaimo's words about photography, the comics frame here functions to "distanc[e], contai[n] and contro[l] its subject" ("Feminist" 198), a nature that is captioned as an inert resource, a landscape at which to gaze, and a site on which to build for human needs. The image in the bottom panel, which shows the coast in the foreground, the La Vieille lighthouse in the middle distance, and the horizon in the background, reappears a few pages later (53). It illustrates a newspaper article, framed within the comics frame as the symbol of a battle that may be already lost. Yet this landscape is viewed again almost one hundred pages later, as the mobilization draws to its end, in the middle of a page where its image of the horizon bridges a panel above with seagulls in the sky and a gathering of militants below, appearing as little more than dots on the land (166). Panoramic and distanced views of the site shift from rendering a way of seeing nature as a resource to a recognition of more-than-human entanglements. The simultaneity of frames gestures toward coextensiveness and connection, the seagulls at the top giving a "matterphorical," to use Lowell Duckert's evocative term (Cohen and Duckert), bent to the bird's-eye view of the militants below.

This image, in being repeated with a difference across the comic, becomes a symbol of the struggle. It is also one of several representations of the horizon, including one that shows Marie and Yvette among militants during a protest on land and sea (57), redrawing the well-known image of a Breton wife at a cliff's edge, a symbol of loss and longing in the face of the hostile sea, into one of hope and possibilities for women as social and political actors and part of a more-than-human Breton landscape. These images of the horizon across the comic serve as a counterpoint to the album's ending, and here it will be useful to draw on Ann Miller's Rancièran analysis of Davodeau's *Les mauvaises gens*. *Plogoff* does not end with Mitterrand's—and therefore, the militants'—victory, but in 2012 with a splash page giving a pithy account of France's continued dependence on nuclear energy. The *récitatif* is combined with an image that is the culmination of a *tressage* network of images of a barn being built on the land of the Mutual Agricultural Land Grouping—serving as a rallying point for an antinuclear demonstration—now abandoned with its message ("the future? it's the concern of us all") faded (71, 117, 190). If this may seem like a rather bleak ending, it also stands as a call to environmental citizenship on the part of Le Lay and Horellou, who since *Plogoff* have continued their graphic exploration of alternative modes of living through solidarity and sustainability, in documentary and fiction. It is in the light of Plogoff as the story of the resistance and victory of unrecognized subjects, but also of France's nuclear energy policy, that the horizons and landscapes seen across the comic may be read as representations of a "dissensual horizon" (Rancière, *Spectateur* 75; Miller), in a *bande dessinée* that draws a "new landscape of the possible" (Rancière, *Emancipated* 103; Miller 133), in which the ecological and the political and the human and the nonhuman are inextricably entangled. This sense of being part of a more-than-human world, the possibilities it opens, and the responsibilities it entails are at the core of my last case study.

Anjela: Sketching Multispecies Stories and Histories of Contemporary Brittany

This last section turns to perhaps the most emblematic of Brittany's female naturalcultural figures, the Brittophone peasant-poet Anjela Duval, as she is reimagined in Christelle Le Guen's 2018 bilingual comic, in which Breton shifts from being a graphic language symbolizing defiance to one of creation.[14] Rather than an adaptation of Duval's poetry or a biography, *Anjela* is an adaptive patchwork of letters and poems forming a first-person narrative. It was published by the association Mignoned Anjela ("Anjela's Friends"), who chose the comics medium for its accessibility as well as its potential to "give life to Anjela's very own words in Breton and French," as part of their aim to preserve and promote her writings. Duval is an important figure in Brittany, along with other women such as the storyteller Marc'harit Fulup

---

14. For a discussion of language in *Anjela* from a postcolonial perspective, see Blin-Rolland ("Breton").

and the singers the Goadec sisters, who are remembered as the "last voices of a disappeared peasant society, last witnesses of a particular relationship to nature and culture" (Thomas 19–20). Duval's poetry reflects her engagement as a Breton nationalist and an "eco-warrior" (Timm, "Eco-Warrior"), a militant for a country that she had seen flourishing and now drained, as she writes in a letter that closes the comic to the prosecutor in the trial of members of the underground independentist movement Front de la Libération de la Bretagne [Breton Liberation Front] (Duval and Le Guen 48–49).

Duval, who lived her whole life on the family farm in the Bro-Dreger/ Trégor province, saw Brittany undergo not only a language shift[15] but also an agricultural shift toward an agro-industrial model. *Anjela* features powerful images of intensive farming with people in hazmat suits and animals trapped in confined environments. This production-driven, exploitative relationship to the nonhuman is evocatively described by the peasant-poet as "a kind of prostitution" (22–23), a phrasing with connotations of unequal gender power relations and one that gestures toward an understanding of human-nonhuman relations in bodily terms. This sense of corporeality is seen again, this time with loving undertones, in "Barzhonegoú-noz— Barzhonegoú-deiz" [Night Poems—Day Poems], where Duval's creative engagement with the land as a peasant and as a poet "matterphorically" (Cohen and Duckert) becomes an erotic encounter with Brittany itself (Duval and Le Guen 37). Nature and nation fuse in the textual image of a woman planting seeds in and creating *with* an earthy body. This earthy body is gendered as male by the French language in Paol Keineg's translation: "celui que j'aime" [the one I love] agrees with the male word for country in the verse below. The Breton is more ambiguous, less unequivocally heterosexual, as the one who is loved in "an hini a garan" could grammatically be male or female, and the word for country is feminine. We find our image of the land as body again, but one whose gender is potentially fluid across languages, and one, crucially, that is fleshy and living.

How does the comic redraw this aliveness and corporeality of the environment and more-than-human entanglements? I already touched upon the idea of nature's graphic texture in relation to *Brigande!*, and in *Anjela* it becomes the matter with which the text is made, as the quasi-palpable strokes of this drawn black-and-white world evoke and recreate the "inter-texturity"

---

15. As Fañch Broudic notes in his 2007 sociolinguistic history of Breton, across the twentieth century Breton shifted from a majority to a minority language in Lower Brittany (the area where it is traditionally spoken), with an estimated 85 percent fall in the number of speakers between the 1950s and the late 1990s (18).

(Lestel) of the human and nonhuman.[16] This line-based texture means that this comic may be productively thought of as, rather than a network of "connectable points," a "meshwork" of "interwoven lines," as theorized by Tim Ingold, in which "every organism—indeed, every thing—is itself an entanglement" (1806). In the intertextual meshwork of *Anjela*, linework therefore takes on "narrative" (Miers) *and* ecological properties, rendering the porosity of the more-than-human rather than the clear outlines of separate beings.

The chapter entitled "Ar c'hleuz" / "Le talus" [The Hedge] (30–33) enables us to explore more closely the graphic transposition of the liveliness of nature and its creative and destructive entanglements with the human. The titular hedge is about to be bulldozed, as was common during the land consolidation process. The text of Duval's poem is narrated from the perspective of the hedge, language articulating its thoughts and emotions, voice forming its body, as in "my back full of thorns" and "on my head my bramble hair." The images do not represent a humanized hedge, but a textured ecosystem with thorns, bramble, and bird forming bundles and knots of entangled lines. On the adjacent page the "great devil" that is the bulldozer rips the bank up, and the layout of horizontally elongated panels, as if stretching rhizomatically (Deleuze and Guattari 9–37) with the hedge, turns vertical, echoing a hierarchical understanding of human-nonhuman relations. In the image the bulldozer is not red as in the text but a solid, deep black, and its defined, sharp spikes contrast with the porous boundaries of the hedge that it is ravaging.

On the next double page, the poem closes with the hedge's soul floating in the dust that is all that remains of it, turning into a cloud carried by the wind to "the heaven of old hedges," a phrasing that clearly draws on Duval's Catholicism but pictures a nonhuman afterlife. In the images, this process is represented not through explicit religious imagery but by a bird turning into a flock, flying high above the ground. On the adjacent page, Duval is drawn thinking about the title she is to give her poetry collection, *Kan an douar* [The Song of The Land]. Through the copresence of the poem and its creative process, and images that stylize rather than humanize the hedge, the graphic version of "Ar c'hleuz" draws the anthropomorphism of the text as something more and something other than a projection of the human onto the nonhuman. It is an act of imagination, neither in a sense of a human injection of meaning and life into inert nonhuman matter nor a way to erase difference but rather a creative reconfiguration of the hedge's own agency. As such, it calls upon the reader to, in turn, see the hedge not

---

16. Lestel is talking specifically of human and nonhuman animals.

as a single, clearly delimited self but as an entangled ecosystem that is alive precisely *as* a hedge that therefore can be killed. This is poetic anthropomorphism but one that arguably goes beyond anthropocentrism to point us toward the "multispecies histories" (Haraway, *When Species Meet* 23) that form the land of Brittany.

Across the intertextured meshwork of the comic, the reader may follow or trace a line back to the double page that I have already mentioned on intensive farming, where bundles of lines are forcefully straightened—in the rows into which pigs and cows are crammed, the geometrical shapes of vast fields, the barriers all around the animals, the comics frames acting as borders between people and cattle (23). The consequences of devaluing the nonhuman, of seeing it as a resource to be exploited, are probably already known to *Anjela*'s readers. The destruction of hedges has led to water pollution, soil erosion, inundations, and loss of biodiversity. As a result of the pollution of the soil and sea through intensive farming, toxic algae regularly cover Breton coasts with deadly consequences, as redrawn in the comic *Algues vertes, l'histoire interdite* [Green Algae, the Forbidden Story], which confronts readers with landscapes of clashing colors, corpses of blue dogs and purple boars on beaches turned bright green (Léraud and Van Hove 18, 54). Read across the text and context, anthropomorphism in "Ar c'hleuz" is therefore not only imaginative but also "strategic" in the way that it "[gives] matter access to articulation" (Iovino 82), narrative and ecological properties of linework and of word and image combining in the creative-destructive story of an entangled hedge as part and parcel of Brittany's more-than-human narratives.

And if the boundaries between the human and nonhuman are in fact porous, what might this mean in turn for the human self? It means that she is a "tissue of knots" (Ingold 11) too, a bundle of lines, embodied and entangled. We see Duval's lined face in close-up and her shoulders rounded by effort in silhouette (10–11); we see her make lines, scribbled on paper (14, 39) and furrowed into the land (33, 37). The comic already productively decenters and multiplies the "I" of the text, as an album that is not "straightforwardly" an adaptation, an (auto)biography, or a translation but a bilingual adaptive patchwork that pieces together a first-person narrative woven out of different texts. The "I" that emerges is also one that sees no firm divide between her human self and the nonhuman, in a comic where a hedge can have bramble hair and a woman can be a fern or "ur radenenn" (2). The opening double page, on which we find this articulation of the self as vegetal, shows Anjela as a child, picking up an insect and laying it on a book, and older Anjela the poet as if looking back, forming a self/portrait of the author as an ecographic woman, drawn by another, and entangled with the other-than-human.

That the album opens with Duval as a reader leads us to think in turn about the human self of the comic's reader and to think ecologically about the cocreative part she may play.[17] It is not that *Anjela* is a "hard" comic to read, but it is a slow one and an open one in which the small amount of text, its often poetic tone, and the texture of the images encourage the reader to combine attention to narrative progression with looking around, (re-)tracing lines across its meshwork. Thinking of the reader as an ecographic cocreator means sharing the "optimistic conviction" that encounters with artworks can "constitute *meaningful* entanglements" with the nonhuman (Garrard 12; Alaimo, "Feminist"). The reader's experience of nature in *Anjela* is mediated through a peasant-poet's own subjective experience as it is reimagined through an art form of hybridity and relationality. It is an encounter that, for the reader, may develop what I would call her "visual ecoliteracy" in text and image, and here also importantly in more than one language. "Ecoliteracy" is a term that has been criticized as too all-encompassing to be useful (McBride et al.), but with its focus on reading, it is suggestive here to think about what visual texts can do and what reader-comic-environment assemblages may form. In the graphic treatment of its subject matter, *Anjela* may point the reader's eye and attention toward the intertextured meshwork of her own world; her own self as a tissue of knots; and the ethical responsibilities, creative-destructive implications, and possibilities for becoming-with that being part of an entangled more-than-human world entails.

Duval's profound sensitivity toward nature in her writings, and her life led on the land and as an independent single woman, have seen her hailed as "an ecological poet before her time" (Timm, "Eco-Warrior") and a woman "ahead of the times" (Le Coadic). Yet as Nelly Blanchard and Mannaig Thomas argue, Duval's iconic status has tended to overshadow or detract from her "obstination in fighting against all societal changes," in particular the fact that her ecological and political commitments for Brittany were combined with conservative positions on gendered issues such as childcare and abortion (45). While Lenora A. Timm rightly points out that readers in search of "overt feminist themes in Duval's poetry will be disappointed" ("Introduction" 30), it has long been clear that nature and nation, the peasant-poet's two key themes, have not somehow existed somewhere outside the realm of gender and are also feminist matters. *Anjela*, a bilingual, woman-authored graphic narrative about an older woman who is defined neither as wife, widow, nor mother, is a text that clearly stands out in the comics landscape

---

17. On the comics reader as cocreator, see, for instance, Balcaen (8).

of Brittany. Moreover, in its ecographic exploration of Duval, *Anjela* redraws the land as a naturalcultural ground that is, importantly, neither fixed nor inert. Adapting Duval and reading *Anjela* may therefore perhaps lead us to think of the dissolution of the human-nonhuman divide and the refusal of a hierarchization of languages and cultures, to trouble binary thinking further, and to trace new lines to cast an outlook on Brittany that productively entangles the environmental, the minor, and the feminist.

Conclusion

In this chapter I have used Breton comics as a lens through which to explore entanglements of women and natures at the crossroads of discourses of femininity, nature/the rural and identity, and more-than-human landscapes and narratives. I have placed Brittany at the center—rather than at the periphery—because the comics medium played an important role in its construction as France's folkloric, feminized, and rural internal Other and due to the recent emergence of women artists in the green-blue graphics that have been part and parcel of the Breton comics field since the 1970s. As such, it is a fruitful locus for the ways in which it makes clear the relevance and necessity of a feminist perspective in ecographics. Entanglement is a term that emphasizes the inseparability of the human and the nonhuman, and it is, I believe, a productive way to bring comics more firmly into these debates because it has evocative textile/textual connotations and relationality at its core. As Posthumus argues, an ecological reading does not aim "to reduce the literary text to a single, political message, but instead attend to its multiple discursive and thematic threads" (158). Reading comics ecologically means dis- and re-entangling knots of nature and culture, exploring the ways in which graphic narratives redraw discourses about the environment, their intertwinements with social categories and ingrained binaries, nonhuman agency, and more-than-human relations and transformations. Interactions between words, images, lines, colors, and frames have led us to consider feminist and environmental questions of landscape, bodies, performativity, toxicity, and agency. As graphic spaces of potentially multiple perspectives, comics may dis- and reassemble gender-nature and human-nonhuman configurations, offer (Breton women) images beyond stereotypes, and suggest modes of becoming that interweave rather than demarcate nature and culture.

A glance at winners of Artémisia prizes in the last few years shows that nature is a subject matter that is being explored by more and more women authors in widely different genres and approaches, including Claire Malary's

2018 *Hallali* (which was published by the Rennes/Rhoazon-based collective L'Oeuf, of which Rouxel is a part), Catherine Meurisse's 2018 *Les grands espaces* [The Great Outdoors], Linnea Serte's 2019 *In-Humus*, as well as Anne Defréville's 2019 *L'âge bleu* [The Blue Age] and Lison Ferné's 2019 *La déesse requin* [The Shark Goddess], which were respectively awarded the "prix de l'environnement" and "prix écologie." While the *bande dessinée* canon is certainly ripe for ecological rereadings, these contemporary albums are signs that comic art has a role to play in the urgent task of placing a renewed focus on creativity at the intersection of nature and culture at a time when it is becoming harder to think of our relationship to the environment as something other than destructive. And in an ecographics that attends to graphic entanglements of the human and nonhuman, women's experiences and engagements with nature are not peripheral but integral to the local and global more-than-human narratives of our world.

Works Cited

Alaimo, Stacy. *Bodily Natures: Science, Environment, and the Material Self.* Indiana UP, 2010.

———. "Feminist Science Studies and Ecocriticism: Aesthetics and Entanglement in the Deep Sea." *The Oxford Handbook of Ecocriticism*, edited by Greg Garrard, Oxford UP, 2014, pp. 188–204.

———. "Trans-Corporeal Feminisms and the Ethical Space of Nature." *Material Feminisms*, edited by Stacy Alaimo and Susan Hekman, Indiana UP, 2008, pp. 237–64.

———. *Undomesticated Ground: Recasting Nature as Feminist Space.* Cornell UP, 2000.

Alaimo, Stacy, and Susan Hekman. "Introduction: Emerging Models of Materiality in Feminist Theory." *Material Feminisms*, edited by Stacy Alaimo and Susan Hekman, Indiana UP, 2008, pp. 1–19.

Baetens, Jan. "From Black & White to Color and Back: What Does It Mean (Not) to Use Color?" *College Literature*, vol. 38, no. 3, 2011, pp. 111–28.

Balcaen, Alexandre. *Manifeste.* Adverse, 2016.

Barad, Karen. *Meeting the Universe Halfway: Quantum Physics and the Entanglement of Matter and Meaning.* Duke UP, 2007.

Barry, John. "Resistance Is Fertile: From Environmental to Sustainable Citizenship." *Environmental Citizenship*, edited by Andrew Dobson and Derek Bell, MIT Press, 2005, pp. 49–74.

Blanchard, Nelly, and Mannaig Thomas. "Entre sous-représentation et sur-investissement: Les femmes dans la littérature de langue bretonne." *Bretonnes? Des identités au carrefour du genre, de la culture et du territoire*, edited by Arlette Gautier and Yvonne Guichard-Claudic, Rennes UP, 2016, pp. 35–50.

Blin-Rolland, Armelle. "A Breton *Bande Dessinée*? Graphic Mosaics of Brittany." *Nottingham French Studies*, vol. 60, no. 2, 2021, pp. 254–71.

———. "Towards an Ecographics: Ecological Storylines in *Bande Dessinée*." *European Comic Art*, vol. 15, no. 2, 2022, pp. 107–31.

———. "'Tu te décolonises': Comics Re-framings of the Breton Liberation Front (FLB)." *Studies in Comics*, vol. 10, no. 1, 2019, pp. 73–91.

Broudic, Fañch. "Langue bretonne: Un siècle de mutations." *International Journal of the Sociology of Language*, vol. 2013, no. 223, 2013, pp. 7–21.

Butler, Judith. *Notes Toward a Performative Theory of Assembly*. Harvard UP, 2015.

Caumery, and J. P. Pinchon. *L'enfance de Bécassine*. 1913. Gautier-Languerau, 1991.

Chute, Hillary. *Graphic Women: Life Narrative and Contemporary Comics*. Columbia UP, 2010.

Cohen, Jeffrey Jerome, and Lowell Duckert. "Introduction: Welcome to the Whirled." *Veer Ecology: A Companion for Environmental Thinking*, edited by Jeffrey Jerome Cohen and Lowell Duckert, U of Minnesota P, 2017, pp. 1–15.

Conan, Renée, and Annie Laurent. *Femmes de Plogoff*. 1981. La Digitale, 2010.

Deleuze, Gilles, and Félix Guattari. *Mille plateaux: Capitalisme et schizophrénie*. Minuit, 1980.

Duval, Anjela, and Christelle Le Guen. *Anjela*. Pollina/Mignoned Anjela, 2018.

Evain, Brice. "La seconde vie de Marion du Faouët." *Annales de Bretagne et des pays de l'ouest*, vol. 121, no. 1, 2014, http://journals.openedition.org/abpo/2731.

Flinn, Margaret C. "Popular *Terroir*: Bande Dessinée as Pastoral Ecocriticism?" *Studies in 20th & 21st Century Literature*, vol. 43, no. 1, 2018, pp. 1–21, https://doi.org/10.4148/2334-4415.2041.

Forsdick, Charles. "Exoticising the Domestique: Bécassine, Brittany and the Beauty of the Dead." *The Francophone Bande Dessinée*, edited by Charles Forsdick, Laurence Grove, and Libbie McQuillan, Rodopi, 2005, pp. 23–36.

Fraser, Benjamin. *The Art of Pere Joan: Space, Landscape, and Comics Form*. U of Texas P, 2019.

Fresnault-Deruelle, Pierre. "Du linéaire au tabulaire." *Communications*, vol. 24, 1976, pp. 7–23.

Garrard, Greg, editor. *The Oxford Handbook of Ecocriticism*. Oxford UP, 2014.

Gautier, Arlette, and Yvonne Guichard-Claudic. *Bretonnes? Des identités au carrefour de genre, de la culture et du territoire*. Rennes UP, 2016.

Groensteen, Thierry. "Paysage." *NeuvièmeArt 2.0*, 2012, http://neuviemeart.citebd.org/spip.php?article803.

———. *The System of Comics*. Translated by Bart Beaty and Nick Nguyen, UP of Mississippi, 2007.

———. *Système de la bande dessinée*. Presses Universitaires de France, 1999.

Grove, Laurence. *Text/Image Mosaics in French Culture: Emblems and Comics Strips*. Ashgate, 2005.

Haraway, Donna J. *The Companion Species Manifesto: Dogs, People, and Significant Otherness*. Prickly Paradigm Press, 2003.

———. *When Species Meet*. U of Minnesota P, 2008.

Hatfield, Charles. *Alternative Comics: An Emerging Literature*. UP of Mississippi, 2005.

Herman, David, editor. *Animal Comics: Multispecies Storyworlds in Graphic Narratives*. Bloomsbury, 2018.

Ingold, Tim. "Bindings against Boundaries: Entanglements of Life in an Open World." *Environment and Planning A: Economy and Space*, vol. 40, no. 8, 2008, pp. 1796–810.

Iovino, Serenella. "The Living Diffractions of Matter and Text: Narrative Agency, Strategic Anthropomorphism, and How Interpretation Works." *Anglia*, vol. 133, no. 1, 2015, pp. 69–86.

Iovino, Serenella, and Serpil Oppermann, editors. *Material Ecocriticism*. Indiana UP, 2014.

Jouitteau, Mélanie. "Bretagne et féminisme, quarante ans à traîner des pieds." *Le peuple Breton / Pobl Vreizh*, no. 670, 2019, pp. 10–12.

King, Edward, and Joanna Page, editors. *Posthumanism and the Graphic Novel in Latin America*. UCL Press, 2017.

King, Ynestra. "The Ecology of Feminism and the Feminism of Ecology." *Healing the Wounds: The Power of Ecological Feminism*, edited by Judith Plant, New Society Publisher, 1989, pp. 19–28.

Kristeva, Julia. *Semiotike: Recherches pour une sémanalyse*. Seuil, 1969.

Le Coadic, Ronan. "Anjela Duval aujourd'hui." *Anjela.org*, 2020, https://www.anjela.org/oberenn/anjela-duval-aujourdhui/.

Le Doujet, Corentin. "BD: Laëtitia Rouxel dégaine *Brigande!*" *Le télégramme*, 18 June 2019, https://www.letelegramme.fr/soir/reserve-telegramme-soir-bd-laetitia-rouxel-degaine-brigande-18-06-2019-12314624.php.

Le Lay, Delphine, and Alexis Horellou. *Plogoff*. Delcourt, 2013.

Léraud, Inès, and Pierre Van Hove. *Algues vertes: L'histoire interdite*. La Revue Dessinée / Delcourt, 2019.

Lestel, Dominique. "Like the Fingers of the Hand: Thinking the Human in the Texture of Animality." Translated by Matthew Chrulew and Jeffrey Bussolini. *French Thinking about Animals*, edited by Louisa MacKenzie and Stephanie Posthumus, Michigan State UP, 2015, pp. 61–73.

MacGregor, Sherilyn. *Beyond Mothering Earth: Ecological Citizenship and the Politics of Care*. UBC Press, 2006.

McBride, B. B., et al. "Environmental Literacy, Ecological Literacy, Ecoliteracy: What Do We Mean and How Did We Get Here?" *Ecosphere*, vol. 4, no. 5, 2013, https://doi.org/10.1890/ES13-00075.1.

Michon, Roland, and Laëtitia Rouxel. *Brigande! Marion du Faouët: Vie, amours et mort*. Locus Solus, 2019.

Miers, John. "Depiction and Demarcation in Comics: Toward an Account of the Medium as a Drawing Practice." *Studies in Comics*, vol. 6, no. 1, 2015, pp. 145–56.

Mignoned Anjela. "Mignoned Anjela Is Celebrating 20 Years of Work!" *Anjela.org*, 2018, https://www.anjela.org/oberenn/?lang=en.

Miller, Ann. "Consensus and Dissensus in *Bande Dessinée*." *Yale French Studies*, no. 131–32, 2017, pp. 109–37.

Porhel, Vincent. "Genre, environnement et conflit à Plogoff (1980)." *Genre & Histoire*, no. 22, 2018, http://journals.openedition.org/genrehistoire/3757.

Posthumus, Stephanie. *French Écocritique: Reading Contemporary French Theory and Fiction Ecologically*. U of Toronto P, 2017.

Rancière, Jacques. *The Emancipated Spectator*. Translated by Gregory Elliott, Verso, 2009.

———. *Le spectateur émancipé*. La Fabrique, 2008.

Rose, Gillian. *Feminism and Geography: The Limits of Geographical Knowledge.* U of Minnesota P, 1993.

Sharp, Joanne P., et al. "Entanglements of Power: Geographies of Domination/Resistance." *Entanglements of Power: Geographies of Domination/Resistance,* edited by Joanne P. Sharp et al., Routledge, 2000, pp. 1–42.

Simon, Gilles. *Plogoff: L'apprentissage de la mobilisation sociale.* Presses Universitaires de Rennes, 2010.

Stephens, John, and Robyn McCallum. *Retelling Stories, Framing Culture: Traditional Story and Metanarratives in Children's Literature.* Garland, 1998.

Thomas, Mannaig. "Anjela Duval *est* la Bretagne?" *Dire la Bretagne,* edited by Nelly Blanchard and Mannaig Thomas, Presses Universitaires de Rennes, 2016, pp. 19–22.

Timm, Lenora A. "Brittany's Eco-Warrior: The Environmental Poetry of Anjela Duval." *Anjela.org,* 2017, https://www.anjela.org/oberenn/brittanys-eco-warrior-the-environmental-poetry-of-anjela-duval-lenora-a-timm/?lang=en.

———. "Introduction." *A Modern Breton Political Poet: Anjela Duval; A Biography and an Anthology,* edited and translated by Lenora A. Timm, Edwin Meller Press, 1990, pp. 1–24.

Williams, Heather. *Postcolonial Brittany: Literature between Languages.* Peter Lang, 2007.

Wylie, John. *Landscape.* Routledge, 2007.

CHAPTER 6

The Feminine Plural in Africa and the Diaspora

Quartets of Women in *Aya de Yopougon* and *La vie d'Ebène Duta*

MICHELLE BUMATAY

If, as the chapters in this anthology suggest, women's role in the cultural field of French-language comics has long been overlooked and understated, one can argue that it is even more so the case for minority women, though this has been changing in the last two decades (McKinney, "Representation"; MacLeod). This chapter aims to highlight the diversity of contemporary female cartoonists by focusing on the work of two women creators originally from Francophone West Africa by comparing the series *Aya de Yopougon* with *La vie d'Ebène Duta*. *Aya de Yopougon,* an ongoing series (2005–10, 2022) is written by Franco-Ivorian author Marguerite Abouet and illustrated by French artist Clément Oubrerie. Though very much a collaborative effort, many downplay Oubrerie's contributions in favor of highlighting Abouet's voice. While it is not my intention to do the same, especially considering that the series' artwork—Oubrerie's contribution—is fundamental to the verisimilitude of the series, for the purposes of this chapter, I will focus on Abouet's narrative decisions (from volumes 1 to 6) since the series' concept

---

I would like to express my thanks to the staff of the Billy Ireland Cartoon Library and Museum and to Maggie Flinn for their work in bringing this volume to press.

stems from her memories.[1] Abouet was born in 1971 and grew up in Abidjan, the economic capital of the Ivory Coast, until the age of twelve when her parents sent her and her brother to live with relatives in France. Originally, she planned to write about her childhood, and she and Oubrerie pitched the idea to editors at the prestigious French publisher Gallimard, who suggested that they age the main character for marketability (D'Almeida). The result, the first volume of *Aya de Yopougon*, launched Gallimard's newly created Bayou collection dedicated to *bandes dessinées* under the leadership of celebrated cartoonist Joann Sfar. Whereas Abouet was born soon after Ivorian independence, Joëlle Epée Mandengue, better known as Elyon's, was born over two decades after Cameroonian independence in Bafoussam. Furthermore, in contrast to Abouet, Elyon's grew up in Cameroon and only lived in Liège, Belgium, while attending art school. In 2009, while a student, she developed the character Ebène Duta on her BD blog. Thanks to crowdfunding, she transformed the blog into a book in 2014 with the first volume of *La vie d'Ebène Duta* (Irène).

As cultural objects, these two series are distinctly different; published as a flagship series in Gallimard's Bayou collection, *Aya de Yopougon* is a high-quality mass-produced collaborative production whereas the blog-to-book *La vie d'Ebène Duta* is a fan-funded self-publishing project. While the former involves subplots and takes time to explore various themes, the latter mobilizes repetition and variation through titled one-page vignettes that often end with a comedic punchline or ironic zinger. Additionally, Abouet and Elyon's represent different generations. Though both series take place after decolonization, *Aya de Yopougon* starts in 1978 at the height of the Ivory Coast's postindependence economic boom, and *La vie d'Ebène Duta* is set in the contemporary moment but centers on Africans living outside of Africa. In spite of these differences, both series challenge Western stereotypes about Africa and Africans and employ similar narrative and textual approaches at the heart of which are questions of gender, sexuality, urban life, and the pursuit of happiness.

Though both series explore a vast range of engaging topics and employ nuanced artwork to combat what Mark McKinney refers to as the "colonial heritage" of French-language comics, for the purposes of this chapter, I am interested in how these series mobilize a quartet of female friends to explore the range of African women's responses to and interactions with

---

1. I discuss in more nuance Oubrerie's contributions and their impact on how *Aya de Yopougon* is framed in "*Aya de Yopougon*: Gender and Identity Formation in the Ivory Coast and in France" in *African Francophone Bandes Dessinées: Graphic Autobiographies and Illustrated Testimonies*.

their respective societies and cultures (McKinney, *Colonial Heritage* 7–8). *Aya de Yopougon* has been likened to the hit HBO television series *Sex and the City* (Harris; McWilliams), and one could easily make a similar comparison for *La vie d'Ebène Duta*; yet the postcolonial context of these two series facilitates a much more complex set of situations and issues around gender than those faced by the group of high-powered New Yorkers. To be sure, four young women spending time discussing their aspirations and love lives has, since the late 1990s, been a popular and a productive vehicle for destabilizing monolithic portrayals of women as little more than objects of desire. This easily recognizable and oft-imitated quartet of female friends stems from HBO's *Sex and the City*, which debuted in June 1998 and ran for six seasons.[2] Capitalizing on the growing popularity of chick lit, *Sex and the City*, Deborah Jermyn argues, "engag[ed] with contemporary third-wave feminist politics" in its formulaic structure and remixing of literary and cinematic precursors (3). For Jermyn, "it was precisely through its quartet of deliberately contrasting, diverse female 'types,' their never-ending analysis of their condition, and Carrie's continual return to the questions that consume them that *Sex and the City* declared its preoccupation with the politics of women's choice(s) at the start of a new millennium" (4). While it is undoubtedly limiting to reduce *Aya de Yopougon* and *La vie d'Ebène Duta* to little more than imitations of *Sex and the City*, such a comparison generates insight into the different preoccupations of African women in postindependence Ivory Coast and African women's experience of the diaspora.

Aya de Yopougon: Yop City, African Modernity, Intertextuality, and Self-Fashioning

Though the title of Abouet and Oubrerie's series is *Aya de Yopougon* (referred to hereafter as *Aya*) and though the covers of the first three albums and the

---

2. In 2016, HBO premiered *Insecure*, created by Issa Rae and Larry Wilson, which once again takes up the popular premise of a quartet of female friends; however, *Insecure* focuses on Black women in Los Angeles and, like *Aya* and *LVDD*, foregrounds the intersectionality of women's identities and explores how this impacts their self-fashioning and interpersonal relationships. Interestingly, HBO also green-lighted Robin Thede's *A Black Lady Sketch Show* in 2019 (coproduced by Thede and Rae) and one of the recurring sketches parodies the female quartet. Initially framed as four Black women friends on a sleepover, subsequent sketches across the three seasons ramp up the absurdity of the friends' supposed situation. At first, the women seem to be the sole survivors of an unexplained apocalypse; due to cast changes from season one to season two, one of the members changes (Skye Townsend replaces Quinta Brunson); and at one point, the quartet are transformed into Muppet versions of themselves.

larger font for Aya's name on every cover suggest that the series closely follows Aya's life, it quickly becomes clear that the setting of Yopougon is an equally central character; put another way, to tell the tale of Aya and her friends is to tell the tale of their specific context and community. The series initially presents as a melodrama focused on the love lives of Aya and her close female friends (Adjoua, Bintou, and Félicité) at the height of the economic boom and modernization known as the Ivorian miracle, but by the second volume and even within the first, the narrative expands outward to other characters, locations, and plot points. In fact, Aya's distaste for drama and her abstention from situations that could produce gossip mean that her plotline and presence are initially rather subdued but pick up when the series shifts to more serious themes in the third volume.[3] Rather, Aya often functions more as a plot device, simultaneously the central kernel to the growing cast of characters and a sympathetic life coach upholding morals and personal growth for herself, friends, and family. This positioning of Aya as the narrative glue can be read in the sepia-toned opening sequence when her voiceover delays her own introduction, a strategy that subsequently places her closest to the description of her neighborhood, affectionately referred to as "Yop City" in imitation of American films. In contradistinction to the almost family-less quartet in *Sex and the City*, the expansion of the cast in *Aya* indicates the importance of family and intergenerational connections as integral to the fabric of everyday life in Yopougon.

Abouet and Oubrerie point to this expansion through two-page schematics in the front matter for volumes 2 through 6; these visualizations of narrative content, beyond offering quick recaps, provide insight into the range of familial structures and hint at the complex ways in which individuals participated in Ivorian modernization. The frontmatter of the second volume is a double-page "cast of characters"[4] featuring portraits and relationships of the households of Aya, Adjoua, Bintou, and young men of interest; Mamadou (at this point in the narrative with no known relations); and Moussa with his parents. Embedded in this schematic are subtle indicators of the socioeconomic mobility characteristic of Youpougon as a popular urban neighborhood, a middle ground between more rural villages and the wealthier, cosmopolitan regions of Abidjan. For example, Félicité, Aya's family's maid, becomes an important character and completes the quartet with Aya, Adjoua, and Bintou. Though she is presented as "la bonne" and does not share the same educational path as the other three women, Aya and her family consider her to be part of their family. Through Félicité's

---

3. For more on how the focus of the series shifts, see Leslie Goufo Zemmo.
4. Unless otherwise noted, all translations are my own.

plotline (like that of her male counterpart, Hervé, who is Bintou's cousin), Abouet demonstrates that at the story's time of rapid modernization, one's socioeconomic origins and level of education were not the sole indicators of social mobility and success. Indeed, it is both comedic and telling that, on the one hand, it is the soft-spoken and shy Félicité who is the only woman from the quartet chosen as a finalist of the Miss Yopougon contest and, on the other, that Hervé, who does not ostensibly stand a chance in competing for women's attention when compared with the handsome Mamadou, succeeds (with Aya's encouragement) at the garage where he works, eventually becoming the owner and therefore desirable. In the fourth and fifth volumes, readers learn that both Félicité and Hervé come from humble beginnings and were born in villages outside Abidjan. When returning home to present baby Aya to his village chief as per tradition, Ignace (Aya's father) runs into an old friend, Zékinan, who has fallen on hard times and who ignores his own daughter, Félicité. Young Félicité helps calm baby Aya, and Aya's parents decide to take her with them, for which Zékinan demands an exchange of goods despite not caring for or looking after Félicité. Hervé's past equally involves an economic transaction. Hervé's backstory is devastatingly tragic though lightened and rendered somewhat comedic when told in his simple and rather matter-of-fact way of speaking. In response to Hervé's mother dying after giving birth, Hervé's father left him with his grandmother who died shortly thereafter. Once reunited with his father, his father's new wife puts Hervé to work. When their cousin Koffi (Bintou's father) shows up to take Hervé off their hands, the new wife demands compensation for all that she is giving up in terms of domestic labor.

What the examples of Félicité and Hervé demonstrate is Abouet's intelligent balance between humor and drama, particularly when it comes to combatting Western stereotypes about life in Africa. Abouet's narrative neither engages in a polemic about polygamy nor casts characters—women and men alike—as "contained within, and restricted by, this binary axis . . . between 'traditional' socio-cultural expectations and 'modern' ideologies," as did the narratives of many early African Francophone women writers (Hitchcott 20). Rather, through the large cast of characters, the series explores the complex ways in which individuals navigate a moment of change. A prime example of this is found in Aya's mother, Fanta, who is described on the second page of the series as both an assistant director at the Singer company and a healer. That Fanta successfully maintains these two careers no doubt serves as a model for Aya who wants to become a doctor—a decision that blends her mother's traditional occupation with professionalization through higher education. Even though the love lives of the main female quartet drive the narrative in the first volume, already by the second volume, Aya's female friends, like her, are equally driven towards personal success independent of men: Adjoua, after giving birth and deciding not to marry Moussa or Mamadou (dramatically revealed to be the baby's biological father), opens her own *maquis* (an open air restaurant-bar); Bintou first runs a dating advice booth then successfully auditions to be a backup dancer for Alpha Blondy on the television show "Super Star Station"; and after being named runner-up for the Miss Yopougon competition, Félicité becomes a spokesmodel. Though we might consider these successes evidence of Abouet's take on African feminism, it is important to remember that "until recently, the reference points for Western feminist and African women activists have been totally different, because Western women were emphasizing individual female autonomy, while African women have been emphasizing culturally linked forms of public participation" (Mikell 4). Ultimately, the core female characters support one another and form strong bonds that assist them in successfully overcoming serious (if serially dramatized) issues, including unplanned pregnancies, child-rearing, rape, corruption, cheating partners, potential conflicts resulting from polygamy, kidnapping, and blackmail.

While male characters are just as important as female characters in *Aya*, textual homages to other feminine series and genres as well as in-text cultural allusions reveal a preoccupation with the role of media in the Ivory Coast as a key tool for self-fashioning. First, while the front matter of volumes 3 and 4 expand and update the cast of characters' schematic, the front matter of the fifth and sixth volumes offers a kaleidoscope of scenes from the previous volume titled "Previously on *Aya de Yopougon* . . ." in imitation of television series' recaps. Instead of *Sex and the City*, a closer comparison and an actual in-text allusion is to the American soap opera *Dallas*, which premiered the same year as the start of *Aya* (1978). As Marla Harris points out, quoting Deborah Kaspin, such uses of Western cultures in *Aya* demonstrates how individuals' appropriation strategies speak to their own situations and interests (123). Economic prosperity and its attendant social mobility rendered the wealthy Ewings of *Dallas* aspirational role models (Adjoua even names her son Bobby after Bobby Ewing). Second, at one point in the fourth volume, Abouet and Oubrerie insert a short two-page photo-roman diagonally framed by two diegetic panels showing Bintou's dating advice booth (figure 6.1). This intermedial shift is not, as Harris suggests, "borrowed from Italian popular culture," or at least not directly (123). Rather, it operates as a *clin d'oeil* to West African women readers who would be familiar with such photo-romans featured in West African women's magazines dating back to the 1950s such as *Bingo: L'illustré africain: revue mensuelle de l'activité noire*

FIGURE 6.1. Left-hand page of two-page spread featuring an intermedial shift to a photo-roman typical of West African Francophone glossy magazines such as *Bingo* and *Amina*. Marguerite Abouet and Clément Oubrerie, *Aya de Yopougon,* volume 4, 2008, p. 22.

(established in 1953), *AWA: La revue de la femme noire* (established in 1964), and *Amina* (founded in 1972). The inserted photo-roman casts Bintou as part of the readership of such glossy magazines while demonstrating their prevalence, popularity, and power as important interlocutors in the fashioning of one's identity.

Recent research by Ruth Bush on *AWA* and Tsitsi Jaji on *Bingo* about the importance of such magazines as crucial sites for the exploration of African modernity and identity construction, especially for African women, sheds light on the narrative and textual strategies at work in *Aya* beyond the photo-roman insert. First, *Aya*'s emphasis on African feminine plurality was previously the guiding principle of *AWA*, as Bush's analysis of the magazine's full title indicates; for Bush, the magazine's title "presents a singular, personified point of identification and aspiration" through metonymy but also "acts as a repository for multiple ideas regarding feminine identity in post-independence francophone Africa" (226). Second, according to Jaji, *Bingo* "displayed a global black consciousness entangled in aspirational consumption, performances of new national and gender identities, and multiple engagements with media" and translated such consciousness "into less elite forms, such as photo-comics, women's pages, reader competitions, personal ads in search of romance, consumer advertising, and the like" ("*Bingo* Magazine" 115). Additionally, *Bingo* facilitated up-to-date international exchanges by republishing "stories that had already circulated in Anglophone magazines, including *Drum, West African Review, Ebony*, and even *Esquire*" (113). Moreover, Jaji underlines how *Bingo* "placed gender at the heart of the projecting modernity" and "encouraged readers to imagine themselves as cultural producers, active participants" of such a project (116). As active participants, Jaji suggests that readers honed what she calls "sheen reading"—the process of "interpreting reflective surfaces whose distortions provided generative openings for improvisations of new identities"—and that such a skill transferred to everyday decisions (*Africa* 116). In *Aya*, this helps account for the many American pop cultural references that serve as touchstones for personal self-fashioning (Yop City, the Miss Yopougon competition, Innocent's adoption of Michael Jackson's style and his styling of African women à la Grace Jones). It also helps us reexamine the significance of *Aya*'s sepia-toned opening that features hallmarks of African modernity in the form of multiple modes of transportation (a man on a bike riding next to a bus), access to technology and electricity (the television and the telephone), and the indispensable importance of photography as a means to perform and demonstrate one's identity (the two framed photographs).

Lastly, another way in which *Aya* alludes to feminine genres is in the bonus section at the end of each volume ("Ivoirian Bonus") that shares local flavors with readers in the form of a lexicon of *nouchi* (Ivorian slang made popular in Abidjan in the 1970s) and recipes introduced by characters alongside tidbits of cultural knowledge about the Ivory Coast. Initially such tidbits teach readers about aspects of women's quotidian experiences but quickly move to more complex issues. This charming approach to cultural difference has even resulted in Abouet writing an actual cookbook, *Delicices d'Afrique*, laden with illustrations and anecdotes.[5] Ultimately, allusions to and imitations of *Sex and the City*, *Dallas*, and photo-roman, as well as the addition of recipes in the bonus section, are but some of the ways in which Abouet's narrative practices imitate her characters' identity-formation strategies.

LVDD: Repetition, Variation, and Comparison

Turning now to the three volumes of *La vie d'Ebène Duta* (referred to hereafter as *LVDD*), it is not surprising to find that recipes and food also play an important role in framing the series and serving as a means of exploring cultural difference, as evident from the back cover's tagline: "Take a spoon of bad luck, a pinch of misunderstandings, all sprinkled with dire straits. Leave to simmer and you get the diary of Ebène Duta, a young black girl living far from her homeland."[6] In contrast to the way *Aya* quickly moves beyond the love lives of the main quartet, *LVDD* revolves around Ebène's relationships through repetition and variation thus making it much more akin to *Sex and the City*. The covers of the three volumes generate a sense of the interpersonal relationships of the main quartet and their love interests. In each case, Ebène's Belgian counterparts flank her, suggesting comparative peers. In imitation of *Sex and the City*, the two Belgians are opposites: the naïve purple-haired Lulu repeatedly misunderstands sexual innuendos while the voluptuous and promiscuous Camille encourages Ebène's pursuit of sexual pleasure. The final member of the quartet, Claire, is repeatedly positioned vertically above Ebène. Claire, a cousin that Ebène had previously not met, arrives in Liège to stay with her while applying for internships. As another Cameroonian living abroad, Claire offers a different kind of counterpoint to

---

5. See Abouet and Maupré's *Delicices d'Afrique*. The blend of storytelling with recipes is a common feminine genre and, within the context of Francophone African female authors, echoes Calixthe Beyala's 2000 novel *Comment cuisine son mari à l'Africain* [How to Cook Your Husband the African Way] and Léonora Miano's 2009 collection of short stories *Soulfood équatoriale*.

6. Translation provided by the promotional tagline of the eBook English version of the first volume.

Ebène. While Lulu and Camille, sympathetic confidants, function as a kind of proxy for Western ignorance about Africa and cultural differences, Claire represents an alternative approach to diasporic life. Though the most petite of the quartet, Claire is portrayed as more experienced, calculating, and self-assured than any of the other women (figure 6.2).

The creation, development, and materialization of *LVDD* attest to the formation of Elyon's as a graphic artist, her digital savvy heavily influenced by her love of manga and anime and with an eye toward branding, and her recognition of her fans. For example, in addition to repeating a similar layout for each cover, each volume is color-coded to match up with the season setting of each volume (fall, spring, summer). Elyon's extends this playful approach to repetition and variation, offering her fans an abundance of her artwork and blurring the lines between the text and the paratext, as with other "BD girly" or "chick BD" that do not hide their online origins (Bozard 39). Each volume starts with a short scene featuring Ebène before announcing the season for each volume with chibi versions of the characters.[7] This is then followed by a separate title page on the back of which Elyon's offers a chibi version of herself at her desk—a self-stylized logo—and the dedication for each volume. At first, Elyon's thanks her Belgian roommate (volume 1), then all the people she encounters in her life (volume 2), and lastly, rather than a dedication, offers a Biblical citation: "'It is better to take refuge in the Lord than to trust in man' Psalms 188:8" (volume 3). It is worth underlining that Elyon's's personal faith becomes increasingly present by the third volume, which contrasts sharply with the premise of the third volume: Ebène's struggle to choose between Mathieu who accepts her as she is and Enzo who, while they were in a long-distance relationship, cheated on her and who encourages her to try to be sexier.

At its core, this series centers on Ebène's experience of the diaspora as a twenty-something. Elyon's playfully blends the everyday trials and tribulations of young women dating with key preoccupations of those living in the diaspora including microaggressions, structural racism, and cultural hybridity. As with the sepia-toned opening of *Aya*, the opening vignette of *LVDD*, entitled "Feeling Blue," introduces readers to Ebène and makes use of a TV show to establish the specific setting and introduce key themes. In contrast to Aya's slightly sarcastic narration, Ebène speaks aloud to no one

---

7. The manga term *chibi*, Japanese slang for "short," refers to a more simplistic and often cartoonish version of a character that typically increases the proportion of the character's head with regards to its body and exaggerates its facial expression. This shift in proportions connotes more child-like emotions and behaviors and is often used comedically.

FIGURE 6.2. All four women hang out at Lulu's apartment to react to Ebène's confession of having slept with Mathieu for the first time. Though the shortest, Ebène's cousin Claire dominates the scene offering her expert advice. Elyon's, *La Vie d'Ebène Duta*, volume 2, 2015, p. 69.

in particular and immediately starts with a curse word to complain about the fall weather in Belgium, effectively alerting readers to *LVDD*'s humor and rather mature content.[8] To cheer herself up, Ebène decides to watch TV and stumbles upon a special report titled "Go Back to Your Country!" In the middle strip, the bubbles for the out-of-frame television combined with Ebène's blushing face and oversized nervous sweat icon suggest that she feels as though she is being singled out by the report. The bottom strip features a panel in which Ebène appears both annoyed and relieved, saying that it was just a joke accompanied by what appears to be a manufactured screen shot of the report underneath which Elyon's includes a footnote to inform the reader that it was not a joke: "Contrary to appearances, this was a televised show released in 2010 on racial diversity and the acceptance of differences." This vignette and its title establish homesickness as the lens through which Ebène experiences living abroad while the vignette's irony speaks to Belgian stereotypes that will inform Ebène's story.

While the overarching narrative arc centers on Ebène's love life, many recurring gags engage with cultural difference and colonially inherited European biases and ignorance through food and misunderstandings, as indicated by the recipe on the back cover. Whereas Camille and Claire serve as a twinned Western/African binary point of comparison for Ebène's dating life, Lulu and Leo (one of Ebène's art school classmates and later one of Claire's boyfriends) function as a balanced approach to social critique. Lulu's light-hearted naïveté—such as when she stresses about having to remember that while South America is a continent, South Africa is a country—is juxtaposed with Leo's unapologetic racism evidenced by his sustained refusal to call Ebène by her name and using "Noire" instead. At one point, in volume 3, Elyon's even draws him wearing a T-shirt that says "White Power Ranger" with the first two words purposefully much larger than the third (39).

Like Leo, many of the characters sport T-shirts featuring American pop culture references, but, as is evident in the extensive use of chibi versions of the characters (as well as Elyon's) in paratextual spaces, global nerd and fan cultures play a much more important role. Lulu's apartment (as seen in figure 6.2) is particularly rich in fan culture: it features a replica of a Fauve statuette (the emblem of the Angoulême International Comics Festival), a giant panda-shaped chair, and a Poké Ball. The global cultural references within the series point to the internet's ubiquity and the fact that laptop computers and cellphones have replaced magazines, televisions, and photographs as

---

8. Elyon's includes a naked chibi version of Ebène on the back cover of (only) the second volume, whose midsection is cheekily covered by the sign she is carrying that features a warning symbol and "+14" to indicate the volume's mature content.

key technology for self-fashioning. Recurring jokes about technology involve Ebène skyping with her mother, Ebène stalking Enzo on Facebook, and ill-timed personal ringtones. All of this underlines that Elyon's can be considered part of the younger generation of Africans that Teju Cole refers to as "digital natives." Rather than hone "sheen reading" via glossy magazines as a strategy for negotiating one's identity, "digital natives," as Cole suggests, mediate their identity through "a piece of glass, usually a touchscreen" in "a space in which everything is possible" (39–40). However, Françoise Vergès reminds us that not everyone in Africa is online and that there remains a technological imbalance between the West and the rest of the world that "is also heavily gendered," going on to point out that "women in African countries are, generally speaking, still even more disconnected than their male mates. What is more, the information technology is totally *man-made*—the programs, the applications, the games, the apps—all are mostly developed by men" (46). In this regard, Elyon's and her work combat such imbalances and normalize the range of African women's experiences. Drawing on *Sex and the City* as a template and playfully exploring repetition, variation, and comparison in *LVDD*, Elyon's balances humor and drama to represent the everyday lives of young African women living abroad.

Community-Building Textual Practices

For both *Aya de Yopougon* and *LVDD*, the main character quartets allow Abouet and Elyon's to present a range of female experiences; at the same time, this defining narrative choice also points to the importance of community for women in West Africa and in the diaspora. In this last section, I'd like to turn to the textual practices at work in these two series that generate a sense of community between the readers, characters, and creators as both series mobilize front matter and bonus sections to pull readers into the characters' lives and to speak directly to them. Though such reader outreach has long been a marketing strategy in American comics, the community-building employed in both series can be seen as a continuation of such practices in West African women's magazines. As Jaji notes, the magazine *Bingo* "facilitate[ed] not only the spread of information and knowledge, but also the construction of new social bonds" through reader engagement; in a section titled "The Readers Write," readers' poetry was published, and there was even what Jaji characterizes as "a pre-Facebook feature" titled "Our Readers Find Each Other" that "helped readers who were trying to reconnect with old friends" ("*Bingo* Magazine" 115). As previously mentioned, each volume of *Aya* ends with an "Ivoirian Bonus" that initially mobilizes characters to address readers. At first, the bonuses are highly gendered, focused almost exclusively on women's daily lives, including Bintou's tips for how to shake your hips while walking and Adjoua's unpacking of the cultural importance of women's *pagnes* and what they communicate.[9] Emboldened by the series' early success, Abouet shifts strategies, and in the fourth volume she speaks to readers without the intermediary of a character; Abouet's coming out in this specific volume, as I've pointed out elsewhere, is not arbitrary.[10] Volume 4 begins with Innocent's arrival in Paris, introducing immigration as a central plotline.[11] Thus, immigration is Abouet's impetus for including her own story of leaving the Ivory Coast and differentiating herself from the series' main quartet.

Elyon's introduces the bonus sections in *LVDD* with another chibi scene and incorporates strategies from her blog to attract and retain fans. To thank them, she includes fan art of the main characters at the end of volumes 1 and 2. Her choices in each volume are far from accidental. First, they speak to the series' international reach by listing the fan's home country with their name; the list of countries spans Europe, Africa, and the Caribbean. Second, in the first volume Elyon's includes fan art by Gabonese cartoonist Pahé (whose own autobiographical series *La vie de Pahé* serves in many ways as an important precursor and corollary to *LVDD*) and Belgian cartoonist Eric Warnauts (her former art school professor). These personal friends and mentors not only offered encouragement but also patronage and legitimation of Elyon's's talent by supplying their fan art (Irène). Elyon's subsequently takes on the same role of patron in the second volume through her choices for fan art winners who, as it turns out, are also budding African artists. Elyon's tells her readers to visit the winners' Facebook pages and shower them with "likes." She also reinforces fan loyalty by encouraging fan art submissions for the subsequent volume. However, at the end of the third volume, there is

---

9. A *pagne*, also known as a wrapper or a loincloth, is a piece of fabric that can be worn in a multitude of ways (a skirt, a dress, a head wrap, etc.). In many African countries, *pagnes* are often made of brightly colored wax-print fabric or traditionally dyed fabrics and, as pointed out in the bonus material of the first volume of *Aya de Yopougon*, *pagnes* and how one wears them can convey a whole range of meanings. For an in-depth analysis of women's *pagnes* in *Aya de Yopougon*, see Ajah and Egege.

10. I made this observation in *African Francophone Bandes Dessinées*, and Abouet later confirmed such a correlation as made evident in Gilles Olivier's "Marguerite Abouet."

11. Though travel to France as a crucial form of cultural capital is introduced in volume 2 when Bintou dates Grégoire, immigration remains an allusive topic as none of the characters have any reason (economic or otherwise) to leave the Ivory Coast, that is, until Innocent decides to no longer hide his homosexuality.

no fan art! This absence seems jarring, but Elyon's fills the space with other material meant to foster fan loyalty and spark community-building.

Wanting to control her brand and ensure that readers understand that though she and Ebène are similar, they are not the same, at the end of the third volume, Elyon's offers a summary of her time as an art student in Liège when she was similar to Ebène. She also provides an updated description of her professional work and a screenshot of an article about the series printed in *Le monde Afrique* with a photograph of her holding the first volume of *LVDD*. This mise en abyme testifies to the success of the series and Elyon's, which she uses to promote cross-cultural conversations. At one point in the text, Enzo runs into a Cameroonian friend living in Liège, and the two speak Camfranglais, thus leaving Lulu, who is with them, as well as certain readers out of the conversation. Rather than provide a translation, the page's footnote informs readers that they will find a translation on page 92. Yet, when the reader turns to that page (located in the bonus section), the translation is absent! In its place, Elyon's promotes a friend's forthcoming Camfranglais dictionary and YouTube channel. She also recommends getting to know Cameroonians living nearby to help with translations, suggesting the ubiquity of the Cameroonian diaspora and leveraging the community-building that launched *LVDD* to generate new connections.

Conclusion

It is strange and yet telling that in many ways Marguerite Abouet and Elyon's as well as their respective series are mirror images. Whereas Elyon's presents her readers with a character living abroad who struggles with the loneliness of living in the diaspora, Abouet paints a portrait of a supportive mix-gendered and multigenerational community. In contrast, the two creators are the exact opposite. Abouet has mentioned that telling and writing stories was a crucial strategy for dealing with the oppressiveness of living within the claustrophobic and isolating four walls of a *chambre de bonne* in Paris (Federici 290). Hence, while her characters thrive within their community, her own experience as a young adult was perhaps much more like Ebène Duta's. Conversely, while Elyon's might have also felt isolated and struggled with the difficulties of being between cultures, her personal trajectory is one steeped in community. In addition to staying in Cameroon through university and thus remaining within a familial and communal context for much longer than Abouet, Elyon's is an active participant in the larger, transnational community of Francophone African cartoonists.

As mentioned, through fan art and other materials in the *LVDD* bonus section, Elyon's demonstrates respect for her cartoonist elders who encouraged her and at the same time continues this crucial function within the growing network of African cartoonists by encouraging, promoting, and even collaborating with younger artists.[12] Elyon's has long been the most visible and often one of the only female cartoonists included at BD festivals dedicated to African BD and at African BD sections of general BD festivals. Moreover, since settling in Brazzaville in the Republic of the Congo, she has taken on a much more proactive role as a cofounder of the Bilili BD Festival that offers a range of events including master classes, conferences, film screenings, video game competitions, and cosplay events.

In contrast, Abouet's success and rise to fame have been and continue to be framed as individual genius, a market tactic applied to other female authors as addressed by Jessica Kohn in her chapter in this volume, "Women Cartoonists: A New Avenue for Understanding a Little-Known Profession?" According to Sandra Federici, Abouet has crafted a public identity in France as an African intellectual engaged with universal themes (291). Moreover, as Frederici notes, while Abouet benefits from large-scale exposure via key French cultural and official institutions such as Gallimard, the Angoulême festival, and national museums (in particular her close collaboration with the *Albums* exposition at the National Museum of the History of Immigration in Paris), she has been noticeably absent from pan-African BD events within France and Africa, considering herself a writer full stop (288).[13] This is not to say that Abouet has not deployed her own strategies for community-building, but her approaches are staunchly situated within existing cultural hegemonies that bifurcate the Global North from the Global South. For example, to ensure a wider dissemination of *Aya* in Africa, Abouet developed her own organization, Des Livres Pour Tous [Books for All], to build new libraries in nonurban spaces in West Africa and worked with Gallimard to publish a smaller-format, more affordable version of *Aya*. Furthermore, the enormous success of *Aya*—translated into twenty-five languages—cannot be overstated and is in itself a form of community-building. A consequence of such success can be read in the role of Elyon's as cocurator of the

---

12. For more information on how African cartoonists mimic writers in their system of patronage as described by Richard Watts in *Packaging Post/Coloniality: The Manufacture of Literary Identity in the Francophone World* (Lexington Books, 2005), see my article "Humor as a Way to Re-Image and Re-Imagine Gabon and France in *La vie de Pahé* and *Dipoula*."

13. For more on Abouet's participation as a key spokesperson for the *Albums* exposition, see my article "African Bande Dessinée Festivals and Competitions."

exposition *Kubuni: Les bandes dessinées d'Afrique.s* for which she worked with the French government as part of President Macron's campaign that 2020 would be the year of Africa. Due to the COVID-19 pandemic, the exposition was pushed back and premiered at the Cité internationale de la bande dessinée et de l'image in Angoulême in January 2021 and has subsequently been held at various Instituts Français in Europe and Africa. The desire to produce BD that speak to the everyday realities in West Africa and the diaspora beyond Western media stereotypes has undoubtedly borne fruit. Like the characters in *Aya de Yopougon* and *La vie d'Ebène Duta*, Marguerite Abouet and Elyon's continue in the pursuit of their personal goals while engendering community and celebrating the diversity of African women.

Works Cited

Abouet, Marguerite, and Agnès Maupré. *Délices d'Afrique: 50 Recettes pour petits moments deconfidences à partager.* Alternatives, 2012.

Abouet, Marguerite, and Clément Oubrerie. *Aya de Yopougon.* Vol. 1. Gallimard Jeunesse, 2005.

———. *Aya de Yopougon.* Vol. 2. Gallimard Jeunesse, 2006.

———. *Aya de Yopougon.* Vol. 3. Gallimard Jeunesse, 2007.

———. *Aya de Yopougon.* Vol. 4. Gallimard Jeunesse, 2008.

———. *Aya de Yopougon.* Vol. 5. Gallimard Jeunesse, 2009.

———. *Aya de Yopougon.* Vol. 6. Gallimard Jeunesse, 2010.

Ajah, Richard Oko, and Letitia Egege. "Deconstructing the Ivorian Vestimentary Traditions: New Fashion, Contemporary Beauty and New Identity in Marguerite Abouet and Clément Oubrerie's Aya de Yopougon." *Wagadu: A Journal of Transnational Women's and Gender Studies*, vol. 18, 2017, pp. 55–80.

Beyala, Calixthe. *Comment cuisiner son mari à l'africaine.* Albin Michel, 2000.

Bozard, Laurent. "Défense et illustration de la chick BD." *Alternative Francophone*, vol. 1, no. 9, 2016, pp. 36–49.

Bumatay, Michelle. "African Bande Dessinée Festivals and Competitions: Participation, Patronage, and Performance." *Research in African Literatures*, vol. 50, no. 2, 2019, pp. 35–48.

———. *African Francophone Bandes Dessinées: Graphic Autobiographies and Illustrated Testimonies.* 2013. University of California Los Angeles, PhD dissertation.

———. "Humor as a Way to Re-Image and Re-Imagine Gabon and France in *La vie de Pahé* and *Dipoula*." *European Comic Art*, vol. 5, no. 2, 2012, pp. 45–66.

Bush, Ruth. "'Mesdames, il faut lire!' Material Contexts and Representational Strategies in Early Francophone African Women's Magazines." *Francosphères*, vol. 5, no. 2, 2016, pp. 213–36.

Cole, Teju. "Do African Digital Natives Wear Glass Skirts?" *Journal of the African Literature Association*, vol. 11, no. 1, 2017, pp. 38–44.

D'Almeida, Xavier. "Marguerite Abouet & Clément Oubrerie: Visions d'Afrique." du9, l'autre bande dessinée, 2006, https://www.du9.org/entretien/visions-d-afrique/.

Elyon's. *La vie d'Ebène Duta*. Vol. 1. Lyon Bande Déssinee Organisation, 2014.

———. *La vie d'Ebène Duta*. Vol. 2. Lyon Bande Déssinee Organisation, 2015.

———. *La vie d'Ebène Duta*. Vol. 3. Lyon Bande Déssinee Organisation, 2017.

Federici, Sandra. *L'entrance des auteurs Africains dans le champ de la bande dessinée Européenne de langue française (1978–2016)*. L'Harmattan, 2019.

Goufo Zemmo, Leslie. "Parcours figuratif de la femme dans la bande dessinée *Aya de Yopougon* de Marguerite Abouet et Clément Oubrerie." *Alternative Francophone*, vol. 1, no. 10, 2016, pp. 156–68.

Harris, Marla. "'Sex and the City': The Graphic Novel Series *Aya* as West African Comedy of Manners." *International Journal of Comic Art*, vol. 11, no. 2, 2009, pp. 119–35.

Hitchcott, Nicki. *Women Writers in Francophone Africa*. Berg, 2000.

Irène. "Interview: Negronews rencontre Elyon's, l'auteur de la bd *La vie d'Ebène Duta*." *Negronews.fr*, 2 Feb. 2014, http://negronews.fr/inspiration-interview-negronews-rencontre-elyons-lauteur-de-la-bd-la-vie-debene-duta/.

Jaji, Tsitsi. *Africa in Stereo: Modernism, Music, and Pan-African Solidarity*. Oxford UP, 2014.

———. "*Bingo* Magazine in the Age of Pan-African Festivals: A Feminist Archive of Global Black Consciousness?" *Nka: Journal of Contemporary Africa Art*, nos. 42–43, 2018, pp. 110–23.

Jermyn, Deborah. *Sex and the City*. Wayne State UP, 2009.

MacLeod, Catriona. "Adopting and Adapting: Ethnic Minority Women's Quest for Identity in the *Bande Dessinée*." *Adaptation: Studies in French and Francophone Culture*, edited by Neil Archer and Andreea Weisl-Shaw, Peter Lang, 2012, pp. 207–17.

McKinney, Mark. *The Colonial Heritage of French Comics*. Liverpool UP, 2011.

———. "The Representation of Ethnic Minority Women in Comic Books." *Women, Immigration and Identities in France*, edited by Jane Freedman and Carie Tarr, Berg, 2000, pp. 85–102.

McWilliams, Sally. "Sex in Yop City: Ivorian Femininity and Masculinity in Abouet and Oubrerie's *Aya*." *The Blacker the Ink: Constructions of Black Identity in Comics and Sequential Art*, edited by Frances Gateward and John Jennings, Rutgers UP, 2015, pp. 45–62.

Miano, Léonora. *Soulfood équatorial*. NiL éditions, 2009.

Mikell, Gwendolyn. "Introduction." *African Feminism: The Politics of Survival in Sub-Saharan Africa*, edited by Gwendolyn Mikell, U of Pennsylvania P, 1997, pp. 1–52.

Olivier, Gilles. "Marguerite Abouet: Innocent d'*Aya de Yopougon*, c'est moi." *Albums des histoires dessinées entre ici et ailleurs: Bande dessinée et immigration 1913–2013*, edited by Gilles Olivier and Vincent Marie, Futuropolis, 2014. pp. 148–51.

Vergès, Françoise. "Digital Africa." *Journal of the African Literature Association*, vol. 1, no. 1, 2017, pp. 45–49.

CHAPTER 7

Revolutionary Comics
Samandal's Feminist Topography of Resistance

ALEXANDRA GUEYDAN-TUREK

Substantial recent attention has focused on women graphic artists from the Middle East and North Africa, or MENA region, both as pillars of the vibrant contemporary comics scene and as active participants in ongoing discourse on civil and women's rights. In her contribution to the 2018 "New Generation: Arab Comics Today" exhibit, comics scholar Lina Ghaibeh situates the rise of female graphic artists in the Mashreq within the broader critical context of grassroots civil movements and protests that have marked the last two decades: "Those women who dare to speak of their intimacy are also those who manifest in the streets and actively take part in the transformational movement in the Arab world. As privileged witnesses of injustices, they carry great political ideals and fight at the forefront to defend their rights" (Collectif AUB 34).

Starting after the civil war that ravaged Lebanon between 1975 and 1990, women have played a prominent role in a series of movements that have worked for change: the 2005 Cedar Revolution leading to the withdrawal of the Syrian army and ending a fifteen-year occupation; the 2011 Intifada

---

I would like to express my thanks for the engagement of the other contributors to this volume, to Carla Calargé for her intellectual generosity, and to Maggie Flinn for her editorial and organizational work.

of Dignity; the 2015–16 protests against a waste-disposal crisis; the 2019 call for the reform of a legal system; and more recently the 2020 antigovernment protests following the collapse of its banking system. Insofar as these movements have pushed back against different types of oppression—classist, confessional, patriarchal, environmental—some have been successful, others less so. Irrespective of the historical details, though, women have been at the forefront of demonstrations in Lebanon that target corrupt systemic reforms to address a culture of discrimination.

Comics production furnishes visible artifacts of these recurring demands for sociopolitical change, creating archives and disseminating important messages—both nationally and internationally. George Khoury (known under the pseudonym JAD) links the engagement of female graphic artists with the transformative potential of this particular visual medium. As Khoury puts it, women artists have "dared to defy the authorities and traditional orthodoxy concerning women's rights, particularly their right to bodily integrity. *The high percentage of female artists specializing in the professional comic book sector is an important indicator of this engagement*" (Collectif AUB 17).[1] Khoury's comment here echoes Hillary Chute's conception of comics as an intimate creative practice where one's body, through the movement of its hand and the lines drawn, translates itself onto the page (Chute 11). This "aesthetic intimacy" (Chute 6) gains in strength when female artists capture their trauma, reimagine their bodies, and share their desires. I want to argue here that these intimate graphic narratives do more than simply straddle the line between the personal and political, becoming creative experiments in re(en)visioning the minoritized gendered self. By creating this bridge between the female body and the body politic, they serve a variety of ends: uplifting marginalized voices, allowing for the public examination of gender and sexuality-related issues, and effecting changes in popular understandings of these issues.

Through the study of shorts from the 2016 Lebanese comics anthology *Ça restera entre nous / Kalf al-bab* [This Will Stay Between Us], produced by the collective Samandal, this chapter investigates how the unfolding sequential form facilitates the questioning of normative representations of gender,

---

1. In reference to the 2016 Angoulême polemic and absence of female artists among the nominees for the Fauve d'Or that year, Lena Merhej (another cofounder of Samandal) notes that the situation in the Arab world also differs due to the gendered nature of the profession: "We don't have any problem of masculine exclusivity in the Arab world. Here, people who work in the art world are mostly women. . . . During art school, there were only two guys in my class" (qtd. in Voitachewski). Translations are mine, unless otherwise noted.

intimacies, and sexualities in the Arab world. I will consider these works in the spirit established by Ramzi Fawaz in *Queer Forms*, where they noted that the comics medium offers a privileged physical structure for the expression of multiple gendered identities and their subsequent plural readings:

> The medium's fundamental creative logic of handmade visual frames arranged in sequence is driven by an additive or proliferative impulse that produces plurality as its visual and conceptual *sine qua non*. Comics frequently require that a single body or object be drawn numerous times across many panels in a sequential strip, so every depiction of that figure will be slightly different, multiplying its representation across space. . . . Seen from this vantage, the unpredictable procession of sequential panels that constitute any given comic strip is ripe for articulation with queerness. (254)

Fawaz is interested in the ability of queer art to "relentlessly display different aspects of gender and sexual existence, thereby making them available to our perception and soliciting collective attempts to produce interpretations of gender and sexuality's manifold dimensions" (36). In the comics medium, the sequential movement both within and across frames accomplishes this with unpredictable associations and unexpected juxtapositions of bodies and meanings. In the spirit of Ramzi Fawaz's structural analogy between the comics medium and queer world-making, I will demonstrate how Samandal's graphic anthology, in its reproduction of successive yet divergent expressions, promotes a diversified range of gendered selves, desires, and intimacies. Pursuing this argument further, I will examine how the very material conditions of the production of Samandal, with the collective's efforts toward a collaborative and more horizontal community and practice, redraws the field of comics in Lebanon as an inclusive and "queer" geography.

Samandal: A Privileged Topography of Resistance

Ça restera entre nous / *Ḵalf al-bab* was produced by a relatively new Lebanese comics collective, Samandal. Created by Fadi Baqi (fdz), Omar Khouri, Hatem Imam, Lena Merhej, and Tarek Nabaa, the Beirut-based collective published its first adult comics magazine in 2007 and has become a key platform for sequential art in the MENA region. Presently in its eighteenth edition, this eponymous comics magazine describes its mission "to lift the stature of comics to that of a mature art form capable of tackling issues beyond superheroes and their baffling hairdos" (qtd. in di Ricco 190). Each new thematic volume investigates contemporary issues through formal experimentation. Consciously rejecting an exclusive vision of Lebanese comics as either Arab or Francophone, it moves toward a more horizontal and inclusive definition of the field of comics. Work from artists in the MENA region is published alongside pieces from peers around the world. Editions are typically trilingual, featuring comics in Arabic, English, and French, to reflect the multilingual character of both the country and the collective's collaborators. As argued in "Le renouveau de la bande dessinée maghrébine contemporaine," multilingualism constitutes a key aspect of the contemporary relational ethics of comics in the Arab world: alongside a series of other linguistic processes (silent narratives, code-switching, marginal notes, and endnote translations) the multilingual nature of these works helps them escape easy categorization. In spite of one language possibly being privileged by the artist within their panels, the comics are designed to be accessible to Arabophone, Anglophone, and Francophone readers alike and should thus be considered *simultaneously* published in three languages.[2]

Samandal released *Ça restera entre nous / Ḵalf al-bab* in 2016, under the lead of Lebanese artist Lena Merhej. The tongue-in-cheek title (translated as "This Will Stay Between Us / Behind Closed Doors") places the works under a faulty pact of secrecy: "focusing," as Merhej explains, "on things left unsaid or things happening behind closed doors." By revealing what has been hidden from the eyes and ears of its readers, Merhej hopes to surface societal wounds related to "questions of sexuality, a broader context for things related to gender, feminism and queerness" (qtd. in Dueben). While the formula for this volume closely resembles its predecessors, critics such as Ghaibeh have highlighted its rather exceptional content: Samandal's 2016 comics "revealed the high interest of young female artists on this topic. Their contribution was not only quantitative (consisting of more than double that of their male counterparts) but also ground-breaking in its rupture with social boundaries, revealing intimate fantasies and using more direct representations where men dared not adventure" (Collectif AUB 37). Here, Ghaibeh clearly articulates the high stakes behind such projects—by bringing intimate experiences into the public space, they can at once reveal taboos and break with their inhibiting forces.

---

2. While the shorts I consider in this chapter were published with inline texts in Arabic or French, the authorial translation is used as it appears in Samandal's volume. To acknowledge the multilingual nature of the collection, however, all titles appear deliberately in three languages with the original title in line with the drawing appearing first.

Subverting Scopophilia: "Éditorial/Al-iftitāḥiyyah"

The volume opens with Merhej's bilingual (Arabic and French) "Éditorial/Al-iftitāḥiyyah" in which she formulates her artistic vision for the volume. Against the backdrop of various women's bodies dancing, Merhej describes (in a voice akin to a first-person manifesto) the urgent imperative to free oneself from social strictures and expectations. She calls for artists and readers alike to find their individual voice and represent their body outside of any cultural hijacking: this serves both to document diverse performances of gender and sexuality and to encourage readers to envision their own body and sexuality differently. The first two pages feature women's bodies on the left-hand side of the page, emphasizing movements of their hips with six small inset panels on the right side of the page that zoom in on different parts of the body (2–3). Despite the differing skin colors of the two female subjects, the hips that appear in small frames are depicted as interchangeable. The potential objectification of the subjects by the (male) gaze is called out by a speech bubble coming from the anonymous hips: "While dancing, I free every single one of my muscles so that their movements follow the cosmic rhythms" (2).[3] The body refuses to remain a silent spectacle on display on the page under the spectator's scopophilic gaze;[4] it asserts its embodied subjectivity as the first-person narrator describes its own pleasure in dancing and its ensuing sense of freedom. As such, the dancing bodies' performance shifts away from the readers to escape objectification and reclaim dance as a transcendental practice.[5]

The bodies are designed to escape objectification, fetishization, or capture: extending beyond the frame, their legs, hands, and elbows occupy the gutter. On the third page (figure 7.1), as the protagonist draws parallels between dancing and drawing, frames disappear altogether: "While dancing, I experience the primordial freedom of movement, a way of inhabiting space. By creating comics, I experience freedom of expression through the interplay of images and text" (4).

The forms taken by the female bodies are unusual, widely varied, and experimental. In the upper tier of the third page, a female body reminiscent

---

3. An exception in its format to the rest of the comics anthology, no English textual version is provided to Merhej's editorial.

4. In Laura Mulvey's terminology, "scopophilia" is the pleasure that derives from looking at a "spectacle." In Mulvey's analysis, the "sexual imbalance" that orders the world dictates that the female be the object of the look while the male subject, who is the bearer of the look, projects his phantasy onto her.

5. We may read this opening as a rebuttal of the Western perception of "oriental dance" as a sexual and erotic practice aimed at tourist consumption.

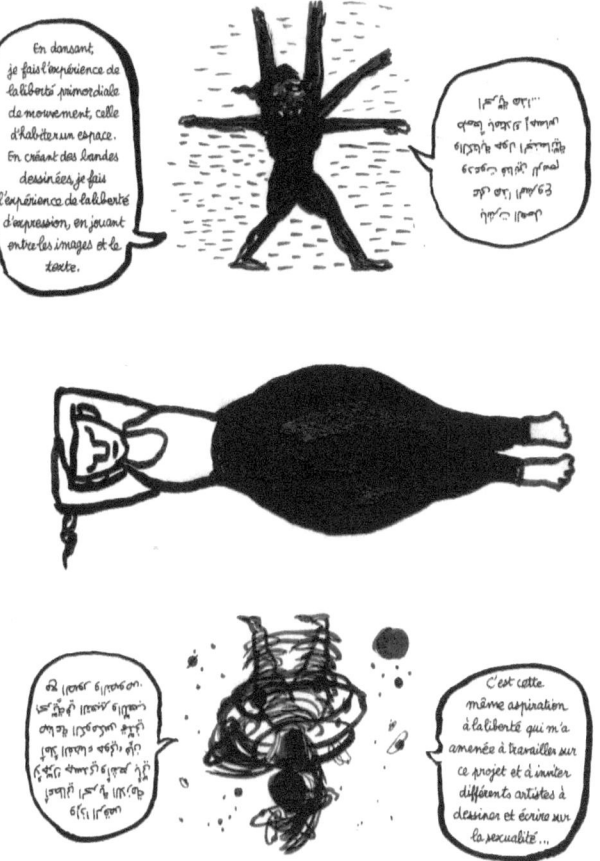

FIGURE 7.1. Lena Merhej, "Éditorial/Al-iftitāḥiyyah," *Ça restera entre nous / Ḳalf al-bab*, 2016, p. 4. © Alifabata/Samandal.

of Da Vinci's Vitruvian man is freed from its square and circle and appears above a voluptuous body in the center panel with a pear shape that emphasizes the female hips so as to resist the pleasure associated with the representation of a petite body. In the bottom tier, a body is depicted with motion lines suggesting a planet's revolution; a solar system in the background seems to announce a Copernican revolution with women at its center.

Near identical iterations of the same figure are used by Merhej to illustrate one subject's varied affects and bodily practices in an attempt to counter any quick moral judgements on the part of the reader. A bare-chested female figure, first encountered on page five, is initially portrayed with her eyes averted. In the following frame, she clutches at her breasts to cover herself, with emanata expressing her embarrassment. In a speech balloon, she defends the right of people to choose their own representation and to be free to embody their values: "The freedom to be . . . what one wishes, and to denounce what one doesn't want" (5). When this same figure reappears in a later panel, she raises her hands and uncovers her breasts in an assertive manner, smiling, with the emanata transformed into motion lines; shortly afterward, three separate frames depict close-ups of her feet, vagina, and nose (8). Instead of being erotic, these representations stress the natural aspect of nakedness, which is detached from considerations of women's desirability and sexuality by Merhej's simplistic style and the sequentiality of this particular episode. The caption accompanying this second set of representations attempts to frame this gesture: "To reclaim our bodies from the pornographic and bulimic mainstream media requires that we speak openly of our personal experience, to our self-identification with it" (8). Merhej is less concerned with the specific nature of these different representations than she is with the subject's agency in those depictions. The shift between these two pages, in other words, isn't about "moral" conservatism or "liberating" nudity. Rather, Merhej acknowledges that both positions can derive from oppressive or positive values alike and that central to our reading is women's agency in adhering to those values.

Merhej's re-visioning of the embodied female subject reclaims the body from its objectified, look-at-edness and places it back at the center of the artwork; it recasts the female body as a speaking subject whose agency determines the state of undress. This is particularly relevant for women from the MENA region whose bodies are enmeshed in overtly political networks of meaning, whether it be at home where they are mobilized as symbols of family honor and virtue or abroad where they are reduced to victims of Arab patriarchy to be liberated. As another of Merhej's female protagonists explains: "Here, in Europe, we know so little about countries from the Arab world. Mass media are overly simplistic and superficial . . . They do not explain the richness and complexity of societies from the South and East of the Mediterranean, nor do they discuss how these societies have changed and what is at stake for them. So many images to redraw . . ." (6; ellipses in original).

As Merhej's subjects gain agency over their expressions, they disrupt the networks of meaning in which they would be traditionally viewed. Merhej continues this destabilization through a technique that Jonathan Guyer calls "the flippy page," where readers of different languages can flip the page 180 degrees to read in either French or Arabic. In the particular page being discussed, Merhej's text is superimposed over the delineated coastline of Lebanon, Egypt, Turkey, and Greece. When reading in French, the map appears upside down with Middle Eastern countries featured in the first tier of the panel (when reading in Arabic, the map is right side up). The feeling of disorientation experienced by the Francophone reader implicitly raises Merhej's criticism of Western-centrism, unsettling a Francophone readers' assumption of knowingness. Following Sara Ahmed's conceptualization of disorientation as a queer rhetoric in *Queer Phenomenology*, the disoriented reader strives to reorient their understanding of the world and the way they inhabit it. Readers will actively engage with the anthology that Merhej introduces, manipulate the material volume, and question what they conceived as established codes; it leads them to discoveries in new languages in the body of the various texts that make up the volume.

Collectively, the aesthetic strategies that Merhej employs (many of them unique to comics) allow her to acknowledge the taboos endemic to particular sociocultural contexts and caution the reader against faulty frames of reading while simultaneously encouraging the reader to embrace multiple alternative portrayals of Arab women. The renewed vocabulary in this art, in turn, permits the artists to treat the body in a revolutionary fashion. Instead of a facile aestheticization of a subversive discourse on genre, intimacy, and sexuality, Samandal's contributors reflect on and experiment with its aesthetic vision *as aesthetics*; it is not subservient to any political cause. This is perhaps most visible in two other graphic shorts, (co)created by female artists, that invite the readers to rethink and re-envision feminine sexuality from the Global South and to consider how innovative forms in comics successfully lend themselves to queering mainstream representations of the body and reconceptualize sexuality, desire, and intimacy in a nonnormative way.

Queering the Body: "Le corps de l'autre / Jasad al-āḵar / The Body of the Other"

"Le corps de l'autre" (113–21) is a joint graphic work by two female artists, Tunisian poet Abir Gasmi and Franco-Tunisian graphic artist Noha Habaieb.[6] Gasmi and Habaieb's short seems to run afoul of the artistic tradition of comics: it consists of a love poem superimposed on a series of seven full-page ink wash paintings that feature abstract visuals. The graphics

---

6. Habaeib is also the cofounder of *Lab 619*, the main Tunisian comic collective. For more information regarding the work of this particular collective with artists from different regions of the MENA region, see Gueydan-Turek (49–50).

simultaneously evoke natural elements, silhouettes, and body parts and are bisected by white and black vertical and horizontal lines distinctly reminiscent of the comics' interframe space. While its very inclusion in the Samandal volume invites us to examine it as a graphic narrative, its distinctively experimental form should give pause to the reader.

The graphic narrative opens with a declaration of intimacy through the equation "Your body, my territory" (121), a juxtaposition that simultaneously imprints and erases the bounds between the lovers' identities. This sense of fluidity is echoed in the broader aesthetics of the full-page panels, stylized so as to defy any definite reading: tree lines from a forest seem to morph into intertwined bodies, grass morphs into pubic hairs. The overlain love poem supports these multiple simultaneous readings: "Hair waterfall constantly renewed / Swollen veins / Greenish intermingling / Beating, Subdermal network / . . . A fiery forest of red hair on the curve of the chin" (121). The unidentified narrator draws a portrait of their loved one with a disjointed catalog of physical attributes that ultimately fail to create a clear picture, paralleling Habaieb's undecipherable illustrations.

Gasmi and Habaieb's short elaborates an erotic cartography that continually plays on a multiplicity of meanings, embracing the ambiguity of the lovers' genders. Readers are led to imagine simultaneously contradictory bodies. While our gaze roams over Habaieb's stylized lines of an indefinite landscape, the text first seems to describe a female lover with her red pubic hair metaphorized as a "fiery forest." In line with that image, the evocation of the chin adjoining the female genitals can be read as a veiled reference to oral sex. Yet, the incongruity of the syntax "fiery forest . . . on the chin" offers an alternative reading, evoking facial hair of a male lover. Both the gender of the lovers and their sexuality are portrayed so as to resist any fixed identification; this is especially true of the short's last two panels, which are concerned with the process of (un)voicing and (un)seeing. The lover's voice trails off, the object of its desire remaining unspoken as language seems to fail: "I want to say it / I want to fantasize / on your hands, / your back, / your neck, / your lips, / your . . ." (121). The ellipsis, which stands in for silences and taboos that have been foisted upon the lovers by their community or society, are supplemented with Habaieb's illustration of hands and feet superimposed onto buttocks, labia, fingers, or male genitalia. This experimental graphic narrative reorients our understanding of possibilities by enabling us to see differently.

The elasticity of this particular short certainly calls to mind "formlessness," a privileged trope that serves to translate heterogeneous aspects of gender and sexual nonconformity in queer theory (Fawaz 6–7). Yet, as

Ramzi Fawaz argues in *Queer Forms*, it is the self-conscious play on the formal codes of the comics medium—visual framing, image-text combination, and sequential organization—that "give[s] concrete shape" to the felt experience of nonnormative erotics and intimacies (248). Comics as "queer forms," Fawaz insists, underwrites a renewed apprehension of gendered and sexual selfhood "neither as an infinitely fluid substance, nor an adamantine identity, but as a type of *shapeshifting*" (10). In other words, although this graphic narrative does not offer a self-contained re-presentation of gender and sexual nonconformity, the very mutability of the graphic work renders nonconforming identities and desires accessible to the reader's perception. The "shapeshifting" aspect of Gasmi and Habaieb's work can be read as a strategic queer world-making, where the subject is both made and unmade through formal innovations. In the spirit of Fawaz's analysis, the reader is denied any closed, singular interpretation: the only stable referent appears to be that of the pleasure and desire.

Re-Visioning Pleasure: "Ahed wa Karīm / Ahed et Karim / Ahed and Karim"

One of the most explicit works in *Ça restera entre nous/Ḵalf al-bab* is Beirut-based Nour Hifaoui Fakhouri's[7] "Ahed wa Karīm," a thirteen-plate comic built around a personal narrative that explores the role of sexuality in a relationship. Nudity, hard-core porn, and orgasm are prominently featured to offer a complex reading of the connection between contemporary intimacy, sexuality, pleasure, and the interplay with pornography. Fakhouri openly admits that uncomfortable moments in her autofictional comics are used "for the reader to face the reality of the body and its pleasure, especially that of women" and push the limits of expression in Lebanon ("Nour Hifaoui Fakhoury").

"Ahed wa Karīm" opens with a sexual encounter between a woman named Ahed and her partner Karim. The layout of the initial fifteen frames in a "waffle-iron" grid imposes a strict symmetry between the two partners: on the right-hand side, close-ups on Karim's face mirror parallel images of Ahed's face on the left. On the next page, however, the flow is

---

7. "Fakhouri" (a variation from the most common spelling, "Fakhoury"—we favor here the spelling provided in the Samandal volume) cofounded in 2017 the *Zeez* collective with Omar Al Fil, Tracy Chahwan, Carla Habib, Nour Hifaoui, and Karen Keyrouz. The comics collective uses the zine format and is named in Arabic after the cicada, a small animal that makes a lot of noise and announces the warmer days.

interrupted as Ahed appears to jolt awake, leaving the reader to wonder whether the encounter really occurred. In the "pillow talk" scene that follows, she recounts to Karim an erotic dream of her visit to a female prostitute. The explicit content of the dream and the exaggerated depiction of the couple's earlier intercourse call to mind pornography, but Ahed's peaceful facial expressions and the couple's intimate kiss during the "pillow talk" scene softens it, recoding sexual pleasure as intimacy and unguardedness. These juxtapositions question the complex and ambiguous place of porn and sexual pleasure within each protagonist's exploration of a liberated sexuality and the couple's intimacy.

Fakhouri follows the dream scene with shared memories of the two lovers' respective sexual awakenings. Portrayals of Ahed are tied to images of symbolic violence paralleling the couple's sexual dynamic, most overtly in the double-splash page representing her nightmare (figure 7.2): Ahed's naked body appears simultaneously as a stripper performing a pole dance, the assistant of a carnival knife thrower, and as a sex doll adopting roles for the pleasure of her lover. While the image of a pole dance may depict Ahed's physical empowerment—her confident athletic pose, disheveled hair, and smile on her face—we cannot read empowerment into the adjacent image of her body strapped to a carnival wheel, surrounded by throwing knives. The proliferating images of Ahed's nude body create an ambivalent portrayal of sex and successively diminish her agency: in the final scripted role, we see Ahed sitting atop a human-size sex-doll box, portrayed as an object for the consumption of a buyer (her partner), who is seated on a throne wearing a crown. The wolf on the back of the throne foreshadows objectification and violence; pleasure and eroticism are replaced by symbols of dominance, submission, and institutionalized gender inequality.

The partners' intimacy appears equally at risk in their daily life. Flashbacks reveal a process of sexual self-discovery that is heavily mediated by technology: Karim's childlike alter ego is seen surrounded by screens, displaying a squirting scene (207). The technological elements of this flashback recall the splash panel used as a title page for the short, where the protagonists' naked bodies are separated by a central blank space broken by cables linking them through their genitals, breasts, hearts, and minds (197). Where the lines extend beyond each body, they connect to computer and TV screens displaying their intimate parts. The plate appears designed to imply that intimate relationships, pleasure, and knowledge are entangled with the overflow of pornographic images. And although Fakhouri may criticize a society in which porn is the only existing vehicle for sex education, she conversely acknowledges its positive role in introducing people to the sensuality of their own bodies.

FIGURE 7.2. The Arabic sentence reads, "When I was young, I used to make up stories." Nour Hifaoui Fakhouri, "Ahed wa Karīm / Ahed et Karim / Ahed and Karim," *Ça restera entre nous / Ḳalf al-bab,* 2016, pp. 200–201. © Alifabata/Samandal.

The final double-splash page partially reconciles the tension between simulated and stimulated pleasure by positioning a new sexual encounter between Ahed and Karim within another "waffle-iron" grid (210–11). Images of genitals appearing repeatedly throughout the short are replaced by close-ups depicting the protagonists' hands clasped together, an intimate kiss, and the intensity of the emotions on Ahed's teary face rather than a close-up of her orgasm. Alongside the criticism of sexuality developed in preceding frames, these images recognize the importance of sexual pleasure to a healthy and close relationship. Fakhouri's short probes the way in which desires and fantasies are shaped by the consumption of porn, but it doesn't appear to make a sweeping statement about pornography; instead, its complex view of eroticism and pleasure reflects the generative potential of sexuality in relating with others and being in the world. In so doing, Fakhouri convokes Linda Williams's notion that "sex is an act and more or less of 'it' may be revealed but . . . it is not a stable truth. . . . It is a constructed, mediated, performed act and every revelation is also a concealment that leaves something to the imagination" (Williams 2). Here, it is the comics' frame—rather than Williams's movie screen—that both reveals and conceals and invites the reader/viewer to a greater imagination of sex and its significance in developing one's identity.

A Feminist Collaborative Ethos

With political imaginaries that distance themselves from gender stereotypes and normative sexuality, Samandal's volume *Ça restera entre nous / Kalf al-bab* challenges the widely disseminated narrative of victimization of Arab women. As Merhej's "Éditorial/Al-iftitāḥiyyah" reminds us, this renewed vision is crucial for MENA-based female artists who, through their creations, must address the faulty images that have shaped the perception of their own life in their country and throughout the world (6). As such Samandal offers a corrective, filling a representational gap in regard to the visualization of women, their intimacies, and their sexualities. But, beyond its graphic output, the very nature of the collective—highlighting a multiplicity of voices, aesthetics, and languages and sharing varied lived experiences—can be said to offer a set of inclusive civic and ethical practices.

Indeed, Samandal's inclusive feminist stance extends beyond the confines of the Arab world, incorporating voices from European and male artists, straight and queer. Alongside Merhej, Fakhouri, Habaieb, and Gasmi, *Ça restera entre nous / Kalf al-bab* features French comic artist Lisa Mandel, Spanish cartoonist Mery Cuesta, and Lebanese artist Joseph Kai. These artists are only a fraction of the ever-growing list of contributors to Samandal, whose international composition reflects the collaborative ethos at the core of the collective and its efforts to redefine comics as a way to build a community and map an alternative understanding of the notion of artistic subjectivity. In sharp contrast to what Sarah Ahmed has termed "a masculinist model of creativity," one that is "premised on withdrawal" and that privileges the fetishization of the individual achievement (*Living* 217), this collaborative network provides a model for intertwined, expanding, and correlational creations. Graphic narratives within this framework are no longer conceived of as isolated works, mirroring the soul of a solitary artist-genius, but rather as networked and relational artworks that connect readers to worlds beyond those on display in their panels. Rather than heroic individual creations, they construct a transnational, inclusive feminist genealogy.

With the growing global popularity of graphic artists from the MENA regions (Gueydan-Turek 46–48), Samandal has gained increasing attention, both locally and globally. This has shifted their role slightly and allows critics to start asking questions regarding their participation in (or influence on) sociopolitical transformations. It would be an overstatement to presume that specific graphic narratives (or even comics as a genre in itself) can usher in widespread social changes—but they can certainly contribute to and shape discourses. Infused with social consciousness and shaped by historical and cultural realities, comics have the ability to make particular issues visible, to address a wide public, and to encourage self-reflection within their audience. From this perspective, Samandal's empowerment of certain artists enables unseen feminist dynamics.

This dynamic, and Samandal's work toward gender equity, extend well beyond its publications. For example, alongside the March 2019 issue titled *Hunna* (a work composed of eight short comics inspired from testimonials of women engaged in community-based activism and whose title is the Arabic feminine plural pronoun for "they"),[8] Samandal organized a workshop to promote gender and social equity. The free program was organized by Samandal contributors Nour Hifaoui Fakhouri and Karen Feyrouz and cosponsored by Oxfam International.[9] It brought together sixteen women and gender-nonconforming participants from Egypt, Lebanon, and the growing Syrian refugee community.

While detailing their accomplishments, these nonfiction, semibiographical, sequential narratives also spoke to the hardships women and gender-nonconforming activists faced in their respective communities. The combined artistic work that resulted from the workshop was exhibited during *Hunna*'s launch, which (symbolically) took place on International Women's Day (March 8, 2019). Oxfam's Gender and Advocacy Advisor, Farah Kobaissy, stated that the goal of this workshop was to equip women from the region with "the skills to tell their [own] stories and to teach them about

---

8. Created by Lena Merhej, *Hunna* was then partially inked by Karen Keyrouz and Nour Hifaoui. According to Keyrouz, this strategy was born of material necessity but became "an asset" and lead to an aesthetic diversity that allowed the three artists to match the uniqueness of each short (qtd. in Negahban). Note that among the subjects whose lives were depicted, *Hunna* also told the story of Samira Khalil, a human-rights activist forcibly disappeared during the Syrian civil war.

9. Oxfam, or the Oxford Committee of Famine Relief, is a confederation of independent charitable organizations working to alleviate poverty and socioeconomic injustice. It has been working in Lebanon since 2006. Samandal's collaborative project with Oxfam came at a somber moment in Oxfam history when a fifteen-month investigation into the sexual exploitation of Haiti's victims of the 2010 earthquake by Oxfam workers was wrapping up. Dubbed the Oxfam scandal, the investigation led to the publication of a report in June 2019 condemning Oxfam's lax culture regarding sexual predation and employees' misconduct more broadly.

drawing and framing and word choice" (qtd. in Negahban). To Feyrouz, though, comics for these women would complete their sociopolitical civic engagement and strengthen their activism. Comics as a political act would bring to light "unheard stories of women silently fighting for change" and disseminate them to create a ripple effect (qtd. in Negahban). Aligning the workshop with feminists' self-empowerment strategies, Feyrouz casts comics as an emancipatory and interventionist practice that allows other women to become agents of change through their creations.

The Hunna workshop is far from unique among Samandal's projects: in a similar spirit, the collective has also organized workshops in public schools and Syrian refugee camps (Guyer). Working alongside nongovernmental organizations to bring visual storytelling pedagogy and accessible sketching techniques to the marginalized subjects, the collective thus seeks to transform (rather than simply inform) contemporary Lebanese society. Building on their visibility on the (inter)national graphic scene, some of the collective's most prominent collaborators have also extended their work into public campaigns to defend women and LGBTQ+ rights. In 2019, for instance, Samandal collaborated with the Lebanese LGBTQ+ rights organization Helem to produce posters for the 2019 International Day Against Homophobia, Transphobia, and Biphobia (IDAHOTB). The project brought together thirteen Lebanese graphic artists—including Tracy Chahwan, Joseph Kai, Karen Keyrouz, Raphaelle Macaron, Lena Merhej, and Barack Rima—to explore "the themes of adversity and acceptance of queer people" through neon- and pastel-colored posters portraying non-cisgender bodies and same-sex couples living their love openly.

Artists at the center of the collective do not work exclusively with Samandal and have also leveraged their visibility from the collective to move into vastly different markets. The Lebanese artist Raphaelle Macaron, for example (a member of Samandal since 2004), became a regular contributor to the French online comics magazine *Bien, Monsieur* [Very Well, Sir] in 2015. The spirit of *Bien, Monsieur* is related (although not identical) to that of Samandal. Its editorial line both privileges a subversive perspective and attempts to bring together the deeply personal with larger political ideals: "To tell our society without reverence, whether by denouncing a current event or a political conduct, or by autobiographical narration." The four sections of the French magazine address themes related to feminism, society, environment, and politics (*Bien*).

Macaron's 2018 contribution to *Bien, Monsieur*, titled "Steak," appeared in the section dedicated to feminism; in it, she tackled the issue of street and sexual harassment. Published as a four-page short, it tells the story of a woman who, while shopping at her neighborhood butcher, overhears a male client complaining nostalgically of a recent past when unwanted sexual advances and emotional abuse were considered harmless fun. As he develops his story, he is drawn so as to increasingly resemble a pig; his speech bubbles are portrayed in full caps, as if to translate his words as loud squeals. He ignores the unease of the speechless female customer; frames depicting him are filled to the brim with close-ups of his corpulent body. The woman, by contrast, is depicted as an outline, viewed from afar, within a relatively bare and mute frame. The drawings reflect the contrast between the two characters: the loud voice and imposing presence of the sexual predator stands in opposition to the nearly anonymous portrayal of the victim who quietly endured the abuse.

Published at the same time as the #BalanceTonPorc movement (the French hashtag equivalent to #MeToo), this short's metamorphosis of the male client into a pig (alongside the pork products in the butcher shop) suggests both a condemnation of toxic masculinity and an expression of solidarity with the larger social current. Despite the aggressive, imposing statements by the customer, the female subject resists his insensitivity: she consumes beef, rather than pork, and when he salutes her with an "Au revoir, mademoiselle" [Good-bye, Miss] in the penultimate frame, she does not return the salutation. Her refusal to acknowledge and reciprocate his salutation becomes a sign of quiet defiance; she resists the process of masculine interpellation through the "mademoiselle," denouncing this word as yet another condescending objectification of her as a woman.[10] This episode rings even truer in the French language, where the term "mademoiselle" was dropped from official documents in 2012 and is falling out of use due to its sexist undertone, which formerly paired the legal status of an unmarried woman with connotations of immaturity and naïveté. Bringing all of these themes together, Macaron's short comics successfully address both the pervasiveness of street harassment and the role played by legislators in confronting it. Coincidently, the issue *Bien, Monsieur* #10 in which Macaron's "Steak" appeared was awarded the Fauve de la BD Alternative in 2018, and a year later Samandal's "Experimentation/Tajrīb" (to which Macaron also contributed) won the same honor.

---

10. Louis Althusser defines the notion of "interpellation" as the process by which a subject is hailed by power, is compelled to answer that call, and by doing so, recognizes one's own subordination, one's own subjection to ideologies in place (174). Among the limitations this theory presents is the sense that the subject's agency appears illusory. Judith Butler is instrumental in articulating Althusser's notion of interpellation with that of agency. In her work on gender theory, she examines the ways in which the subject can answer the hailing in unexpected ways or refuse to answer it altogether. These alternatives are conceived by Butler as performative acts that constitute the subject, rather than scripts that are already predetermined.

Conclusion

Taken together, the work produced by Samandal in *Ça restera entre nous / Kalf al-bab* is notable for its use of diverse formats to explore a wide range of feminist ideas that do not tiptoe around taboo issues or promote any sanitized idealization.[11] Designed simultaneously for both local and international audiences, Samandal appears to embrace the role that John Johnston has referred to as the "public educator" (178). Johnston introduced the term in a discussion of Tahrir Square graffiti, arguing that visual street art has the potential to promote a "critical public pedagogy" through both its palimpsestic engagement with contemporary discourses and its interactions and recontextualization with surrounding graffiti (189). While unauthorized drawing on a public wall clearly differs from the fixed sequential presentation of Samandal's collective productions, Johnston's analysis of networked, intertextual processes of creations and inter-artistic engagements remains relevant. Samandal's collaborative ethos, among diverse artists and across widely differing publics from different geographical and linguistic backgrounds, provides evidence of a "critical public pedagogy" (178). Viewed in this light, Samandal contributes to what Egyptian comics critic Sara Shaker has termed "adult comics artivism": that is to say "a type of activism that can disclose political, social and cultural issues in an attempt to bring change" (209).

Works Cited

Ahmed, Sarah. *Living a Feminist Life*. Duke UP, 2017.

———. *Queer Phenomenology*. Duke UP, 2006.

Althusser, Louis. "Ideology and Ideological State Apparatuses (Notes towards an Investigation)." *Lenin and Philosophy and Other Essays*. Translated by B. Brewster, Monthly Review Press, 1971, pp. 127–86.

Bien, Monsieur. Edited by Elsa Abderhamani and Juliette Mancini, https://revue-bien-monsieur.fr/.

Chute, Hillary. *Graphic Women: Life Narrative and Contemporary Comics*. Columbia UP, 2010.

Collectif AUB. *Nouvelle génération: La bande dessinée arabe aujourd'hui / New Generation: Arab Comics Today*. Alifbata, 2018.

---

11. Jana Traboulsi, another prominent contributor to Samandal, embraces broader political stands. In a series of double-plate drawings, published in the Lebanese newspaper *As-Safir* and partially reprinted in *L'humanité*, Traboulsi denounces Israeli war crimes during the 2014 Israel-Gaza conflict.

di Ricco, Massimo. "Drawing for a New Public: Middle Eastern 9th Art and the Emergence of a Transnational Graphic Movement." *Postcolonial Comics: Texts, Events, Identities*, edited by Binita Mehta and Pia Mukherji, Routledge, 2015, pp. 187–203.

Dueben, Alex. "An Interview with Samandal." *The Comics Journal*, 18 Dec. 2015, http://www.tcj.com/an-interview-with-samandal/.

Fawaz, Ramzi. *Queer Forms*. New York UP, 2022.

Gasmi, Abir, and Noha Habaieb. "Le corps de l'autre / Jasad al-āḵar / The Body of the Other." *Ça restera entre nous / Ḵalf al-bab*, Alifabata/Samandal, 2016, pp. 113–21.

Gueydan-Turek, Alexandra. "Le renouveau de la bande dessinée maghrébine contemporaine: Vers une éthique relationnelle." *Nouvelles études francophones*, vol. 34, no. 1, 2019, pp. 45–59.

Guyer, Jonathan. "War, Romance, and Everyday Life in Beirut's Emerging Alt-Comix Scene." *Atlas Obscura*, 9 Sept. 2019, https://www.atlasobscura.com/articles/middle-east-alternative-comics.

Hifaoui Fakhouri, Nour. "Ahed wa Karīm / Ahed et Karim / Ahed and Karim." *Ça restera entre nous / Ḵalf al-bab*. Alifabata/Samandal, 2016, pp. 197–212.

Johnston, John. "Democratic Walls: Street Art as Public Pedagogy." *Translating Dissent: Voices from and with the Egyptian Revolution*, edited by Mona Baker, Routledge, 2016, pp. 178–93.

Macaron, Raphaelle. "Steak." *Bien, Monsieur*, no. 10, 2018, pp. 39–42, https://www.raphaellemacaron.com/steakbien-monsieur.

Merhej, Lena. "Éditorial/Al-iftitāḥiyyah." *Ça restera entre nous / Ḵalf al-bab*. Alifabata/Samandal, 2016, pp. 2–9.

Mulvey, Laura. "Visual Pleasure and Narrative Cinema." *Screen*, vol. 16, 1975, pp. 6–18.

Negahban, Behbod. "Entretien: Comics Shows Arab Women's Struggles." *The Daily Star*, 16 Mar. 2019, p. 12.

"Nour Hifaoui Fakhoury." *Cité Internationale des Arts*, https://www.citedesartsparis.net/en/nour-hifaoui-fakhoury.

Samandal Collective. *Ça restera entre nous / Ḵalf al-bab*. Edited by Lena Merhej, Alifabata/Samandal, 2016.

Shaker, Sara. "Gender Binaries and Sexual Violence in Adult Comics during Post-Revolutionary Egypt." *Kohl: A Journal for Body and Gender Research*, vol. 3, no. 2, 2017, https://pdfs.semanticscholar.org/5880/b0e34a517cfd7fb416f5df46d9491f62ffb1.pdf.

Traboulsi, Jana. "Des affiches pour Gaza: L'envoi de Jana Traboulsi." *L'humanité*, 13 July 2014, p. 14.

Voitachewski. "Samandal, deuxième rencontre." *du9: l'autre bande dessinée*. Feb. 2017, https://www.du9.org/entretien/samandal-deuxieme-rencontre/.

Williams, Linda. *Screening Sex*. Duke UP, 2008.

CHAPTER 8

Unveiling IVG

Representations of Women's Experiences of Abortion in the *Bande Dessinée*

CATRIONA MACLEOD

Legislation to restrict abortion rights based on gestational age was introduced in nine of the United States in 2019. This was followed in June 2022 by the decision of the United States Supreme Court to overturn the *Roe v. Wade* legislation that had guaranteed the federal right to abortion access for almost fifty years. In France, where abortion[1] is legal up until twelve weeks after conception, the most recent legal changes have appeared to support abortion rights. In 2015, François Hollande's left-wing government abolished the seven-day "reflection period" required prior to the abortion procedure. In early 2017, this same Parti-Socialiste-led government criminalized the dissemination of false antiabortion information online. Nevertheless, public attendance at the annual *Marche pour la vie*—the demonstration protesting abortion held in Paris—has risen continually since its inauguration in 2005 and now attracts, according to its organizers' estimates, some 50,000 marchers (Leclair). As the debate over maintaining abortion access rages in the United States and the *Marche pour la vie*'s fundamental principal of a "comprehensive abolition" of abortion in France appears to be attracting

---

1. In France, abortion, or *avortement*, is also known as *l'interruption volontaire de grossesse* [voluntary interruption of pregnancy], or IVG.

more support and attention every year, the political discourse surrounding the abortion debate appears to be increasingly binary. Ever less nuance appears in public debate between the definitive stances currently known as "pro-choice" and "pro-life."

In 1971, four years before the decriminalization of abortion in France, 343 women famously signed their names to the manifesto written by Simone de Beauvoir and published in the *Nouvel observateur* admitting to having had an abortion, putting themselves at risk of criminal proceedings, not to mention public judgment. Now, almost fifty years later, and four decades after the legalization of abortion in France, in the US, and more in the UK, the taboo nature of admitting to abortion remains. Mallary Allen explains that having an abortion carries a "discreditable stigma" (43), that is, it is an act that is socially devalued but can also be hidden from others. As such, informational control—meaning carefully choosing when to speak about abortion experiences, most often resulting in keeping silent—is an effective stigma management strategy (44). When women *have* chosen to reveal abortions publicly, such testimonies have often continued into the present day to incite negative responses, or silence, thus ensuring the cyclical nature of the stigma despite the legal changes of the '70s and the progress of women's rights movements since these landmark decisions. Annie Ernaux has revealed, for example, that following the publishing of her text *L'evènement* [The Event] in 2000, which told the story of an illegal abortion she underwent in the 1960s, the media, accustomed to welcoming a new Ernaux work with interviews and reviews, adopted an unofficial but uniformly adhered to code of silence regarding this text (Frappier and Frappier 67). As impactful as the manifesto of the 343 women was, decades on, abortion remains for many a shameful secret.

The *bande dessinée* (the French-language graphic novel) was famously associated with the campaign for abortion rights in the 1970s in France: the satirical cartoon by Cabu that followed the week after the *Nouvel observateur* manifesto, cheekily captioned "who knocked up the 343 sluts of the abortion manifesto?" and showing the face of antiabortionist politician Michel Debré replying, "It was in the name of France!,"[2] was so widely read and circulated that it has become synonymous with the original protest text. However, the intersection of abortion being an experience that most directly affects women, the paucity of women artists in the *bande dessinée* prior to the new millennium, and the pervasive culture of silence continuing to surround the experience has meant that abortion narratives have not multiplied in the

---

2. All translations are my own.

bande dessinée as it has grown to become an adult-directed, sophisticated medium. This tide has begun to turn in the most recent years, however. *Des salopes et des anges*, written by Tonino Benacquista and Florence Cestac and published in 2011; *Le choix*, published in 2015 and created by Desirée and Alain Frappier; and *Il fallait que je vous le dise*, written by Aude Mermilliod and published in 2019, all take abortion as their principal theme. Between them, they provide historical and contemporary accounts of abortion before and after its legalization, they comprise both fiction and life narrative, and they swing from explicit and tragic to light-hearted or darkly humorous. This chapter will examine these works, analyzing how they visually and textually depict the abortion experience and how they respond to the taboo that they are breaking, simply by virtue of existing. It will examine how the first two works, in their use of both visual and narrative key tropes, clearly adhere to one side of the pro-choice/pro-life debate and how the most recent, *Il fallait que je vous le dise*, draws on stylistic features of the *bande dessinée* form as well as specific narrative devices to add nuance to the normally strict dichotomy that governs this ultimate "unsayable" of contemporary women's experiences.

In her 2015 study of abortion experiences recounted online, Mallary Allen notes that the highly recognizable political and public split between pro-choice and pro-life positions shapes the way that the few women who do tell their abortion stories frame these narratives. "As a cause gains public attention," she says "formulaic understandings become widespread, and those with ambiguous experiences of an issue learn to emphasize those elements of their biographies most consistent with dominant social movement stories" (45). The tendency to shape stories about abortion into recognizable categories is further heightened by the discreditable stigma attached to the procedure: this means that because of the controversial nature of the admission, those women who do share their stories are particularly susceptible to the emphasis of parts of their experience that correspond with socially recognizable motives or contributing factors.

In her primary source analysis, Allen studies one hundred firsthand abortion accounts from each of two different online fora made for the very purpose, one designated as specifically pro-choice and one as pro-life. She finds that the personal experiences recounted on the pro-choice website consistently emphasize young age, singular abortions, responsible use of contraceptives that unexpectedly failed, serious contemplation of the abortion prior to it, and middle-class goals like education, career, and marriage taking precedence over "irresponsibly" bringing a life into the world (47). Fulfilling these criteria results in what Rayna Rapp in 2000 referred to as a "good abortion" (qtd. in Allen 47). Stories of terminations from the pro-life forum appear markedly different. They foreground the suffering of the woman—both mental and physical, during and long after the procedure—a retrospective focus on the "selfishness" of their decision, accounts of falling victim to profit-driven doctors and clinics, and a focus on repentance (often religious) for having chosen to, as they see it, deny the chance of life (47, 56). While the threat of social condemnation impinges on women generally to stay silent regarding their abortion experiences, women who have undergone the procedure but still, or later, consider themselves pro-life "assert that the pro-choice movement does not want women to talk about their abortions lest the 'truths' of suffering be known" (56). Regardless of political or ethical stance, the complex layering of pressures on women to remain silent regarding abortion renders each recounted experience an important act of testimony on what can be a pivotal decision in the lives of affected women.

Des salopes et des anges was published following the forty-year anniversary of the 343 manifesto and is dedicated to its signatories and to Simone Veil, the health minister who fought for and succeeded in legalizing both contraception and abortion in France. Its paratext thus establishes it as a pro-choice work. This position is then borne out in both parts of its narrative. The book begins with a five-page historical outline of antiabortion laws and the corresponding punishments for breaking them as well as the various ways women through the ages have themselves attempted to end their pregnancies with often fatal results. The narrative proper then begins: a fictionalized tale of three women of differing ages and lifestyles, prior to the legalization of abortion in France, who travel to London with a coachfull of other women seeking the procedure that is already legal in the United Kingdom. The final pages of their story are interspersed with panels depicting Simone Veil's ultimately successful appeals to the French parliament to legalize abortion. The intent of this *bande dessinée* is clearly to remind its readership (or, indeed, to inform younger readers for the first time) of the consequences of an abortion ban, the manifestation of this intent ranging from snapshot images of hemorrhaging or death due to unsafe clandestine abortions to the longer-form narrative depiction of the stress and indignity of having to travel en masse alongside strangers to other countries to safely undergo the procedure. Artist Cestac's signature style—the bulbous nose, exaggerated facial expressions, and bold colors—lends a comic lightness to the strip that clashes with the gravity of the subject matter. This juxtaposition reminds the reader that the exceptional situation these women find themselves in is as truly lived as any comedic mishap that might more readily be expected of this artistic style and that their lives continue after it.

The title, *Des salopes et des anges*, is both a reference to the Charlie Hebdo *Manifeste des 343 salopes* [Manifesto of the 343 Whores] caricature, which is referenced and reproduced visually during the historical introduction (Benacquista and Cestac 6), and to the so-called *faiseuses d'anges* [angel makers]—women who performed clandestine terminations on other women prior to the legalization of abortion, using the necessarily unsophisticated (and, hence, high-risk) methods visualized in the *bande dessinée*. The title also poses the question of female stereotypes and of the relation between conflicting notions of "idealized womanhood" in the modern world and how these notions are associated with the opposing stances of the abortion debate. The division of women into the binary categories of "Madonna" and "whore," or, indeed, *ange* and *salope*, based primarily on their sexual behaviour (whether perceived or real) is many centuries old.[3] Mary Ferguson, in her work on female stereotypes in traditional narratives, denotes the selfless mother type (a version of the Madonna extreme) to be one of the key, most-recognizable tropes of womanhood. She states that "in every age woman has been seen primarily in her biological, primordial role as the mysterious source of life" (4). Bernadette Jacobs confirms this, stating of the child*less* woman that, to varying extents over time, she has cross-culturally been regarded as "unnatural" and even as a figure to be feared (68). The woman who elects not to become a mother by terminating a viable pregnancy, then, constitutes the most extreme challenge to the traditional notion of womanhood, this confrontation encouraging the understanding of women who choose abortion as *salopes* or whores and also sometimes criminal and unstable.

The narrative formulas defined by Allen in her research respond to the challenge posed by abortion to differing interpretations of women's roles in the twenty-first century. That which emerges from the pro-life testimonies remains close to the traditional notion that motherhood is an essential part of the female experience (such narratives are focused on regret, suffering, and often supported by references to Christian faith [47, 58], once again bringing the discourse on women back to the notion of the Madonna). The ideal woman figure who emerges from the pro-choice stories is responsible with her sexuality and relationships, and her personal fulfillment is synonymous with middle-class values of education and career success (Allen 60). In line with the latter, Benacquista and Cestac's text shows abortion to be a necessary element of a feminist, white, middle-class ideal of womanhood. Among the coachload of women traveling to London for a termination, only one woman is shown to be Black. She does not speak but is noted to have

---

3. For example, see Tischkoff.

been raped in a refugee camp (17), further separating her experience from that of the white "norm." All the other women are white and often intellectual in their references—whether literary as in "I'm not crying, I'm reading *La Princesse de Clèves*" (26) or political as in "[cashmire] is a wool made by bourgeoise ex-colonialists" (30)—and are frequently smartly sardonic in their internal commentary, in spite of their emotional distress. Although one of the three main characters, Odile, herself a political activist and a contributor to the Mouvement pour la Liberté de l'Avortement et de la Contraception (MLAC; Movement for the Legalization of Abortion and Contraception), decides to keep her baby at the last minute, she elects to stay in England, the country which would have allowed her termination, the reader understanding that this is her final act of abortion-supporting protest. The other two women, Maïté and Anne-Sophie, flourish in their lives after their abortions. Maïté is emboldened by her experience to assume a more powerful role in her relationship with her partner and goes on to have three children and a successful career after they are married. Anne-Sophie returns home following her trip to London and immediately informs her flabbergasted husband that she will be taking up her political science studies once more. It is noted that, although the three women remain close in the following years, their common experience in London is never again mentioned between them. The album closes with the artists' narration revealing that although Maïté now considers Anne-Sophie and Odile her closest friends, the only souvenir of her trip to London[4] she has kept is a customized T-shirt, symbolic of her feminist awakening, stating that Jean-Paul, her boyfriend who originally pushes her into having a termination, is an idiot (46). Not all elements of *Des salopes et des anges* corresponds to the middle-class understanding of the "good abortion" as defined by Allen and Rapp: Anne-Sophie, for example, falls pregnant due to an unfaithful tryst, a narrative element more associated with pro-life abortion stories, which often regretfully reflect on previously lived "illicit lifestyles" (Allen 55). However, in spite of the differences established between the women—for example, Odile doesn't go through with her abortion, and Maïté does but goes on to have three children once married, while Anne-Sophie already has two children and doesn't have more after her termination—all the women conform to the "stock character" of pro-choice rhetoric in that the fact of having the choice to terminate or not, and actively using that choice, empowers them to pursue specific "feminist and middle-class goals."

---

4. The ambiguity of the French word "souvenir," meaning both a keepsake object and a memory, is played upon intentionally by Benacquista and Cestac here.

Le choix by Désirée and Alain Frappier is another *bande dessinée* narrative that falls clearly, as its title "The Choice" would suggest, into the pro-choice category. This story is written in the first person, but it is only revealed near the close of the story that the narrative "I" is the adolescent voice of the female scriptor, Désirée. A well-documented and resolutely serious work in contrast to Benacquista and Cestac's wryly humorous style, *Le choix* uses writer Désirée's firsthand experience of abortion to emphasize two main points: the lifelong emotional and developmental consequences for a child who grows up with parents that did not want to have them and the ubiquity of illegal abortion in the pre-Veil era in France. The first is shown principally through Désirée's recounting of her childhood experience in a dysfunctional and sometimes violent family environment before and after she learns, from her mother's confession, that her birth had not been wished for. The second is relayed intra-narratively—Désirée herself, her mother, her roommate Mathilde, and her boyfriend's mother are all noted to have undergone abortions during the story—and via instances of testimony from medical professionals, journalists, widowers, and survivors of illegal abortions appearing near the close of the book, among which is the estimation of a gynecologist who worked in pre–Veil law France that as many as one in two women had clandestine abortions prior to the legalization of the procedure (70).

While in Benacquista and Cestac's text it is the latter's comic, almost grotesque style that undertakes the pro-choice task of "normalizing" the IVG process, bringing it from the status of exceptional and unspeakable into a real, lived experience for many women, in *Le choix*, the structuring of panels plays this same role alongside the narrative and testimonial elements previously noted. One striking example of this comes in a double page near the start of the story as Désirée, a teenager in the 1970s, gets involved with the MLAC after being inspired by a friend. The left page of panels is drawn in the standard minimalist realist style of the *bande dessinée*, showing the MLAC militants discussing the significance of everyday language in the context of pregnancy and abortion in among images showing them organizing themselves to administer illegal terminations using a modified bicycle pump (32). The right page eschews the standard architecture of strips and panels entirely and presents a large black-backed splash page showing Simone Veil standing at a lectern below the seated President of the Assemblée Nationale, addressing parliament on the need for a change in the abortion law (figure 8.1). This page is rendered in a much more detailed, realistic style, with the use of dark gray and shadowing giving the images the air of grainy black-and-white photos from a news report. The juxtaposition of these pages, one set against no visibly identifiable background and over eight panels,

FIGURE 8.1. Désirée Frappier and Alain Frappier, *Le choix*, 2015, p. 33.

featuring women and men of the MLAC calmly huddled together discussing who will take a turn at assisting the performance of illegal abortions, and the other, one single image of two isolated figures, set, despite the grainy quality of the image, against the opulent surroundings of the Assemblée, opposes clearly the difference between the reality of lived experience for women and the slow pace of legal response which, up until this point, had apparently ignored the dangerous consequences of the abortion ban.

Although each of the three texts examined in this chapter focuses on different elements of the issue of abortion, all three feature the face and words of health minister Simone Veil. The sites that hosted the testimonies studied by Mallary Allen are American in origin; the findings she deduces, while seeming clearly to fit transnational pro-choice discourse, must also be considered as such. One thing, therefore, that may be added to a specifically French pro-choice ideology would seem to be the consistent holding up of Simone Veil as a hero of the feminist and proabortion (these two sociopolitical stances often being conflated) movements. The focus on Veil in the modern-day abortion debate in France is already somewhat predetermined as the 1975 law that guaranteed access to abortion and still exists today, officially titled "The law of 17 January 1975 concerning the voluntary termination of pregnancy," is known more commonly in France as the "Veil law." The recognition of the legislation as the effort of a specific politician is an interesting feature of the French history of reproductive politics; it contrasts with the linguistic focus in the United States, for example, on the female *citizen* who challenged the illegality of abortion (the "Jane Roe" of the oft-cited *Roe v. Wade* Supreme Court decision of 1973). Veil's interment in the Panthéon in 2018, establishing her status as a "great citizen who has earned national recognition,"[5] and the other trappings of state-sponsored hero worship such as having streets and hospitals named after her, are further proof, alongside their recent consolidation of the Veil law by abolishing the pretermination "reflection period" as noted above, of the French government's left-leaning policy slant in direct opposition to the generally right-wing shift visible in Western abortion discourses of the last twenty years.

Each of the *bandes dessinées* studied here also consolidate and defend Veil's status as a hero within their own narratives (and paratextually, in the case of Cestac and Benacquista's text, which is partially dedicated to Veil).

---

5. The 1885 decree that clarified the Panthéon's postrevolution function as a place of burial for the great citizens of the Republic in actuality specified it as a resting place for "great *men* who have earned national recognition" (my emphasis). The first woman to be interred was Marie Curie in 1995. There are, at time of writing, six women buried in the Panthéon alongside seventy-five men.

In *Le choix*, for example, Veil's campaign to legalize abortion is presented in a further contrasting double page, immediately following that analyzed above, in which she is introduced to the story standing at a lectern in the Assemblée. The left-hand page of this second example continues in the same reportage style. It contains a column of text in its center that explains the finer detail of the proposed law being heatedly debated in the Assemblée. Veil's depiction on this page is presented both visually and textually in line with several well-known tropes of heroic narrative. A small footnote explains her overcoming of incredible personal odds as it notes that Veil and her family, of Jewish origin, were deported to Nazi-led concentration camps in 1944, resulting in the death of both parents and her brother. The visual setting of Veil's clearly defined image directly opposite one of a group of watching female citizens at the top of the page (separated only by the column of text) further establishes her as champion of the people and opposes her against the images of her antagonists: shadowy, unidentifiable male politicians who stand alone against black backgrounds, displaying aggressive stances and speaking emotionally charged words against the legalization of abortion. A quotation at the bottom of the page establishes Veil as courageous, even at personal expense: she states, "I could never have imagined the hate that I was going to provoke, the monstrosity of some of the politicians' words, or their rudeness towards me," these words appearing next to the drawn sign of a swastika that is noted to have been scrawled on Veil's apartment building. The opposing, right-hand page returns to the standard, minimalist visual style of the *bande dessinée*, indicating that the narrative proper has once again begun. Veil's heroic victory in parliament is described as "like the declaration of the end of a war" (35); and religious symbolism, such as the image of sunlight spreading out over a statue of the Madonna, is used to convey the enormity of its consequences. The middle column of the previous page does admit to the Veil law's limitations—its expectation of a reflection period and suggestion that abortions should be privately funded by all women with the necessary means—but it also presents these elements as Veil's carefully calculated concessions in order to secure the larger, decisive victory. No other politician is named in this sequence, thus presenting the successful passing of the law as the result of Veil's sole effort and her as a solitary, selfless hero.

Des salopes et des anges and *Le choix*, published in 2011 and 2015, respectively, align themselves with established pro-choice rhetoric in several ways, but both clearly underline the importance of Simone Veil's political campaign to legalize abortion and focus largely on the pre-1975 reality of clandestine terminations in order to underline the danger of a potential future return to illegal abortions. *Il fallait que je vous le dise*, by Aude Mermilliod, published in 2019, presents a twenty-first-century, firsthand account of having a termination. This narrative is less clearly movement aligned than either of the preceding *bandes dessinées* discussed and, fairly unusual for the recounting of a contemporary abortion experience, expresses notions key to both pro-choice and pro-life rhetoric.

Mermilliod frames her narrative with explicit references to its autobiographical veracity via a preface at its beginning and a photograph of herself at its conclusion, in contrast to *Le choix*'s cautious, piecemeal approach to revealing Désirée Frappier's place as narrator. The preface underlines the essential difficulty of expressing the abortion experience and refers to the *bande dessinée* as the format that finally enabled her to succeed: "[I tried to] express my experience in words, but maybe if it can't be said, it can be drawn" (3). From the first pages of the story, Mermilliod is careful to align herself with the pro-choice conditions that Allen and Rapp have noted currently render an abortion "more acceptable." Six pages into the narrative as she is starting to wonder if she might be pregnant, she notes that she is using adequate contraception and that she has no money and no stable relationship with the possible baby's father (21). Her future choice to have an abortion is thus established, even before her pregnancy is confirmed, as "responsible" given the circumstances. The issue of her personal responsibility for falling pregnant—or rather her lack of *ir*responsibility—is repeated several times over the next few pages as she learns that she actually is pregnant. The 0.6 percent fail rate of the coil is explicitly stated (23), and her use of what should have been effective contraception is repeated twice more (24), thus clearly establishing the pregnancy as something that has happened *to* her despite her best efforts. The insistence of authors of pro-choice abortion accounts that they are victims of their circumstances while showing a strong sense of self-responsibility is a key feature of the accounts that Allen analyses in her work (49). Allen notes that in direct response to the apparently growing public discomfiture with unrestricted abortion access since the mid-90s, pro-choice discourse has become increasingly apologetic and keen to emphasize those narrative elements that appear to justify a termination while also defensively underlining the concerned women's responsibility and "reverence for the abortion issue" (44).[6] Despite the carefully expressed beginning of *Il fallait que je vous le dise*, however, there are several instances of this *bande dessinée* narrative that stray far from the standardized

---

6. Jeannie Ludlow, in her article on abortion in Diane Noomin's comics, also discusses the "rightward shift in abortion discourse in the 1990s" (192) and the modification of pro-choice rhetoric in order to compensate.

pro-choice rhetoric and use the textual-visual mix of the *bande dessinée* to add nuance to the so-often polarized abortion discourse.

The first is the short sequence depicting the ultrasound Aude has to undergo in order to date her pregnancy properly prior to its termination. Rosalind Pollack Petchesky writes of the importance of the development of ultrasound technology from the 1960s onward in the shifting of understanding pregnancy in the public (nonmedical) imagination, taking it from a mysterious and internal feminine process, to externally visible and, thus, possessable and governable by men as well as women. The ultrasound image, particularly in the hard-line antiabortion stances of the 1980s, would become a prominent visual tool of pro-life supporters eager to defend the notion of "fetal personhood." As Pollack Petchesky also states of ultrasound images in her article, however, "from their beginning, such photographs have represented the fetus as primary and autonomous, the woman as absent or peripheral" (268). The ultrasound image separates the fetus from the mother, who is never identifiable in the picture. In the two-page ultrasound sequence in Mermilliod's narrative (32–33), the artist shows an imagined version of herself standing in front of the ultrasound pictures that are being projected onto the doctor's screen while her "real" character-self lies back. She draws unrealistically large images of the six-week fetus (figure 8.2) as a nod to the visual power of the ultrasound image and the often intensely emotional effect it has on those looking at it. Her drawing of herself in front of the over-sized fetal image uses the flexibility of representation of the sequential art form to reintroduce the body of the pregnant woman into the ultrasound process, breaking down the over-simplified "baby" (pro-life) or "mother" (pro-choice) exclusionary division of focus in abortion politics. Aude stares up at the images of her womb in a series of panels that recall the viewing of a creature in an aquarium. The fetus is a fascinating sight that she reaches out to touch, at once familiar but also unknown, and too young at this stage to resemble a human baby. The colors used in this sequence—the fetus stands out, rendered in bright white strokes against a brown background—render the uncanny presence in her womb almost spectral. This impression is heightened as its image abruptly disappears to be replaced by a black panel representing a turned-off screen just as Aude reaches out to touch it. The colors and positioning of the characters in this sequence show the complexity of this viewing experience for Aude. The "otherness" of its appearance, Aude's fascination and its sudden disappearance all indicate Aude's uncertain relationship to the fetus, thus questioning the definitive stances of pro- and antiabortion positions, which appear to increasingly allow for no ambivalence and expect that a termination is either "good" or "bad," wanted or unwanted.

FIGURE 8.2. Aude Mermilliod, *Il fallait que je vous le dise*, 2019, p. 33. © Casterman. Used with permission from the author and Editions Casterman.

Perhaps the most memorable sequence in *Il fallait que je vous le dise*, and the one which most clearly questions the rhetorical norms associated with the abortion debate, is the scene depicting the procedure itself. Later in the narrative, Mermilliod lets a doctor and writer, Martin Winckler, recount the abortion process from a medical perspective. In these pages the reader is given considerable detail about how the procedure used to and currently works; changing attitudes toward the procedure as a practice from within the medical community; and, like the other *bandes dessinées* noted, a recounting of the fight for its legalization in France and Veil's importance therein, once again confirming her heroic status as a firm feature of specifically French pro-choice discourse.[7] It is in depicting her own personal experience of abortion, however, that Aude engages the medium's particularity and the audience's engagement to greatest effect. Abandoning the standard panel and strip layout that is seen in most other pages of the *bande dessinée*, when depicting the termination she undergoes, Mermilliod instead uses a fluid structure without clearly delineated panels and incorporates minimal dialogue and progressively less bodily imagery, instead emphasizing the sensations felt during the procedure (see figure 8.3). In a striking double splash page (52–53), the reader first sees portions of Aude's body surrounded by clouds of red and gray color. Vertical black lines depict the tensing of her body and multiple repetitions of the letter "R" indicate the sound of the aspiration machine used in the procedure. The impression of the termination's never-endingness is conveyed across the double page by the lack of visual linearity, and the striking red, leaking over the depictions of her body like blood stains, is an effective nonverbal indicator of her suffering. It is, however, the multiple iterations of the "RRRRR" onomatopoeia that most clearly draw the reader's attention—the endless repetition and varying sizing of this textual sound work to draw the eye. Overleaf, a second double page concludes the depiction of the termination and again relies on onomatopoeia to represent Aude's experience. This sequence shows the doctor taking the jar of matter extracted from Aude's body through a door into a darkened room. The shockingly frank textual sounds "chloub" and "fsssh!!!" that emanate from the dark room through sound bubbles indicate that this matter has been disposed of in a toilet, flushed away.

Onomatopoeia in francophone and Anglo-American sequential art often convey by their simple presence a certain legerity, a reminder of the medium's juvenile roots in stories of "noisy" children's adventures. Karin Kukkonen, in *Studying Comics and Graphic Novels*, confirms this and states that sound effects have been eschewed by sequential narratives seeking to convey a tone of maturity, due to their association with the outdated impression of the "infantile and hyperbolic nature of comics" (25). Mermilliod's self-reflexive use here of a normally light-hearted classic comics feature clashes grotesquely with the seriousness of the subject matter: Aude's physical and emotional pain and the entirely undignified means of disposing of the fetal remains, within earshot of the patient, who later relives the noises in

---

7. It should be noted here that Aude's story mostly takes place in Brussels. The medical education of General Practitioner Winckler (real name Marc Zoffran) and his ensuing, staunchly pro-choice practice begin, however, in France.

FIGURE 8.3. Aude Mermilliod, *Il fallait que je vous le dise*, 2019, p. 52. © Casterman. Used with permission from the author and Editions Casterman.

a traumatized flashback (59).[8] The setting of the abortion experience within the everyday as seen in Benacquista and Cestac's work is pushed to extremes here by Mermilliod. The eminently familiar sound of a toilet flushing, associated with the riddance of human waste, contrasts completely with the "reverence" for abortion currently required by standard pro-choice discourse, instead layering it with grotesque, scatological auditory symbols. The lack of sensitivity involved in the abortion procedure undergone by Aude and her difficult physical and mental experience of it, conveyed by both the "RRRR" and "chloub" and "fshh!!!" onomatopoeia, correspond most readily to the suffering often highlighted in the pro-life abortion stories analyzed by Mallary Allen in which almost every testimony describes "painful procedures, cruel or insensitive staff and/or unsettling sights or sounds" (56).[9]

Given their general understanding as unsophisticated and somewhat infantile tools, onomatopoeia remain understudied elements of the sequential art form. However, it is clear that the use of onomatopoeia demands, by their very nature, a high level of participation from the reader. As textualized sound can only approximately depict real auditory sound, suggesting what kind of noise is being heard by the characters in a panel rather than reproducing it realistically, a hefty margin of interpretation is left open. The onomatopoeia therefore becomes an invitation to the reader to fill in the necessary gap created by the visual representation of an auditory experience. In *Il fallait que je vous le dise*, then, Mermilliod does not spare her readers the pain of her termination experience but instead asks that they engage with it and go through it with her as they imagine the sounds that she scribes.[10] Such direct appeal to the reader's active imagination can only be interpreted as a call from the artist to the reader to reflect intentionally on the reality of an often unrepresented, stigmatized experience both as it is happening in the middle of the narrative, where it is shown as painful and traumatic, and then again at the end when Mermilliod expresses her continuing gratitude

---

8. In recounting this aspect of her lived experience, Mermilliod's narrative once again corresponds to an element of pro-life rhetoric. Accusations of mishandling of fetal remains by Planned Parenthood in 2015 in the United States, for example, became part of a larger political push to defund the organization, often associated with the administering of abortions.

9. In contrast, the pro-choice narratives analyzed either do not directly discuss the termination procedure or emphasize the caring nature of clinical staff involved (Allen 56).

10. In this way, something of a parallel can be drawn between Mermilliod's narrative testimony and the comic strip depictions of abortion by US comics artist Diane Noomin in the 1990s. Jeannie Ludlow states in an article on this theme in Noomin's work that "not interested in normalizing abortion through denial or dismissal of discomfort, Noomin instead invites her readers into the tension, the ambivalence that characterizes abortion experience" (201).

that she was able to make the choice (163), thus resetting the understanding of the procedure as painful but necessary. The ambivalence that the reader is asked to confront critiques the current understanding of abortion in the popular imagination. Neither side of the political dichotomy, and their accompanying tropes and vocabulary insisting on polarized extremes, appears to fit her experience.

All three *bandes dessinées* studied here clearly support, in different ways, legal rights to abortion, and all were varyingly positively received, albeit unexceptionally.[11] However, while *Des salopes et des anges* and *Le choix* might be described as classically "pro-choice," consistently displaying the features identified by Allen's study of real-life testimonies, *Il fallait que je vous le dise* appears to intentionally defy categorization by problematizing the definitive schism between the currently held, largely pan-Western pro-choice and pro-life stances. Notably, in undertaking this problematization, Mermilliod draws heavily from specific features of the sequential art medium—particularly its graphic flexibility and use of color and onomatopoeia. If Mermilliod is right and what cannot be said might be able to be drawn, *Il fallait que je vous le dise* suggests that the sequential art medium has the potential to become a contributing factor in eventually breaking or, at least, in diminishing the taboo of openly considering the lived reality of abortion. If they wish to create legislation that best suits both the ethical considerations associated with abortion and the experience of women who might wish to undergo it, this is something to which lawmakers should surely pay attention.

Works Cited

Allen, Mallary. "Narrative Diversity and Sympathetic Abortion: What Online Storytelling Reveals about the Prescribed Norms of the Mainstream Movements." *Symbolic Interaction*, vol. 38, no. 1, 2015, pp. 42–63.

Benacquista, Tonino, and Florence Cestac. *Des salopes et des anges*. Dargaud, 2011.

Feguson, Mary A. *Images of Women in Literature*. 3rd ed., Houghton Mifflin, 1981.

Frappier, Désirée, and Alain Frappier. *Le choix*. La Ville Brûle, 2015.

Jacobs, Bernadette. *Childfree Women: An Archetypal Perspective*. Pro Quest, 2007.

Kukkonen, Karin. *Studying Comics and Graphic Novels*. Wiley/Blackwell, 2013.

---

11. Requests for sales figures for each publication were not returned. However, a survey of the online presence of each *bande dessinée* reveals a certain level of success for each, in particular for *Il fallait que je vous le dise*, which has been most referenced outside of specialist *bande dessinée* print and online sources (referenced or reviewed on mainstream French news sites *Le Parisien* and *France Info*). This text was also short-listed in 2020 for the Prix Artémisia, a range of awards given in France to female-created graphic novels.

Leclair, Agnès. "Bioéthique: Le 'Marche pour la vie' rassemble des milliers de manifestants." *Le Figaro*, 18 Jan. 2019, https://www.lefigaro.fr/actualite-france/2019/01/18/01016-20190118ARTFIG00201-bioethique-la-marche-pour-la-vie-veut-gonfler-ses-troupes.php.

Ludlow, Jeannie. "Graphic Abortion: The Grotesque in Diane Noomin's 1990s Abortion Comics." *Feminist Formations*, vol. 31, no. 2, 2019, pp. 181–204.

Mermilliod, Aude. *Il fallait que je vous les dise*. Casterman, 2019.

Pollack Petchesky, Rosalind. "Fetal Images: The Power of Visual Culture in the Politics of Reproduction." *Feminist Studies*, vol. 13, no. 2, 1987, pp. 263–92.

Tishkoff, Doris. *Madonna/Whore: The Myth of the Two Marys*. AuthorHouse, 2005.

PART 3

REPRESENTATIONS AND HISTORY (HERSTORIES)

CHAPTER 9

The Face of Women in Early *Bandes Dessinées*
Töpffer, Cham, Musset, Gustave Doré

JACQUES DÜRRENMATT

TRANSLATED BY MARGARET C. FLINN

Scholars have frequently commented upon the negative and problematic status of women in Franco-Belgian *bandes dessinées* before the arrival of the first real popular heroines in the 1960s (e.g., Barbarella, Natacha, Yoko Tsuno, Cellulite, etc.).[1] Until that generation of heroines, female *bande dessinée* characters were, at best, marginalized (to the point of absence) or more often grotesque (we might think of Madame Fenouillard and her daughters, Bécassine, la Castafiore, etc.). In this essay, I am interested in the degree to which we can consider this negative situation to stem directly from the very first *bandes dessinées*, those created in the 1830s through the 1850s.

It has been difficult for historians to determine exactly who the audience was for these very early *bandes dessinées*. We do know that Rodolphe Töpffer invented his "littérature en estampes" to make moral lessons more attractive to the students taught at the boys' school he had founded in Geneva.[2] The quickly expanding circulation of those albums necessarily would have led to some female readership—however, precise evidence of that readership remains lacking. Thus, David Kunzle very aptly asks:

---

1. Translations of quotations in this chapter are done by Flinn, except where a published translation is indicated.
2. See Renonciat (261–62).

Who, indeed, was the audience? Töpffer appealed to older children, sophisticated adolescents, adults with the heart of children, adults who like to laugh—children still, of a kind. . . . We must imagine not just schoolboys but whole families gathered round albums of caricatures. We who read in isolation cannot imagine these shared pleasures, Dickens read aloud, Töpffer crowded over, the ricochet of laughter. (*Father* 126)

Sisters and mothers were certainly part of these circles, but one nonetheless tends to suspect that from the outset, this sort of story would have been tinged with an air of prohibition for the female readership. Commentary provided by David Kunzle on the appearance of the first woman caricaturist, Marie Duval, supports this conclusion:[3]

> The ways in which women pursing an artistic career could be undermined were compounded in the case of caricature, a more thoroughly male-dominated profession even than painting. Caricature, as a major branch of magazine illustration, provided a livelihood for a large number of western European artists during the 19th century. All, with the exception of Marie Duval, seem to have been men. This is not hard to explain: "Woman's nature" was considered antithetical to the aggressive polemical and critical nature of so much journalism in general and caricature in particular. ("Marie Duval" 26)

Furthermore, Marie-Ève Thérenty has shown how press readership of the era was also subjected to strictly gendered divisions:

> In the nineteenth-century daily newspaper, the boundaries between the different sections correspond to a normative and prescriptive gendering of the news that reproduces social divisions by defining public space as predominately masculine and private, marginal space as mainly feminine. Political and diplomatic sections are addressed towards men, while the newspaper sections dedicated to the home, to intimacy and the society pages address women. This gap also corresponds to the separation of different temporal regimes: the exceptional, or the event, are male business, while women's business is the repetitive, the banal, the prosaic. Sections are often demarcated by extremely precise gender indicators: prescriptive descriptions of readership that should help avoid any error in guidance as to target audience. These readership contracts can be supplemented by prescriptions

---

3. Duval, though born to French parents, had her entire career in England in the 1870s. For more about the life and career of cartoonist Marie Duval, see Grennan, et al.

internal to the family home, as is shown in this excerpt from Zola's *Pot-Bouille*, where fifteen-year-old Angèle reads the *Gazette de France* behind her *Histoire sainte*: "Angèle," he said, "what are you doing there? This morning, I crossed out the article with a red pencil. You know very well that you are not to read the crossed-out parts." "Papa, I was reading what was next to it," replied the young girl. (254)

From Thérenty's work, we can deduce that the publications specialized in caricature that began to appear at the end of the 1840s in the satirical press—sometimes with a very political dimension—were read by a primarily masculine public.[4] (These included the first serial comics, notably, under the pen of Nadar). This confrontation of two different ways of being in the world is perfectly illuminated by Alfred de Musset's representation of it in his only attempt at *bande dessinée* (for a private readership), inspired by Töpffer, around 1840. George Sand, the preeminent woman writer of the era, is represented bearing the features of her refined character Indiana, pen in hand. Meanwhile Viardot, a real-life friend of Musset and Sand, comes to ask her advice about the difficulties he has encountered while trying to marry a young woman called Pauline. In a most excessive example of caricature, Viardot sports a massive nasal appendage that is simultaneously phallic and grotesque. Indeed, it is so large that he must rest it on Indiana/Sand's writing table and then her shoulder.

In French, disappointment can be expressed with the expression "avoir le nez qui s'allonge" [to have a lengthening nose], thus the visual pun. But what is striking above all is the opposition in style: two distinctive spaces, two modes of reading and writing. As Mireille Dottin-Orsini notes:

> Indiana . . . has the more spectacular role. She appears, smoking a pipe, in panel 9, while the rejected Viardot recounts his misfortunes, his long nose dripping with tears. A long Oriental sword in her belt, she swears on her chibouk (a small houkah) to deploy her eloquence to repair the engagement. We know the strength of George Sand's persuasiveness: she managed to convince Musset's mother (who didn't like her much) to accept the lovers' trip to Venice. She has large dark eyes, a rounded headband, a luscious mouth; three times we see her saber in hand. She cuts a fine figure, even when smoking under the nose of the Garcia ladies. Attending the wedding (a civil ceremony, given the groom's opinions), she is particularly beautiful, her profile standing out from the long dark hair spread over her

---

4. On the appearance of these publications, see Dürrenmatt, "Nadar."

shoulder. If Pauline sometimes seems silly, there is no caricature in the case of Indiana—quite the contrary, even if Musset had good reason to resent her [Sand]. But his brief series of drawings leaves us with a most lively and amusing portrait of the energetic novelist. (106)

Three options are thus present as representational possibilities for women in this period. The first sacrifices women to a public of men by subjecting them to caricature, most often through reduction to an immediately recognizable type (the Shrew, the Grand Dame, the Old Maid, etc.). The second seems to respect women through a pseudo-idealization or modest effacement. But that pseudo-idealization begs the question as to whether this treatment depriving women of real integration to graphic worlds is not in fact as much or more damaging than the first option. The third option (inspired by Shakespearean or farcical drama) humorously interrogates apparently irreducible gender differences by representing the effects of the inversion of expected binary gender roles and characteristics. In this chapter I will focus successively on each of those three options, which are all constitutive of the first French comics.

Between Caricature and Idealization

From a physical point of view, the paragon of caricatural representation of women is the "Ugly Woman" while from a behavioral point of view it is "The Innocent." The former abounds in literature of the era. She often has a masculine appearance with a prime example being la Grande Nanon in Balzac's *Eugénie Grandet*.[5] The latter is characterized by extreme naïveté, often to the point of stupidity, like Félicité in Flaubert's *Un cœur simple*.[6] This is the antimodel, most often a secondary character, that we find in the first *bandes dessinées* explicitly destined for a readership of young girls that appear in the periodical *La semaine de Suzette* in 1905.[7] The immediately famous Breton servant girl Bécassine exemplifies this naïve type and serves as an extension

---

5. La Grande Nanon is described as a "female built like Hercules, planted as firmly on her feet as a sixty-year-old oak on its roots, with powerful hips, a broad back, a carter's hands, and a study honesty as unassailable as her untarnished virtue" (Balzac, *Eugénie* 19).

6. In a preparatory draft, Flaubert sketches the character as: "profound ignorance. No desire for knowledge. She had but one need, to love," and he speaks of her "demi-somnolence, similar to that of animals or plants" and her "scattered and profound ideas—thinking as if in a dream" (*Trois contes* 262n83).

7. See Couderc.

of the moralizing mission of Töpffer.[8] It is in fact the whole of society, all genders included, abusing the dominant pejorative clichés of women that Flaubert notably echoes in his *Dictionnaire des idées reçues*:

> YOUNG LADY: Utter these words with diffidence. All young ladies are pale, frail, and always pure. Prohibit, for their good, every kind of reading, all visits to museums, theaters, and especially to the monkey house at the zoo. (92)
> CHAMBERMAIDS: Prettier than their mistresses. Know all their secrets and betray them. Always undone by the son of the house. (22)
> MODESTY: Women's great jewel. (64)

Even cartoonist Marie Duval herself was not kind to women, tending to deform all bodies as if to deny her own identity.

We could imagine that *bandes dessinées*' sequentiality would allow for play in the evolution of characters, including in the sense of character development. But this is not the case: from its beginnings, the ninth art demonstrates a penchant for fixity that takes a long time to dissipate (Tintin and Astérix do not age, and they have no developmental character arc to speak of). Even if their lived experiences are often traumatic, more often than not characters come through various stories unchanged.[9] This fixity is even truer for secondary characters, a status held by the vast majority of female characters. Töpffer is so uninterested in women that he almost always reduces them to stereotype, and in so doing, ironically, shrouds them in mystery. Thus, Monsieur Vieux Bois chases after an unattainable "animated object," and when Madame Crépin offers her head to be palpated by the physiognomist Craniose, the latter ends up by refusing to say anything of his discoveries, implying there was nothing to find.

Almost all the albums produced by Töpffer and in his wake are thus stories of male protagonists. The era's only story centered on a woman—or in fact, two women—is Cham's *Deux vieilles filles vaccinées à marier*.[10] The

---

8. Bécassine's name is made by adding a diminutive suffix to the noun "bécasse," which in French designates a bird considered easy to trick and catch. From the Middle Ages, "bécasse" also meant a stupid or ridiculous appearing woman.

9. We should note as exceptions Töpffer's opportunist Albert, who passes from a state of adolescence to that of bearded revolutionary to end up as a perfect lady-killer, and Cham's Barnabé Gogo, who we follow in perfect coming-of-age fashion from childhood to death: his extraordinary physical growth condemns him to end up by literally outgrowing the panel.

10. A digitized version of this text can be found through the Bibliothèque Nationale de France: https://gallica.bnf.fr/ark:/12148/bpt6k91104170.image.

character of the unmarriageable old maid haunts nineteenth-century literature, inviting various forms of mockery (Sagaert 91–97). In this case, the two young women are mocked through the modifier "vaccinated." We must note that Cham includes this characterization that, in the book's very title, compares the old maids to cattle on the auction block.[11] The old maid often exemplifies physical or moral ugliness, like Cousine Bette in Balzac's eponymous novel.[12] The desire for women's liberation was comparable to what happened in the United States in the same era and also can be noted in the position of certain unmarried feminists during the revolution of 1848. These women, mocked by Flaubert through the character of Vatnaz in *L'éducation sentimentale*, remained rare in *bande dessinée* or caricature, however.[13] Politically active women appear mainly as the figure of the bluestocking, cruelly caricatured by Daumier.[14] For his part, the frankly and resolutely misogynist Barbey d'Aurevilly associated bluestockings with literature: "It was from the time of Madame Sand's novels that we started to see swarms of all kinds of books of poetry and prose about the inequality between men and women, penned by feminists, and at that time, the bluestocking appeared" (xvi).[15]

In fact, for his adaption of Fénelon's famous *Télémaque* (itself inspired by the *Odyssey*) Cham chose to represent Nausicaa as a bluestocking. This is the first figure that appears in the album's opening, and one might wonder about the burlesque inversion insofar as the nymph, famous for her exceptional beauty and powers of seduction, is a priori the very opposite of both the old maid and the rancorous intellectual. On the second page, the reader is told that Calypso is gifted with "Napoleonic intelligence," which from the pen of a royalist such as Cham is no compliment. Through a phenomenon we might qualify as metonymic, the very principle of literary adaptation leads to a slippage of the "book-like" character of the album toward the character that opens it. Her ungratifying physical appearance leads

---

11. Vaccine: "A particular virus endowed with the capacity to protect from smallpox, so-named because it was initially collected from the pustules that sometimes form on cow udders, called cow-pox" (Littré).

12. "A peasant woman from the Vosges in the full meaning of those words, thin, dark, with shiny black hair, thick eyebrows joined by a tuft of hair, long, strong arms, large feet, one or two warts on her long, monkey-like face—that, in brief, is a portrait of this spinster" (Balzac, *Cousin* 34). For an in-depth analysis of this "woman who is not one," see chapter two in Mehta.

13. See Berend; Bem.

14. "*Bluestocking*. Term of contempt applied to women with intellectual interests" (Flaubert, *Dictionary* 19). See also Planté.

15. For more details, see Del Lungo and Louichon.

Nausicaa to be doubly damned: first, by belonging to more or less dusty high culture, and second, by her failure to hang on to Ulysses.[16]

The two old maids in Cham's *Des vieilles filles vaccinées à marier* are not in fact typed as bluestockings. Rather, the artist choses to use a well-known burlesque opposition between two opposite physiologies: tall thinness vs. short plumpness. Recalling the famous contrast between Don Quixote and Sancho Panza, this opposition was popularized by Gustave Doré's engravings and Daumier's paintings in the 1850s and '60s and returns quite notably in burlesque cinema with Laurel and Hardy and then again in *bande dessinée* with Astérix and Obélix (with the slight variation of course that Goscinny and Uderzo juxtapose a tall, "husky" man and a small, skinny one).

What is interesting in *Des vieilles filles* is not that it offers something new in the representation in women but rather that Cham ironically exploits what is imposed on women in bourgeois society with its extremely coded behaviors. In the album dedicated to the misunderstood artist Barnabé Gogo (condemned to become a caricaturist because he was unable to bend himself to the era's aesthetic rules), Cham thus presents an exhibition of student work that allows him to showcase the naïve originality of the young artist. In this exhibit, under the sober titled of "A Woman," he introduces a caricatural reprise of a painting that marked the spirit of the era and that made itself rapidly known in artistic milieus thanks to its radicality: "Venus Rising from the Sea—A Deception" (*Un génie* 23). This work by Raphaelle Peale was exhibited in Philadelphia and then Boston in the 1820s and was immediately widely reproduced in engravings. In it, one sees an apparently nude woman's body, nearly obscured by a sheet hanging loosely on a line and painted in trompe-l'œil. In this painting Peale reinterprets the question of the representation of the female body, specifically the nude. While calling into question the way art has exploited the female nude so that a heterosexual male public could satisfy its scopophilic desires while contemplating socially acceptable mythological and historical paintings, Peale also mocks the extreme modesty that led contemporary puritanical Americans to cover nude paintings with sheets. Cham's ironical redrawing of "Deception" immediately sets up what will be the limits of *bande dessinée* faced with the female nude and, at the same time, the problems that arise from the representation of the feminine in caricature in general. By ironically playing with

---

16. The meager public success of such adaptation lead to a near complete abandonment of the practice by the editor Aubert before the final attempt represented by *Les travaux d'Hercule* of Gustave Doré in 1847. Indeed, what public would there be for such a scholarly questioning of literary authority at the time?

the prescriptive "decency" demanded by a large segment of the public (and notably the feminine public), Cham already backs the infant ninth art into a blind alleyway of representational double binds.

First, Cham ironically imitates a kind of illustrated book in style at the very beginning of the nineteenth century and just revived by his own editor, Philipon: this type of book (as *Les portes et fenêtres*) presents itself in the form of a series of doors and window that a cutout allows the reader to open in order to discover scenes of all sorts, including some erotic ones. Cham purifies the voyeuristic *dispositif* by rendering it deceptive: the doors bear the inscription "NO PUBLIC ENTRY," which does not prevent the addition of a comic note by making each door a different size, corresponding to that of the two sisters (*Deux vieilles* 5). Giorgio Agamben defines *dispositif*, which he borrows from Foucault, as "everything that which, in one way or another, has the capacity to capture, to orient, to determine, to intercept, to model, to control and to assure the gestures, conduct, opinions and discourse of living beings" (31). Recalling that definition, we can see how the artist makes his page into a squared-off *dispositif*. By canceling the reader's freedom to see or not see what is behind the doors, he affirms the superiority of the new art to suggest via lack, directly in line with Töpffer, who affirms that *literature en estampes* is an art of lacuna. But in so doing, he also denies the male reader the opportunity to see what and when he presumably wishes (and no doubt feels entitled).

Second, Cham radicalizes the visual impairment by entirely emptying the representation, such that the *bande dessinée* finds itself literally denuded through a blank panel. The pretext of this innovation is decency, according to the caption of the empty space, which reads: "These ladies being at the table, I would be afraid to show them to the reader, lest we disturb them" (*Deux vieilles* 13). For his part, Gustave Doré would also offer blank panels several years later in his *Histoire de la Sainte Russie* in order to show "colorless" events without "encumbering" the reader with "too boring drawings" and to "prove that a skilled historian can soften everything without skipping over anything" (7). The play on words in the adjective "colorless" (*"incolore"*), which denotes the blankness of the panel and connotes the indigence of its potential content also works very well for Cham. Nonrepresentation doubtless has less to do with what could be indiscrete in representing women in the process of eating in a *bande dessinée* (which does them no service by continually caricaturizing them) as it does with the desire to show the vacuity of numerous novelistic representations and descriptions of women. Thus, the women are less the object of satire than they are subjects of all the series of dinners that make up so many novels of the era, often providing cheap filler for books. A similar denunciation of novelistic facileness can be found in the devastating *bande dessinée* adaptation that Cham offers of Victor Hugo's *Les misérables*.[17]

Third, and finally, by diving into the context of the bourgeoisie, Cham evokes the veiled Venus of Peale in an eminently burlesque gesture where both woman and man are hidden behind large napkins and thus are brutally reduced to being equally invisible (*Deux vieilles* 41). In their case, it is the *dispositif* in two sequential panels that allows for radical and exciting effects. The entire album also can be seen to play with continual variation on the theme of representation through absence, which will conclude with one final possibility: the disappearance in a puff of smoke of that which had no other existence than being a pretext for reflexivity. The "gentleman" ends up himself being literally nothing but the shadow of himself (46). This reduction of his own work and everything it represents to a mere pipe dream is perfectly coherent with Cham's marginal position in the artistic field.

In her very recent album *Gousse & Gigot*, Anne Simon seems to take up Cham's two characters, even if certain critics have rather seen in these two physically very different sisters an homage to the descriptively named Ficelle [thread] and Boulotte [chunky]. These are a famous pair of adolescent girls from French youth literature that appeared in Georges Chaulet's 1960 series *Fantômette*, which offered the first female heroines to whom French girls and boys could equally relate.[18] It is difficult to know if Anne Simon was aware of Cham's album: the text has not been reprinted since its original publication but is readily available online. The *bande dessinée* museum in Angoulême holds the unpublished works of Cham and does dedicate significant space to his art—Simon did part of her training in Angoulême, so plausibly would have at least been aware of Cham in general terms. In any case, *Gousse & Gigot* reprises the idea of sisters looking to find a place in the world but gives them a decidedly feminist inflection. Come hell or high water, the sisters manage (sometimes at the cost of committing murder) to take their destiny in hand. In so doing, they refuse "family life." The page that follows Gousse's murder of her lover/fiancé eradicates the traditional petit

---

17. See Dürrenmatt, "*Les misérables*" and chapter 5 of Kunzle, *Cham*.

18. On the influence of this series on numerous French artists and intellectuals, Thomas Clerc writes, "Theoreticians of literature often forget what our aesthetic formation owes to our childhood reading: we are more marked by our favorite heroes than by the official literary canon. Later admiration of masterpieces derives from these formative readings: it's thanks to *Fantômette* that I was able to read Stevenson, Sarraute, and Pessoa. Academic literature (that which gets taught in schools and universities) tends to obscure that primary relationship to works, which will in turn allow a transition towards adult literature."

FIGURE 9.1. Anne Simon, *Gousse & Gigot*, 2020, n.p.

bourgeois model of marriage and is constructed in a particularly effective manner (figure 9.1). The first panel reproduces the size difference between the sisters: the difference becomes materially realized in the panel's background and symbolically realized in the supplicant position of the smaller of the two sisters. The two other panels give even more importance to Gousse, finally showing her in profile like a silhouette portrait on an ancient coin with a brutal hair-color change going from sky blue to a tawny brown. The two speech bubbles that are on the top and bottom of the vertical panel correspond to the symbolic aggrandizement. They assert the young woman's definitive revolt: "After all, family life is not for me" and "I don't care to have a husband and it bugs the shit out of me to have to go for a stroll with him every Sunday." In one fell swoop, the whole project of "two old maids up to be married off" is repudiated. Instead of gently effacing themselves, Gousse and Gigot resolutely affirm themselves, killing off their potential suitors. The indirect object "me" that ends the first line of dialogue becomes the subject "je" at the beginning of the second bubble, and when she again becomes an object ("of me"), it is in a construction that brutally and "vulgarly" rejects all external (male?) regulation of her actions: "it bugs the shit out of me to have to . . . ." Gousse and Gigot realize what the two "vieilles filles" cannot even imagine as they are condemned at the end of the book by the refusals of the men they tried to marry and their mother's negligence: "The two unfortunate ones with no dowry could not marry, lived a very long time and had no children" (Cham, *Deux vieilles* 51). Simon's text thus enacts an effective contemporary riposte to Cham's problematic old maids.

Masculine/Feminine, Feminine/Masculine

Let's now return to Alfred de Musset's drawn narrative. In the panel that follows the violent confrontation between two representational styles, and at the moment of launching a counterattack against the lack of hurry of "these ladies" to marry their daughter Pauline, George Sand is the one who goes off to war wearing the spurs and saber of an eager cavalier. In the eighteenth-century development of caricature, Susan Sontag saw one of the first manifestations of camp. In her seminal work on the topic, she wrote, "Camp is the triumph of epicene style. The convertibility of 'man' and 'woman,' 'person' and 'thing,' . . . the question isn't, 'Why travesty, impersonation, theatricality?' The question is, rather, 'When does travesty, impersonation, theatricality acquire the special flavor of Camp?'" (9). One of the possible interpretations here would be naïveté ("y croire"), another would be the text's positioning at the border between parody and self-parody, and yet another would be that there is something outsized in an ambition that somewhat fails but that also escapes pretension. The extraordinary twists and turns of early *bande dessinée* are campy while their characters are *too* campy. And for all that, Töpffer resolutely believed in the interest and beauty of his work and was flattered by Goethe's compliments of it. For Cham, the question is more complicated because, as Kunzle indicates, his life as a voluntarily fallen aristocrat appeared eccentric and more or less incomprehensible to his contemporaries, such that everything that he produced remained essentially invisible to serious critics of his era (*Cham*). It is thus difficult to say what the contemporaries of those authors really saw when, from a contemporary perspective, we see camp.

The campiest of camp in Musset's Sand drawings (and also in similar caricature/early *bande dessinée*) is the "epicene" affirmation of the slippage between masculine and feminine. The cult of androgyny that characterized the early nineteenth century certainly plays a role here, but the exquisite bodies painted by Girodet are not camp: they are too perfect and therefore participate in the renewed search for ideal Beauty.[19] The cross-dressing games of Byron and his friends, or in France of Mérimée as Clara Gazul or Aurore Dupin as Georges Sand, are not camp either because of their over-seriousness.[20] *Bande dessinée*, however, like B-pictures later, is liberated from a certain number of obligations and constraints and therefore offers the most delirious reversals possible for a mass public audience—as noted, essentially male—which can no doubt thereby purge its anxieties faced by the progressive rise in power (an incremental rise with each revolution) of the so-called "weaker" sex.

We can easily understand George Sand rendered masculine by Musset, but Töpffer goes farther. In *Monsieur Pencil*, it is the household maid that continually acts as the man of the house, taking all initiative and completing all actions rendered necessary by various incredible events thanks to her common sense—a common sense that her fearful master is completely lacking. This type of reversal is not especially original since it evokes some of Molière's comedies. In these plays, the maids are famous for their uncompromising vision of their employers' flaws as well as those of the men who exploit those flaws (for instance, Dorine in *Tartuffe* and Toinette in *Le malade imaginaire*). However, Töpffer takes this type to a whole new level. Even more surprising is his *Le Docteur Festus*. In this text, men and women are forced by events to cross-dress and thus change their visible gender. Above and beyond comedic and burlesque effects, Töpffer takes advantage of this topos to question the status of women in a society where one is only protected by clothing. Thus, all Milady needs to do is dress in the mayor's male uniform and immediately soldiers follow her. As to the mayor himself, he

---

19. On androgyny, see Solomon-Godeau; and on the painter Girodet, see Lippert.

20. On Byron, see chapter 8 of Buffoni. For a psychoanalytical analysis of Mérimée, see Clancier.

at first quickly regains his clothing. Yet, when he once again loses it later in the album, he finds himself permanently transformed by the experience: he is both feminized and "effeminate" and happy to be so. Here we should note that Töpffer is simultaneously parodying—fairly scandalously and voluntarily naïvely so—the pose of the famous Giogione's *Sleeping Venus* used to establish the canon of feminine beauty. The character of the mayor, once he again becomes masculine, ends up, by radical inversion, foundering in a pseudo-military, hyper-virile hysteria that leads to his death. These successive gender reversals are clearly not only burlesque but also eminently campy. What we see throughout Töpffer's drawings is comparable to what will be seen in early cinema or later in American B-pictures: the noninstitutional character of these art forms (and the absence of self-censorship that follows therefrom) allows the artist to grasp the otherwise unrepresentable in its most raw form. We might still dream of what would have happened if a woman would have usurped this privilege even if the probability of which was, for reasons already evoked, almost null.

All of this of course comes from a masculine point of view, one which was no doubt fascinated and terrified by the possibility of crossing to the other side, and was, moreover, haunted by the specter of feminine virility. This latent hostility is illustrated by the literal explosion of Elvire in Töpffer's *Mr Cryptogramme*, wife of the eponymous antihero, who pursues her husband with overactive enthusiasm. Doré expanded this horizon by trying to take the feminine point of view in his inventive *Des-agréments d'un voyage d'agrément* (15–17). In this text, César gives his wife Vespasie a telescope, thus allowing her to "voir rond" (figure 9.2), literally, to "see round." This extraordinary focalization allows for a series of visual inventions that limit vision to abstraction and thus open new spaces of creation, which are much more than decorative, for the emerging art form. Admittedly, this discovery happens under the aegis of affirming the naïveté of Vespasie (along the lines of the discussion of camp above), but what is more important is that, contrary to other moments where originality comes through superimposition or cross-outs, the round panels that reproduce the optical *dispositif* become the means of poetically reinventing a reality that is, after all, quite prosaic. The men seen through the lorgnette are enclosed in a circular panel: a first in an art that had always privileged squares and rectangles. We might wonder if this change in form needs to be read—apart from the optical *dispositif* that motivates it in narrative terms—as a declension of the stereotypical opposition between feminine roundness and masculine angularity.

In the interior of these circles, the masculine figures are progressively reduced to more and more enigmatic traces. They ultimately appear to make

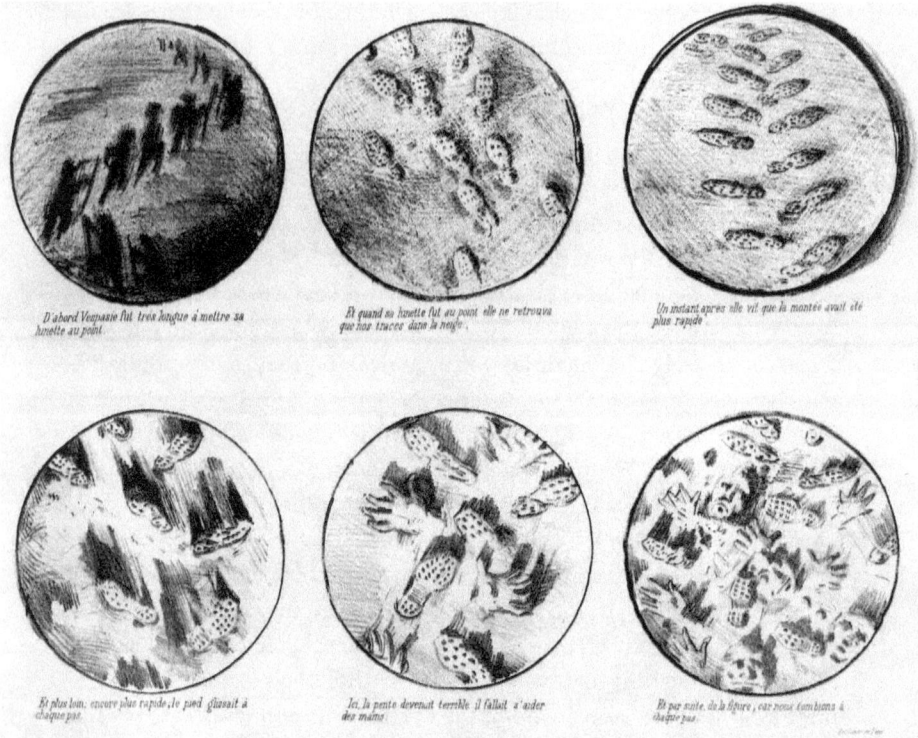

FIGURE 9.2. Gustave Doré, *Des-agréments d'un voyage d'agrément*, 1851, p. 15.

up an incomprehensible graphism in the image of an idea very common since the Renaissance: that animal tracks in snow or mud were one of the possible origins of the idea that lead to writing. In this way, the female gaze tries in a different fashion to read the signs that are offered to the world, thus becoming both metaphorical and euphoric. This new hermeneutics, very close to what Victor Hugo would propose a few years later in deciphering German landscapes, opens heretofore unheard of perspectives for the *bande dessinée*. Such invention happens on the condition of not trying to imitate men, like the bluestockings who appear later on in the album (mocked for the intellectual "suffering" that they impose upon themselves), and remains subordinate to the point of view of the male main character, who begins "for the first time" to appreciate the "poetic serenity" of his spouse (43).

In her essay on "The Beginnings of the *Bande Dessinée*," Patricia Mainardi has quite rightly observed that unfortunately for the history of the *Bande Dessinée*, Doré, like Cham before him, abandoned the medium. Early *Bande Dessinée* artists found their work ill-paid and undervalued, so it is no surprise that they so often took their talents elsewhere. Soon after the publication of *Sainte Russie*, Doré's illustrations to Rabelais were published and were greeted with such acclaim that he decided to devote himself henceforth to the more prestigious media of painting and book illustration. After this initial period of innovation, *Bandes Dessinées* actually became more conservative . . . [but] Doré, who, by deliberately transgressing all the newly established *Bande Dessinée* traditions, established it as a subversive medium that obeys no rules, a definition still applicable today in the twenty-first century. (150)

The triple heritage of the treatment of women by the early *bande dessinée* (caricature, deletion, and camp) would remain until the 1960s the dominant mode of thinking about and using female characters in French and Belgian comics. *Tintin* is quite representative of that difficulty of giving a real place to women in narratives largely designed for boys. The only female character, la Castafiore, is a masculine and ugly woman who understands nothing that happens around her and is always singing (much to the chagrin of the other characters) a very narcissistic song from *Faust*, a nineteenth-century French opera: "Ah! I launch to see myself so beautiful in this mirror," a sentence which has become well known and associated with futility and stupid selfishness. The character looks like a man in drag and is excessive in all her speech and actions and yet is, at the same time, somehow abstract insofar as she never really takes part in the actions unfolding around her. Many scholars have tried to understand, often by searching in Hergé's life and family history, the reasons for this extraordinary treatment of the feminine, but the main reason is perhaps pure inheritance of a tradition that imbued the quasi-totality of the *bande dessinée* industry at the time.

What could be subversive and demarcated itself from such a tradition in early *bande dessinée* began timidly to be rediscovered in the 1960s, with the republishing of some of Töpffer's and Doré's works, at the very moment that female *bédéistes* began to gain a very progressive foothold within the ninth art. It would be very tempting to think this rediscovery played a role at the time, though I regretfully conclude it obviously did not. However, many Francophone graphic novelists, especially some prominent women authors like Anne Simon and Catherine Meurisse, have now, thanks to museums, exhibitions, and new editions, not only engaged with ironical treatment of the clichés of early *bande dessinée* but also the way it used camp and interrogated its literary contemporaries, finding in the complexities of those early representations at least the seeds of models to follow in the present-day reinvention the of women's representation in the ninth art.

Works Cited

Agamben, Giorgio. *Qu'est-ce qu'un dispositif?* Translated by Martif Reuff, Rivages, 2007.

Balzac, Honoré de. *Eugénie Grandet.* Translated by Sylvia Raphael, Oxford UP, 1990.

———. *Cousin Bette.* Translated by Sylvia Raphael, Oxford UP, 2008.

Barbey d'Aurevilly, Jules. *Les bas-bleus.* Victor Palmé and G. Lebrocquy, 1878.

Bem, Jeanne. "La vieille fille et son histoire, chez Flaubert et Maupassant." *Flaubert—Le Poittevin—Maupassant: Une affaire de famille littéraire,* edited by Yvan Leclerc, Publications de l'Université de Rouen, 2002.

Berend, Zsuzsa. "'The Best or None!' Spinsterhood in Nineteenth-Century New England." *Journal of Social History,* vol. 33, no. 4, 2000, pp. 935–57.

Buffoni, Franco. *Il servo di Byron.* Fazi, 2012.

Cham. *Des vieilles filles vaccinées à marier.* Aubert, 1842.

———. *Un génie incompris.* Aubert, 1841.

Clancier, Anne. "Mérimée et le travestissement." *Prosper Mérimée: Écrivain, archéologue, historien,* edited by Antonia Fonyi, Droz, 1999, pp. 191–96.

Clerc, Thomas. "*Fantômette*: L'anti-héroïne de mon enfance." *Libération,* 1 Nov. 2012, https://next.liberation.fr/culture/2012/11/01/fantomette-l-antiheroine-de-mon-enfance_857561.

Couderc, Marie-Anne. *La semaine de Suzette: Histoire de filles.* CNRS Editions, 2005.

Del Lungo, Andrea, and Brigitte Louichon, editors. *La littérature en bas-bleus.* Classiques Garnier, 2010.

Doré, Gustave. *Des-agréments d'un voyage d'agrément.* Aubert, 1851.

———. *Histoire de la Sainte Russie.* Bry Aîné, 1854.

Dottin-Orsini, Mireille. "Une 'bande dessinée' autobiographique d'Alfred de Musset." *Littératures,* no. 78, 2018, pp. 95–107.

Dürrenmatt, Jacques. "*Les misérables* sont-ils solubles dans la BD ou le défi de Cham." *Choses vues à travers Hugo,* edited by Claude Millet et al., Université de Valenciennes, 2008.

———. "Nadar: Naissance de la bande dessinée politique." *Et la BD Fut! Le magasin du XIXe siècle,* no. 5, 2016, pp. 85–91.

Flaubert, Gustave. *Dictionary of Accepted Ideas.* Translated by Jacques Barzun, New Directions, 1967.

———. *Trois contes.* Classiques Garnier, 2018.

Grennan, Simon, et al. *Marie Duval: Maverick Victorian Cartoonist.* Manchester UP, 2020.

Kunzle, David. *Cham: The Best Comic Strips and Graphic Novelettes 1839–1862.* UP of Mississippi, 2019.

———. *Father of the Comic Strip: Rodolphe Töpffer.* UP of Mississippi, 2007.

———. "Marie Duval: A Caricaturist Rediscovered." *Woman's Art Journal*, vol. 7, no. 1, Spring–Summer 1986, pp. 26–31.

Lippert, Sarah. "The Iconography of Girodet's *Endymion*." *Romantic Rapports*, edited by Larry H. Peer and Christopher R. Clason, Boydel and Brewer, 2017, pp. 96–120.

Littré, Émile. *Dictionnaire de la langue française*. Vol. 4, L. Hachette and Cie, 1863.

Mainardi, Patricia. "The Beginnings of the *Bande Dessinée*." *L'art de la caricature*, edited by Ségolène Le Men, Presses Universitaires de Paris Ouest, 2011, pp. 133–50.

Mehta. Brinda J. *Corps infirme, corps infâme*. Summa Publications, 1992.

Musset, Alfred de. "Untitled." 1840.

Planté, Christine. "Les bas-bleus de Daumier: De quoi rit-on dans la caricature?" *La caricature entre République et censure: L'imagerie satirique en France de 1830 à 1880; Un discours de résistance*, edited by Philippe Régnier, Presses Universitaires de Lyon, 1996, pp. 192–202.

Renonciat, Annie. "Un théoricien de la 'littérature en estampes.'" *Töpffer*, edited by Lucien Boissonnas et al., Skira, 1996.

Sagaert, Claudine. *Histoire de la laideur feminine*. Imago, 2015.

Simon, Anne. *Gousse & Gigot*. Misma, 2020.

Solomon-Godeau, Abigail. "Male Trouble." *Constructing Masculinity*, edited by Maurice Berger et al., Routledge, 1995, pp. 69–76.

Sontag, Susan. *Notes on "Camp."* 1964. Penguin, 2018.

Thérenty, Marie-Ève. "Pour une histoire genrée des medias." *Questions de communication*, no. 15, 2009, pp. 247–60.

Töpffer, Rodolphe. *Mr Crépin*. 1837.

———. *Mr Cryptogame*. J. J. Dubochet, 1846.

———. *Monsieur Pencil*. 1840.

———. *Les portes et fenêtres*. Aubert, 1835.

CHAPTER 10

The Amazons of Dahomey in French and African Comics

MARK MCKINNEY

Introduction: Exemplary Shifts in Representing African Amazons

The roles of women from (former) French colonies in comics have undergone a radical transformation in the last few decades thanks to a shift from colonial to postcolonial cultures, as well as challenges to male domination, in France and its former colonies. This chapter examines those changes through a historical genealogy of a single character type in comics: the Black woman warrior, or "Amazon," from Dahomey. Africanist historian Robin Law pointed out that "this was a purely European terminology; in Dahomian vernacular usage, the female soldiers [from Dahomey] were called simply *ahosi*, or 'king's wives'—a term applied generically to all women associated with the royal palace; or alternatively, *mino*, meaning 'our mothers'" (245–46). Law also noted in 1993, the "convention [of calling these soldiers 'Amazons'] is current today among francophone natives of Dahomey" (245). My primary focus here is on a figure often called "the Amazon" in comics and elsewhere.[1]

---

1. Hereafter in this chapter I will use the term without quotation marks.

My analysis charts a telling evolution in representative imagery from key vantage points. I will begin my genealogy by analyzing the Amazon from Dahomey in French cultural forms, including comics, around the time of the French conquest of Dahomey. I shall then turn to two postcolonial French comics featuring Amazons that exemplify a major shift in representation, a partial turning away from demeaning imagery in colonial comics. However, the postcolonial comics nonetheless reproduce some features of colonial-era representation, including the colonial eroticization of Amazons and an orientalist disregard for historical accuracy. My first example, from François Bourgeon's multivolume *Les passagers du vent* [The Passengers of the Wind], a very successful series of comics whose first five albums are about the trans-Atlantic slave trade before the French Revolution, depicts Amazons as beautiful, proud, and dangerous warriors in the service of an African king in precolonial Dahomey who sells Africans to European slavers. The second postcolonial French comic featuring Amazons, *La Vénus du Dahomey* [The Venus from Dahomey], by Stefano Casini and Laurent Galandon, is set at the close of the French conquest of Dahomey in the late nineteenth century. The story, which is the first comic book (in two volumes) featuring an Amazon, follows her from the African port city of Cotonou to Paris. It is one of many colonial and postcolonial "exhibition comics," a genre that features the display of non-European characters in a variety of related shows, spectacles, or performances in colonial-era Europe, including colonial exhibits at World's Fairs, freak shows, and cabarets (McKinney, *Colonial*). A subset of those comics has focused specifically on the exhibition of Black African women, often heavily eroticized. After analyzing comics by French cartoonists about Amazons, I shall turn to how African cartoonists have represented them in a few recent comics. Their representations constitute a second radical shift, this time toward celebrating Amazons as warrior heroines of Dahomey in ways that are not especially eroticizing, certainly not as much they have been in postcolonial French comics. We shall see that this latest shift is due to several factors, including differences in authorship (who writes and draws), intended audiences, and publishers. The changes in depictions of African Amazons are exemplary of general trends within French-language comics, as old representational paradigms become obsolete, with the end of French colonial mastery of certain narratives about Africa and Africans and the increasing prominence of women cartoonists and of people of African descent in creating comics in France and beyond. I now begin my genealogy by surveying colonial-era representations of Amazons from Dahomey.

The Myth of African Amazons in French Colonial Culture

African Amazons were depicted as ferocious and fanatical soldiers, or else as titillatingly exotic and erotic, in French colonial culture of the late nineteenth and early twentieth centuries. Representations of these women were rooted not so much in Dahomean reality as in the imperialist and gendered, male-dominated culture of France. For the French, the Amazons constituted a salient feature of a bloody, ruthless African culture needing French pacification and civilization. So, for example, French colonial administrator Jean Bayol cited the sacrifice of enslaved people at the funeral of King Glele, Béhanzin's father and predecessor, as a reason for initiating French military and diplomatic actions that triggered the First Franco-Dahomean War in 1890 (Schneider, *Empire* 46). However, historian William H. Schneider also notes the concurrent "French support of Porto-Novo, a rival state near the coast, [which] had antagonized relations with the Kingdom of Dahomey, the traditional power in the hinterland" (44–46). Clearly, French military action was far from disinterested. During the Second Franco-Dahomean War, from 1892 to 1894, *Le petit journal* [The Little Newspaper] strongly supported French military action against Béhanzin's kingdom (47–49). For Schneider, "social imperialism, the idea of empire for the masses . . . was the basis for the newspaper's overall pro-colonial policy, and . . . it greatly affected the portrayal of West Africa that appeared in the newspaper" (60).

During the 1890s, many other media venues and cultural forms helped spread procolonial, exoticizing representations of Dahomey and its peoples in France, including novels, posters, prints, songs, theatrical plays, and other live performances. For example, *Négripub: L'image des Noirs dans la publicité*, a study of Blacks in French advertising, reproduces a color advertisement by Lucien Lefèvre promoting the play *Au Dahomey* [In Dahomey] in 1892 (figure 10.1). The poster's two parts suggest a radical contrast between African savagery and French civilization (Bachollet et al. 45). The top half shows Amazons half-naked and looking ferocious, with rifles and curved daggers in hand, running or dancing wildly in front of their king and a statue probably meant to represent the god of war. The bottom half depicts French soldiers in immaculate white colonial uniforms and helmets heroically fighting Béhanzin's army.

Sylvie Chalaye argues that this play about the French conquest of Dahomey participated "in the shaping of a *colonial culture* in France" (117). She also indicates that related plays, reviews, pantomimes, and other live performances on the same topic were produced all around France during this time (298). Chalaye and other scholars discuss the participation

FIGURE 10.1. An exoticizing and eroticizing, procolonial depiction of Amazon warriors in a color advertisement by Lucien Lefèvre promoting the play *Au Dahomey* [In Dahomey] in 1892. Lucien Lefèvre, *Théâtre de la Porte St. Martin. Au Dahomey: Pièce nouvelle à grand spectacle*, 1892 (60 × 42 cm; lithographic print; color). Digital image graciously provided by the Ville de Paris / Bibliothèque Forney (City of Paris / Forney Library); cote AF 44544.

of troupes of Dahomeans in some of the performances, for example, the departure of "African 'warriors'" to Europe even "before the first [French] offensive of 4 March 1890," for a tour of European and American cities (Preston-Blier 136).[2] Dahomeans were also exhibited in 1891 at the Jardin zoologique d'acclimatation [Zoological Garden of Acclimatation] (henceforth simply "Jardin") in the Bois de Boulogne [Boulogne Woods] at the western edge of Paris. On that occasion, Jean-Camille Fulbert-Dumonteil (1, 3) described the Amazons in a pamphlet:

> These famous women warriors of a strange and legendary type, who appear to us like a chimerical vision, in I know not which troubling vapors of an African mirage, are there, under our eyes, with their picturesque uniform, their murderous weapons, their dances and their games, simulacra of combat, their wild and valiant appearance.

The pamphlet also contained two illustrations featuring the women warriors: one brandishing a sword, on the front cover, and another holding a dagger (15). For Fanny Robles, this pamphlet and other representations of Dahomean Amazons at the end of the nineteenth century participated in a process of othering that combined the threat of savage violence, reduced, however, by the French defeat of the Dahomeans, with an "erotic apprehension, ultimate mode of visual or literary consumption, of the exposed subjects" (8). She finds in this representation of the Dahomean Amazons a version of the fin de siècle representation of the femme fatale in European literature and art (8–11).

Suzanne Preston-Blier, an art historian specializing in African art, speaks of a veritable "myth of the 'Amazons' of Dahomey" created through and around the French wars there and developed by touring performances:

> From 1890 to 1925, these exhibitions of "Amazons" left such a mark on mentalities that they helped reinforce the prejudices of millions of Western spectators regarding the "hierarchy of races" and sexes, and of national identity. In Europe, many of these spectacles unfolded in places where animals were also exhibited. (136)

Preston-Blier notes that the four-month performance of a troupe of Dahomeans, including Amazons, in 1893 at the Champ-de-Mars in Paris drew "2.7 million of the curious, an absolute record for an ethnological exhibition"

---

2. All translations are my own.

(138; see also Schneider, *Empire* 142). Quoting Thomas Theye, Preston-Blier argues that the "the power of fascination exerted by the Amazons incontestably came from the erotic charge of the spectacle" (140). The pleasure the Dahomeans afforded was sometimes not only visual but also tactile according to a German critic whom she quotes and who describes white spectators touching and caressing the performers' bodies. Preston-Blier goes on to note that erotic, exotic European pleasure was heightened by the Amazons' clothing and lack thereof:

> It happened that the women posed naked, and they usually performed scantily clad, wearing a *bustier* decorated with shells, a pair of shorts and a wrap skirt made of cloth—a costume that, we will have understood, had nothing in common with the outfit of the "Amazons" of Dahomey. The male clothing was no less provocative. (140)

Pictures taken of such performers form part of the famous anthropological photographic collection of Roland Bonaparte: men and women of at least one such troupe posed seated, alternately clothed and with naked chests, in photos taken from front and side positions, as is typical in imagery used by Western science to racialize or otherwise diminish various groups, often colonized subjects and people of color.[3] Similar imagery was published in *Le petit journal*, for example, in a colored print representing Béhanzin and his Amazons on the front cover of the April 23, 1892, issue (figure 10.2). Again, Preston-Blier states that this clothing was not in fact what the Amazons wore in Dahomey. Moreover, some already suspected at the time that Africans taken to Europe and America by Western promoters to appear as authentic representatives of specific ethnic groups were often not so, a suspicion that Schneider (*Empire* 146) and Law (245) deem to be well founded.

Five cartoons or short comics about Amazons and King Béhanzin by Henriot (Henri Maigrot) and Paul Léonnec were printed in 1892 and 1894, around the time of the Second Franco-Dahomean War, in *Le journal amusant* [The Amusing Newspaper], one of the primary French periodicals featuring comic strips and cartoons during the nineteenth century. They contain elements already described above in other representations of Amazons. For example, "Offres et demandes d'emploi" [Job Offers and Applications] by Henriot (1892) is a collection of ten loosely related cartoons of which two feature Dahomeans out of work after Béhanzin's defeat, one advertising some "beautiful and superb opportunities" and depicting two physically

---

3. Available at https://www.photo.rmn.fr/.

FIGURE 10.2. A colored print representing King Béhanzin and four Amazons on the front cover of *Le petit journal*, April 23, 1892. In the background, two human skulls on poles suggest barbaric cruelty. Béhanzin and one Amazon are bare-chested, adding an eroticizing note. The Amazons wear clothing whose historical accuracy has been disputed. Digital image scanned from an original print publication in the author's collection.

hideous Amazons looking for work as maids but eating and abducting white children. Béhanzin himself is a cannibal, eating his African nurse during his youth in "Béhanzin intime" [Intimate Béhanzin] (1894), a thirteen-panel strip recounting the youth, defeat, and exile of the king, compared unfavorably with Napoleon in the conclusion. Cannibalism appears too in "Béhanzin et les femmes" [Béhanzin and the Women], another strip by Henriot (1894) on the following page, where the king has children cooked daily. The strip satirizes the devotion of Béhanzin's wives to him upon his departure into exile (they swim after him in shark-infested waters as he leaves in a French gunboat), given his prior mistreatment of them and even execution of those who displeased him, according to the cartoonist. "Chez Béhanzin" [At Home with Béhanzin], by Léonnec (1892), depicts Amazons both barebreasted and fully clothed alongside their sanguinary king, who is tricked by van Tricule, a European explorer, and François, his assistant. Cannibalism is a typical, widespread feature of colonialist humor about Africans in French and Belgian cartoons and comics, including by canonical cartoonists Alain Saint-Ogan and Hergé, and ranging far beyond. So too is the trope of the clever European captive hoodwinking violent African captors, often cannibals. The representation of Béhanzin's Amazons as dangerous and ugly, masculinized Black women is a variation on the colonial grotesque that one finds in Hergé's *Tintin in the Congo* and elsewhere but also in English caricatures of Zulus during the English war on them in South Africa in the late 1870s (Robles 6).[4] Representations of the Amazon figure return in postcolonial comics, but with significant, symptomatic shifts.

The Ambivalent Return of the Amazons in Postcolonial French Comics

In recent years French cartoonists have returned to colonial history, including the slave trade and the conquest of Dahomey, for stories both compelling and relevant to postcolonial France. They often foreground colonial documents, including images, as a basis for recovering a forgotten colonial past and suggesting the authenticity of a story that may be highly fictionalized. However, they also often fail to critique the colonial ideologies and practices that shaped the histories and documents that they rework. Even attempts to critique colonial culture may be compromised by readership expectations and commercial pressures in comics publishing, for example, to lace books

---

4. On the colonial grotesque, see McKinney, *Postcolonialism*.

with exoticism and sexual eroticism to sell them better. That is true of my two examples: *Les passagers du vent* and *La Vénus du Dahomey*.

Bourgeon's multivolume *Les passagers du vent* has been an influential fictional comics saga about the triangular slave trade between France, West Africa, and the Caribbean in the eighteenth century and the slave-plantation system in the Americas. It was serialized by the publisher Glénat in its magazine *Circus* beginning in 1979, with accompanying book publication of the first five volumes (1979/80–84). Over a decade ago, the author stated that each volume in the saga had sold about one million copies and that there had been about eighteen translations (Bourgeon, "François Bourgeon"). The series, featuring a strong white female French protagonist, critiques the slave trade and depicts some of the horrors of the Middle Passage across the Atlantic and of slavery in the plantation system of French America (Marshall 161–63). Bourgeon represents the barbarity of European slavers but also brutality by Africans: for example, King Kpengla supplying enslaved Africans to Europeans in volumes 3 and 4 and presiding over the torture and execution of unfaithful wives by feeding them to an army of fire ants in volume 4 (13–14). Bill Marshall rightly views the engagement by the series with "the *contested* memory of the slave trade" as ahead of its time within popular cultural forms (161–62). He also usefully situates Bourgeon's series within a wider French coming-to-terms with France's participation in the trans-Atlantic slave trade, enslavement on plantations in the Americas, and contemporary memory of those historical facts (161–67). Marshall notes that Bourgeon foregrounds his historical documentation before the beginning of his fiction in volume 3, *Le comptoir de Juda*, as a way of legitimizing comics and helping to produce what Roland Barthes called the "reality effect" (159, 163).[5]

Although the series has been celebrated as expertly documented and historically faithful to the period in which it is set (Thiébaut; Tramson), in some ways Bourgeon's documentary approach is less historically or culturally accurate than it might first appear. The artist displaces copied colonial imagery in both time and place (Gauthier 56–58, 61; see Bourgeon, 4: 3), a recurring practice in postcolonial comics that recalls a colonial-era orientalist approach in art and literature (Porterfield; McKinney, *Redrawing* 39–41). Bourgeon does this with colonial-era imagery depicting Amazons. In his study of Bourgeon's series, Michel Thiébaut (65) reproduces one of Roland Bonaparte's 1891 photographs of "Dahomean Amazons" used by Bourgeon as a model for an Amazon in the court of King Kpengla in 1781 (Bourgeon

---

5. See also Fresnault-Deruelle.

4: 10.4).⁶ Thiébaut approvingly notes that this photo and another one, "certainly from later, give great authenticity to his evocation" (65). The statement is openly contradictory. In sum, the cartoonist redrew a photo taken in 1891 of an African woman, presented in Paris as an Amazon, who might or might not really have been from Dahomey and whose purportedly Indigenous clothing was probably neither the authentic original nor a faithful replica, as a model for a woman in a story set in Abomey over a century earlier, during the reign of one of Béhanzin's ancestors. Looking through the series of Bonaparte's photos of the Dahomean troupe in Paris, one finds additional examples that probably served as visual models for other characters in Bourgeon's story.⁷ Moreover, there is considerable overlap between the eroticism and exoticism in nineteenth-century traveling shows featuring Dahomean performers in Europe and how Bourgeon depicts Black Africans in his series, notably the characters Aouan and Alihosi, an African man and woman, respectively, who play important secondary roles in the series, but also more minor African characters, including Amazons (e.g., 4: 6, 10, 21.1). True, eroticism is a major mechanism across the entire series, in which Isabeau (or Isa), the white French female protagonist, plays the primary role, including erotically, with other white, male and female, French and English characters in supporting ones (Marshall 163).

I now turn to what appears to be the most extended representation of an African Amazon in postcolonial comics, the two-volume *La Vénus du Dahomey* [The Venus from Dahomey], which Casini and Galandon published in 2011 and 2012. It critiques colonial racism and sexism but in an ambivalent way. Here too the artists rely on colonial-era documents. For example, the end papers of both volumes of the comic contain a blurry, enlarged photograph taken in a park, probably the Jardin in Paris, showing European children sitting on a platform strapped to the back of an elephant, with two keepers standing on either side, suggesting a nostalgic perspective on the colonial era that the album's story contests, although the latter contains historical distortions, beginning with the dates of the fiction. It opens in autumn 1887 and rapidly moves to reenactments in the Jardin of the defeat of Béhanzin and his Amazons in their last combat against the French colonial army, composed mainly of Senegalese riflemen led by French officers (1: 3.1, 12–13,

---

6. In Bourgeon's *L'heure du serpent* (10.4), the Amazon on the right appears in photos 17-568747, 17-568748, 17-586299, 17-591859, and 17-592083 at https://www.photo.rmn.fr/; see also Thiebaut (65).

7. For example, photo 17-591890 as the model for the woman on the far left in Bourgeon (4: 10.4) and photo 17-591868 as the model for the woman second from the right (4: 21.1) at https://www.photo.rmn.fr/.

15.4; 2: 3.2).[8] However, the Dahomean king ascended to the throne in 1890 and finally surrendered to the French in January 1894. The motivation for the discrepancy of the timeline is not obvious, but the warped chronology indicates that the fictional overrides historical accuracy.

Casini and Galandon may have been inspired by the film *Vénus noire* [Black Venus], by Abdellatif Kechiche (2010), the Tunisian French film director, and its comic book adaptation by Kechiche and cartoonist Renaud Pennelle (2010), published under the same title. Both recount the story of Saartjie Baartman, nicknamed the "la Vénus hottentote" [Hottentot Venus]. The two comics have several similarities, beginning of course with their titles, which suggest that a Black African woman is playing the role of the Roman goddess of love, beauty, and sex. In both *La Vénus du Dahomey* and *Vénus noire*, a Black woman is taken from Africa to Europe to participate in a series of exhibitions and performances that follow a degrading, downward trajectory, including the threat of rape in *La Vénus du Dahomey*, prostitution and rape in *Vénus noire*, erotic and exotic exhibitions in freak shows in both comics, and ultimately the tragic, untimely death of their protagonists. Although the Black female protagonist repeatedly resists physical and sexual violence,[9] predatory white men use substance addiction to dominate and exploit her: heroin dependence in *La Vénus du Dahomey* and alcohol in *Vénus noire* (Hendrick Cæzar, an Afrikaner showman who exploits Baartman, plies her with alcohol to subjugate her, a technique he explicitly describes).[10] In both stories, prominent French scientists, supported by scientific organizations and institutions, examine the bodies of African women in ways that degrade, exoticize, and eroticize them in order to advance racist theories supporting white supremacy. In *Vénus noire*, they include Etienne Geoffroy Saint-Hilaire, Georges Cuvier, Henri-Marie Ducrotay de Blainville, and the Muséum d'histoire naturelle de Paris,[11] whereas in *La Vénus du Dahomey* no famous scientists are named, although French anthropologists and a doctor engage in similar activity (1: 17.6, 26, 29–30). As the film does, the comics version of *Vénus noire* reworks direct quotations from Cuvier about Baartman. However, much is unknown about the life of Baartman, and Kechiche's film has been critiqued by Anne Hugon, Delphine Peiretti, and Christelle

---

8. Page and panel numbers to the two volumes appear in this way throughout this chapter.

9. See, for example, Kechiche and Pennelle (51, 53, 104, 106–10).

10. Kechiche and Pennelle (77; see also 32, 37, 53, 56, 76–78, 87, 90, 96–98, 106, 108, 112–15).

11. Kechiche and Pennelle (6–15, 100–108, 120–30); on this history, see, for example, Schneider, "Les expositions ethnographiques."

Taraud, three historians specializing in African colonial history, for filling in the historical unknown with hypersexualized representations of the protagonist, for example, by including a lengthy orgy in a libertine Parisian salon, "a pornographic scene as unhealthy as it is superfluous, and especially historically questionable" (179). Corresponding scenes are shorter and less sexually explicit in the graphic novel version (Kechiche and Pennelle 90–99, 120–21), thereby avoiding some of the pitfalls of the film. This may be to reach a younger audience with the graphic novel version. Kechiche and Pennelle include a page of text outlining what is known about Baartman and containing a photo of her plaster cast and four colonial-era images: two satirical cartoons and two other drawings of her (130). Pennelle also explains his working method, including a reliance on "paintings or prints of the time" (131).

By contrast, in *La Vénus du Dahomey*, Casini and Galandon include no paratextual material designed to historically authenticate their story other than the photographic image on the end pages, perhaps because they were not aiming very closely for historical veracity and instead took considerable liberties with their fiction. Other possible sources of inspiration include Daeninckx's *Cannibale* (2002) and its comic book adaptation (Reuzé and Daeninckx 2009) about Kanak from New Caledonia exhibited in Paris in 1931; the documentary film *Zoos humains* (2002) [Human Zoos] by the ACHAC group (Association pour la Connaissance de l'Histoire de l'Afrique Contemporaine [Association for the Knowledge of the History of Contemporary Africa]), which includes the film "Baignade de nègres" [Bath of Negroes] by the Lumière brothers, filmed in the Jardin in 1896 (a passage in the comic where an African boy dives for coins thrown by spectators strongly resembles the Lumière film [1: 10–11, 18]); and *Zoos humains*, a scholarly collection of essays first published in 2002. *La Vénus du Dahomey* has a characteristic blend of postcolonial French approaches to colonial-era themes in comics, as we shall now see.

The Amazon as Superhero and Victim in *La Vénus du Dahomey*

Diamanka is a kind of Black superhero, drawn with a corresponding aesthetic: she is tall, strong, muscular, and beautiful. However, her accession to protagonist status is qualified by her eroticization and exoticization. The cartoonists liberally display Diamanka in various states of undress as the subject of voyeuristic curiosity of the French, especially, but not only, men.

The cartoonists critique white male voyeurism and racial science in a passage set in the Jardin in which anthropologists and a medical doctor named Fernand de la Fillière are attempting to advance science, no doubt of a racist variety, by examining the Dahomean troupe in a scene based on historical events and documents. They include the anthropological photographic and collecting activities of the sort that produced Bonaparte's collection of photographs (1: 29–30).[12] Ocularized panels represent Diamanka's almost naked body like a visual blazon, with close-ups of her neck and shoulders, hips and crotch, and breasts. The images conflate three or more different viewing perspectives, blurring boundaries between scientific documentation and pornography: first a camera operator takes photos of Diamanka standing in front of a white sheet, wearing only a skimpy loin cloth and looking at him, while Fernand and a white-jacketed scientist look on from behind the photographer; and then another white-jacketed scientist seated in from of Diamanka, still standing, examines her many scars up close through a magnifying glass while Fernand stands behind her, gazing at her. She puts up with the white men's attention until Fernand, still behind her, puts his finger into a scar on her shoulder, a gesture clearly mixing eroticism with pseudo-scientific curiosity, and suggesting the white man's sexual penetration of the Black woman (it also recalls an earlier groping by Saint-Juste, a Frenchman who purchased Diamanka's freedom from prison in Cotonou to bring her to Europe and to feature in his show reenacting her army's defeat by the French colonial forces). When Diamanka defends herself by grabbing Fernand's arm forcefully and angrily, a French scientist in a white jacket calls her "a real savage" (1: 30).

However, Fernand is captivated by Diamanka, returning frequently to the Jardin to observe her, scantily clad, practice her military art, take a pain endurance test (1: 37–38), and later perform a Vodoun dance (1: 40–41). He prefers doing this to spending days with his wife (1: 36). He also brushes off his wife's sexual advances at night and goes instead to his office to gaze at an almost naked Diamanka in the photo taken for the anthropologists (1: 39). As the story's title suggests, Diamanka incarnates the figure of "Black Venus" (Nederveen Pieterse 181–87; Berliner 194–204). Later, in a cabaret where Diamanka is exhibited, the American owner, Willy Chance, presents her as a conflation of exotic and colonial stereotypes: "The intrepid warrior! The invincible Amazon! The cannibal from Africa! The serpent tamer! The Venus from Dahomey!!!" (2: 27). Throughout the story we repeatedly see

---

12. See Zaborowski; Schneider, *Empire* 125–36.

Diamanka's gaze become angry when she is molested or humiliated, indicating her resistance to exoticization, erotic voyeurism, and exploitation (1: 8, 12, 16, 18, 30, 37–38; 2: 8, 10–11, 44–46). After having been liberated from the cabaret, she rejects the imposed French identity of Venus and reclaims her original role of Amazon (2: 43). Diamanka's final heroic charge against her French pursuers next to the Seine River in Paris, with her now clothed again, implicitly puns on "heroisch," the German term used to refer to "heroin" in the story (1: 31, 48; 2: 11): she symbolically throws away a basket containing the substance before heroically charging the police. Her suicidal gesture is cast as a liberating resistance to colonial and sexist violence, an epic feat that she orders Djiba, her young brother who has accompanied her to Europe, to recount: "Someone will be needed to tell the tale of the combat of the last Amazon from Dahomey . . . Go, Djiba!" (2: 45; ellipsis in original). Of course this is also the cartoonists' storytelling activity.

Through the experience of Diamanka and Djiba, the cartoonists reconstruct a version of what Edward Said (216, 244, 256) called "the voyage in," in this case of the colonized to the French colonial metropolis, a journey both geographical and intellectual. Reconstructing the voyage in is especially relevant in France today where people of Black African descent now constitute a significant portion of the population. From the outset of their story, Casini and Galandon suggest that the arrangement that Chance and Saint-Juste make with the African performers they bring to Europe is akin to enslavement (1: 5). The only African character who finds his situation substantially improved in Paris is the albino, who notes that Chance "takes care of 'his monsters'" and that he is better off with the American in Paris, where we see him working as a doorman at the cabaret (2: 24), than in Dahomey, where he was rejected and even beaten because of his albinism: "Here we lack nothing, we are respected . . . with our differences" (2: 33). Despite its language recalling civil rights discourse from 1980s France, his statement is hardly a ringing endorsement of the freak show's treatment of human difference, suggesting instead that one bad situation has been replaced by another that is only marginally less so. The cartoonists therefore critique colonial displays of defeated and exoticized African others in humiliating human zoos and freak shows. However, they do so with considerable ambivalence.

Despite the cartoonists' goal of condemning French colonial culture, some colonialist representations go unexamined. For example, their depiction of Vodoun arguably strives for historical authenticity, including through the fact that the religion originated in Dahomey and surrounding areas. However, it is highly sensationalized in the narrative where it acts as an exotic, occult, and negative force, leading ultimately to the death of two women, one French and one African.[13] In the first of the story's two Vodoun episodes, Diamanka dances in a rainstorm at the Jardin while Africans look on from inside the enclosure to which they are normally confined, and Fernand gazes at her too, perhaps from outside the fence (1: 40–41). The dance ends with Diamanka crawling through the mud. The word "Dangbé" appears fourteen times in black-outlined, orange-and-yellow capital letters on the double page. They straddle the gutter, partly crossing panel borders and entering the image space. There is no visual indication that any character is physically chanting the word. The word's meaning is only supplied later, when Diamanka asks Fernand why "Dangbé," the python, a "god in our homeland," is confined to a glass terrarium in his office (2: 7).

Later, Diamanka finds herself alone in the office after having received a strong dose of heroin from the doctor. This time "Agbo" is repeated four times, apparently chanted, in lettering similar to that of the earlier "Dangbé," across the top of a sequence of three images depicting African objects collected by Fernand (a lion's skin and head, carved wooden masks, and weapons) and the terrified face of Diamanka, gazing at the python (2: 13). An editorial note at the bottom of the page informs us that "Agbo" is the "nickname of the Amazons in Dahomey." In an inset panel, we see Diamanka looking up with only the whites of her eyes showing, indicating she is again in a trance (2: 13.7). The python commands her to free it from the terrarium and then open the office door. Its speech is contained in balloons shaped like those of an earlier conversation between Diamanka and Djiba (1: 23–25), indicating that its words are in her African language. The snake's speech and his physical transformation into a creature half-human, half-snake suggest that the whole scene consists of subjective images focalized by Diamanka, no doubt still under the influence of the heroin injection. The snake, now loose in the house, frightens Marthe, Fernand's wife, so much that she falls backward off a balcony headfirst onto the patio below, smashing her head and dying instantly (2: 12–15). Vodoun, therefore, leads indirectly to the death of both Marthe and Diamanka, who apparently caught a pulmonary infection while dancing in the rain and mud (1: 40–41, 42.5), which led Fernand to inject her with heroin as an experimental remedy, thereby creating her addiction, her later subjugation through it to Chance at the cabaret, and her suicidal revolt in the conclusion.

---

13. Vodoun also plays an important role in Bourgeon's *Les passagers du vent*, especially volumes 3 and 4, but see also 5: 34.5.

In the comic, Vodoun mediates between the Amazon and animality at the heart of the category of "savage" by making Diamanka more animal and anthropomorphizing an animal (Diamanka is also associated with a black panther that she frees from the zoo early in the story, later killed by Saint-Juste, and with the lion in Fernand's office [1: 23–28; 2: 13.1, 30.6]). In *La Vénus du Dahomey*, Vodoun is an occult force that indirectly kills two women, a role not atypical in Western literature and media (Shohat and Stam 202–3). We could also see the destruction wrought by Vodoun and by Diamanka as an Amazon in Paris as a return of repressed colonial violence that strikes both colonizer and colonized in the colonial metropolis. An encounter between colonized and colonizer creates havoc in the story, structures the narrative, and is associated with a confusion of the categories of savage and civilized, African and European, female and male.

La Vénus du Dahomey ambivalently, alternately critiques and celebrates a European savior figure in Fernand de la Fillière, the primary carrier of the colonial white man's burden and a sort of perverse Dr. Livingstone. He tries to prey sexually on the vulnerable Diamanka (2: 7–8) and treats her as a medical subject by injecting her with heroin and taking notes about its effects on her, even though he saves his own son Eugène from an opium overdose when the young man smokes it in a Parisian den with Saint-Juste (2: 31–35). On the other hand, he also tries to send Diamanka home to Dahomey (2: 19–21) and later to keep her from being killed after her escape from the cabaret (2: 40, 46). The white savior trope at the end of the story also functions ambiguously. By then, Fernand's ties to women have been severed through the deaths of Marthe and Diamanka. He has also disavowed his son, Eugène, who is a figure of the romantic painter and perhaps therefore a negative alter-image of the cartoonists themselves. Eugène's first reaction to Diamanka is racist: he calls her a monkey (1: 43.6). He is devious, dissolute, and fails to live up to his father's expectations of success either as a surgeon or a painter. The artist, after having his first painting exhibition panned by a famous Parisian art critic (2: 35–36), punches him and is called a monster (2: 36). He is symbolically castrated when the Amazon amputates his hand (2: 44) and then abandoned by his father (2: 47). The amputation is justified both immediately, by Eugène's attempt to bludgeon Diamanka with a club (2: 44), and a bit more distantly, by the arrangement that Eugène and Saint-Juste force on Chance in a conversation overheard by Djiba that sparks the boy's killing of Chance and his escape with his sister from the cabaret (2: 41–43). When Eugène sees Diamanka in Chance's cabaret act, he becomes enraged that the person he holds responsible for his mother's death and whom he deems a monster (2: 15) is so successful (2: 36–37). Determined to punish the virginal Amazon, or to destroy the Amazon in her (2: 40.9), Eugène gives Chance a new supply of heroin for Diamanka, stolen from his father (2: 34.1, 39.3), in exchange for allowing the young Frenchman to rape the Amazon while she is helpless to fight back, right after taking a drug dose (2: 41). Overhearing the plot, Djiba bursts in to protect his sister. He brandishes a revolver he stole from the albino, kills Chance who thinks a "dirty little Negro" is incapable of using the weapon, and locks up Saint-Juste and Eugène while critiquing their colonialist language and evil deeds: "You take us for savages, but you are not worth more than hyenas!" (2: 41–42). He then takes the cash and heroin lying on Chance's desk, gets his sister, and leaves the cabaret.

The story ends somewhat surprisingly with quasi-paternal bonding between the white French doctor and the African boy, who together make the voyage out, or back, to Africa with Djiba implicitly taking Eugène's place next to Fernand. The cartoonists depict the doctor's relationship to Djiba as ambivalent: Djiba accuses Fernand of harming Diamanka by getting her addicted to heroin (2: 38) but then acknowledges his helpful warning that Eugène is trying to harm her (2: 40.9). However, the doctor's trip with Djiba to Dahomey may not just be kindly paternal or solely disinterested but also a flight from scandal in Paris. This is prepared first by gossip between three well-dressed French women in a cemetery where Fernand appears to be looking at Marthe's grave, perhaps just after her burial. The women surmise that Fernand's wife died not in an accident but instead killed herself because "her husband was sleeping with a Negro woman!—And under their roof, to top it off!" (2: 16.2). The story's final panel, in which Fernand is apparently reading about Diamanka in *Le petit journal*, indicates that the Amazon's last combat is national news and suggests that their scandalous relationship is widespread knowledge in France, where he has no doubt become a pariah (2: 48.5). The voyage to Africa is probably therefore a journey into exile for Fernand whereas it means going home for Djiba. The reference to *Le petit journal* also serves as an authentifying gesture, suggesting to readers that the story, if not actually true, is at least historically plausible and that the cartoonists built it on both real events and bona fide documents from the colonial past.

La Vénus du Dahomey contributes to a general awareness of too often marginalized histories of what accompanied brutal French colonial conquest, including exploitative trips by colonized Africans to France, collaboration there between racist social science and popular spectacle, and colonialist voyeurism. With Diamanka, the story features a resisting African woman traveling to France during the colonial era, a rarity in French comics. However, the story is ultimately unsatisfying as a critique of colonial culture because of how it represents African religious beliefs and traditions and an African woman, who is still heavily eroticized and is finally killed and replaced by a white Frenchman. By contrast, comics by African cartoonists, to which I now turn, shift the representation of Amazons from Dahomey in key ways.

African Comics about Amazons

Three comics by African cartoonists about Amazons from Dahomey are representative of significant new trends in French-language comics. Those tendencies include the arrival and establishment of African cartoonists in Europe, collaboration between African cartoonists originally from different countries (and between African and French cartoonists), support of African comics by public and international institutions, a pedagogical role for comics about Africa and Africans, retelling stories of anticolonial resistance (among other African histories and memories), and a readership at least partly outside of Africa, in Europe and beyond, for comics by Africans. Another major factor in shifting comic strip narratives about Africa and Africans is the appearance of women of African heritage as authors of comics, of whom scriptwriter Marguerite Abouet is the best known.

The first of the three comics about Amazons is "Les couleurs de la mémoire" [The Colors of Memory] (2006), an eight-page story drawn by Héctor Sonon and scripted by Florent Couao-Zotti, both of whom are from Benin. Sonon draws editorial cartoons and comics and is a painter. Couao-Zotti is an accomplished writer who has published many novels, including with the major French publisher Gallimard. "Les couleurs de la mémoire" engages with history through a frame narrative about a contemporary archeological dig that yields up the magical bracelet of Adefemi, an enslaved woman of royal Yoruba lineage in the court of Glele, king of Dahomey and father of Béhanzin. A wise old man (and retired teacher) who sees the bracelet tells Adefemi's story to the archeologists attempting to reconstruct the past. He says that a Fon prince fell in love with her. King Glele's refusal to accept a foreign princess in his court meant that she would be sold and deported as a slave to Brazil. However, before being taken onto the ship, Adefemi leads a revolt and is shot, but her body magically disappears. In contrast to the impossible French-African mixed couple found in *La Vénus du Dahomey*, there is here an impossible African-African mixed couple that highlights how tensions between African societies left Africa vulnerable to European colonialism. An African woman archeologist hearing this oral history calls Adefemi "an Amazon," indicating that she served in the military unit of the Dahomean king before being sold to European slavers. The story was published in *Africalement* [Africally], an issue of the magazine *Afrobul* [AfroSpeechBalloon], edited by Alix Fuilu, a cartoonist originally from the Democratic Republic of the Congo, and published by Afro Bulles Editions, located in the northern French city of Tourcoing. The stated goal of *Afrobul* is "to make known the Africa of comics." "Les couleurs de la mémoire" thematizes the recovery of a memory and history of African resistance to the colonial slave trade and specifically the contribution of African women to it. It represents this retrieval and reconstitution as a wholly African endeavor in which African anthropologists learn from an African oral historian.

The second work is *Les femmes soldats du Dahomey* [The Women Soldiers of Dahomey] (2014), a seventeen-page comic scripted by Sylvia Serbin, a French Caribbean journalist and historian who spent several years in Africa, and drawn by Pat Masioni, an accomplished cartoonist from the Democratic Republic of the Congo. A UNESCO booklet published online in both French and English in a series on the history of women in Africa, *Les femmes soldats du Dahomey* recounts the history of Dahomey's Amazons in both precolonial and colonial history, dealing with issues such as the triangular Atlantic slave trade, which Dahomey helped supply, and the French conquest of the country. Throughout the story, the authors use the term "woman soldier" instead of "Amazon" and gloss the Fon term "Agon'dijé" [Get out of there! Make a space for me!] on the back cover. The comic strip is part of a series designed to "pay homage to African women and honor their memory," according to the last page. It notes that King Ghezo helped constitute the Amazons as a fighting force in part through forced conscription of war captives from other kingdoms. The comic strip history ends by connecting the precolonial Amazons to women soldiers in postcolonial Benin (figure 10.3).

Couao-Zotti, who scripted "Les couleurs de la mémoire," also wrote the script for *Gbéhanzin* (2015), a full-length comic book based on an original idea by Sonia Houenoude and Couao-Zotti, drawn by Constantin Adadja and published in Cotonou, Benin. *Gbéhanzin* takes a biographical approach to history by telling the story of the king, beginning with his accession to the throne and continuing with his resistance to French conquest, defeat, exile in Martinique and then Algeria, his death there, and the repatriation of his

FIGURE 10.3. Here, the cartoonists pay homage to the woman soldiers of the Kingdom of Dahomey (*far right*), connecting them to female soldiers in the present-day army of the Republic of Benin (*far left*). The cartoonists connect the two generations by referring to the enduring memory of the former and to their dances, songs, and legends. Pat Masioni and Sylvia Serbin, *Les femmes soldats du Dahomey*, 2014, p. 21.

remains to Dahomey years later.[14] Although *Gbéhanzin* is primarily about the king, it devotes several passages to glorifying the courage, prowess, and devotion of Dahomean Amazon soldiers (7.4, 42–45, 48, 52–53, 56–58, 67.4).[15] The authors use both "Amazon" and "agodjiée" to refer to the women.

These three comics recuperate and rehabilitate African history in different ways and thematize that process in their stories and in paratextual material. In an interview with Michelle Bumatay, Masioni, now based in Paris, explained that he had visited Benin in 2009 to do independent research on the Amazons and was contacted by UNESCO in 2012 to draw *Les femmes soldats du Dahomey*. However, all three comics indicate recourse to colonial-era visual documentation, *Gbéhanzin* most strikingly through several photographs of the king reproduced in the end papers and redrawn on the book's

---

14. The comic takes sides in an ongoing dispute over the surrender of Béhanzin and the transfer of power. This has present-day ramifications because there are two different sovereigns in Abomey with competing claims to the throne (Boko).

15. Elsewhere, I have written about another comic featuring Béhanzin, this time scripted by Yvan Alagbé, a French cartoonist of Benin heritage (McKinney, "Rappels").

back cover. The Amazons' dress in *Gbéhanzin* is close to Bourgeon's drawings in *Les passagers du vent*, suggesting a common source. In their foreword to *Les femmes soldats du Dahomey*, the authors state that the images are based on "historical and iconographic research" but that they are "an artistic and visual interpretation and . . . not intended to be an exact representation of events, persons, architecture, clothing, hairstyles or accessories of this period" (4). They modeled the Amazons' clothing on that of a lurid colonial-era print of an Amazon holding a severed head, blood dripping from it, that is reproduced in the online pedagogical module associated with the comic book, where it is credited to Frederick Forbes, a British naval officer who wrote about two missions to the King of Dahomey in the mid-nineteenth century.[16]

Conclusion

Ending her study "Scenes of Empire: Representation of Ethnographic Spectacles in European Literature and the Visual Arts at the Time of the Colonial Conquests," Robles argues that the difficulty of identifying with the mixed audience and especially with the figure of Sarah (or Saartjie) Baartman in the film and comic book versions of Kechiche's *Vénus noire*, because we are given little access to her thoughts or speech, "permits the inauguration of a new type of visual consumption: that of a spectator (man or woman) of the third millennium, paradoxically called upon to face her or his own look and curiosity." Her observation applies to all the postcolonial documents about Amazons analyzed here insofar as they imply a range of reading motivations and solicit diverse reading strategies structured around and through the figure of the African Amazon. In the postcolonial French comics studied, recuperating the history of the African Amazon helps highlight the preconquest kingdom of Dahomey, African resistance to French colonization, and key aspects of French colonial culture, including colonial eroticism and the production of racism through the physical and social sciences. In contemporary French comics, eroticism is in part a legitimizing tactic, marking comics as meant for adults, not children (Miller 22). However, in stories about the colonial era, this often entails transferring colonial eroticism into comics from other arts and media, such as painting, photography, or prose fiction, as I have argued elsewhere (*Colonial*; *Redrawing*). That is clearly the case in both *Les passagers du vent* and *La Vénus du Dahomey*. This erotic dimension is

---

16. The image appears on a plate in Forbes (22–23).

less salient in the postcolonial African, or Franco-African, comics discussed here. Their authors represent Amazons primarily to help recall European colonial violence (including the slave trade), armed anticolonial African resistance, and the place of women in preconquest African societies. In their comics, Amazons also serve to bridge colonial rupture and imagine continuity between preconquest and postliberation African society.

Works Cited

Bachollet, Raymond, et al. *Négripub: L'image des Noirs dans la publicité*. Somogy, 1994.
Berliner, Brett A. *Ambivalent Desire: The Exotic Black Other in Jazz-Age France*. U of Massachusetts P, 2002.
Boko, Hermann. "Au Bénin, la vie du grand roi Gbéhanzin en bande dessinée." *Le monde Afrique*, 3 May 2016.
Bourgeon, François. "François Bourgeon, interview intégrale: 3e partie." Interview by Olivier Delcroix. *Le Figaro* blog, 16 Dec. 2009; https://blog.lefigaro.fr/bd/2009/12/francois-bourgeon-interview-in-1.html.
———. *Les passagers du vent, Volume 3: Le comptoir de Juda*. Casterman, 1994.
———. *Les passagers du vent, Volume 4: L'heure du serpent*. Casterman, 1994.
———. *Les passagers du vent, Volume 5: Le bois d'ébène*. Casterman, 1994.
Casini, Stefano, and Laurent Galandon. *La Vénus du Dahomey, Volume 1: La civilisation hostile*. Dargaud, 2011.
———. *La Vénus du Dahomey, Volume 2: Le dernier combat*. Dargaud, 2012.
Chalaye, Sylvie. "Entertainment, Theater and the Colonies (1870–1914)." *Colonial Culture in France since the Revolution*, edited by Pascal Blanchard, et al., translated by Alexis Pernsteiner, Indiana UP, 2014, pp. 116–23.
Couao-Zotti, Florent, and Constantin Adadja. *Gbéhanzin*. LAHA, 2015.
Daeninckx, Didier. *Cannibale*. 1998. Verdier, 2002.
Forbes, Frederick E. *Dahomey and the Dahomans: Being the Journals of Two Missions to the King of Dahomey, and Residence at his Capital, in the Years 1849 and 1850, Vol. 1*. Longman, Brown, Green, and Longmans, 1851, https://archive.org/details/dahomeydahomansbooforb.
Fresnault-Deruelle, Pierre. "L'effet d'histoire." *Histoire et bande dessinée: Actes du deuxième Colloque international éducation et bande dessinée, La Roque d'Antheron, 16–17 février 1979*. Objectif Promo-Durance; Colloque International Education et Bande Dessinée, 1979, pp. 98–104.
Fulbert-Dumonteil, Jean-Camille. *Guerrières et guerriers du Dahomey au Jardin zoologique d'acclimatation*. Imprimerie Dubuisson et Cie, 1891, https://gallica.bnf.fr/ark:/12148/bpt6k1037736g.
Gauthier, Guy. "De l'imagerie d'une époque à sa représentation aujourd'hui." *L'histoire . . . par la bande: Bande dessinée, histoire et pédagogie*, edited by Odette Mitterrand and Gilles Ciment, Syros, 1993, pp. 55–61.

Henriot [Henri Maigrot]. "Béhanzin et les femmes." *Le journal amusant*, no. 1959, 17 Mar. 1894, p. 7.

———. "Béhanzin intime." *Le journal amusant*, no. 1959, 17 Mar. 1894, p. 6.

———. "Offres et demandes d'emplois." *Le journal amusant*, no. 1891, 26 Nov. 1892, p. 2.

Hugon, Anne, et al. "*Vénus noire*: Posture politique et imposture historique." *Vingtième siècle: Revue d'histoire*, no. 111, 2011, pp. 177–80.

Kechiche, Abdellatif, and Renaud Pennelle. *Vénus noire*. Emmanuel Proust, 2010.

Law, Robin. "The 'Amazons' of Dahomey." *Paideuma: Mitteilungen zur Kulturkunde*, vol. 39, 1993, pp. 245–60. *JSTOR*, https://www.jstor.org/stable/40341664.

Léonnec, Paul. "Chez Béhanzin." *Le journal amusant*, no. 1862, 7 May 1892, p. 3.

Marshall, Bill. "Imagining the First French Empire: *Bande Dessinée* and the Atlantic." *Bande Dessinée: Thinking Outside the Boxes*, special issue of *Yale French Studies*, edited by Laurence Grove and Michael Syrotinski, nos. 131–32, 2017, pp. 151–67.

Masioni, Pat. "Interview with Artist Pat Masioni." Interview conducted by Michelle Bumatay. *YouTube*, uploaded by Michelle Bumatay, 19 Oct. 2020, https://youtu.be/m64QeWoQAAg.

Masioni, Pat, and Sylvia Serbin. *Les femmes soldats du Dahomey*. UNESCO, 2014, https://fr.unesco.org/womeninafrica/sites/default/files/pdf/Les%20femmes%20soldats%20du%20Dahomey_Femmes%20dans%20l%27histoire%20de%20l%27Afrique_Bande%20dessinée_0.pdf.

———. *The Women Soldiers of Dahomey*. UNESCO, 2014, https://en.unesco.org/womeninafrica/sites/default/files/pdf/The%20Women%20Soldiers%20of%20Dahomey_Women%20in%20African%20History_Comic%20Strip_0.pdf.

McKinney, Mark. *The Colonial Heritage of French Comics*. Liverpool UP, 2011.

———. *Postcolonialism and Migration in French Comics*. Leuven UP, 2021.

———. "Rappels croisés de la colonisation dans *Qui a connu le feu* (2004) d'Olivier Bramanti et Yvan Alagbé." *Bande dessinée francophone et colonisation*, special issue of *Outre-mers*, edited by Philippe Delisle, vol. 104, nos. 392–93, 2016, pp. 161–86.

———. *Redrawing French Empire in Comics*. The Ohio State UP, 2013.

Miller, Ann. *Reading Bande Dessinée: Critical Approaches to French-Language Comic Strip*. Intellect, 2007.

Nederveen Pieterse, Jan. *White on Black: Images of Africa and Blacks in Western Popular Culture*. Yale UP, 1992.

Porterfield, Todd. *The Allure of Empire: Art in the Service of French Imperialism, 1798–1836*. Princeton UP, 1998.

Preston-Blier, Suzanne. "Les Amazones à la rencontre de l'Occident." *Zoos humains: XIXe et XXe siècles*, edited by Nicolas Bancel et al., La Découverte, 2002, pp. 136–41.

Reuzé, Emmanuel, and Didier Daeninckx. *Cannibale*. Emmanuel Proust, 2009.

Robles, Fanny. "Scènes d'empire: Représentation des spectacles ethnographiques dans la littérature et les arts visuels européens au temps des conquêtes coloniales." *Synergies Canada*, no. 3, 2011, https://journal.lib.uoguelph.ca/index.php/synergies/article/view/1365.

Said, Edward. *Culture and Imperialism*. Vintage Books, 1994.

Schneider, William H. *An Empire for the Masses: The French Popular Image of Africa, 1870–1900*. Greenwood Press, 1982.

———. "Les expositions ethnographiques du Jardin zoologique d'acclimatation." *Zoos humains: XIXe et XXe siècles*, edited by Nicolas Bancel et al., La Découverte, 2002, pp. 72–80.

Shohat, Ella, and Robert Stam. *Unthinking Eurocentrism: Multiculturalism and the Media*. Routledge, 1994.

Sonon, Héctor, and Florent Couao-Zotti. "Les couleurs de la mémoire." *Afrobul: Africalement*. Afro Bulles, 2006, pp. 11–18.

Thiébaut, Michel. *Les chantiers d'une aventure: Autour des Passagers du vent de François Bourgeon*. Casterman, 1994.

Tramson, Jacques. "La bande dessinée de fiction historique: Deux visions 'documentées' de l'Afrique." *La bande dessinée*, special issue of *Notre librairie*, no. 145, 2001, pp. 82–89.

Zaborowski, Sigismond. "Visite aux Dahoméens du Champ-de-Mars." *Bulletins de la Société d'Anthropologie de Paris*, series 4, vol. 4, 1893, pp. 327–38, https://www.persee.fr/doc/bmsap_0301-8644_1893_num_4_1_5445.

CHAPTER 11

Catel

Portrait of the Twenty-First-Century Feminist Artist and Author of Drawn Biography

ISABELLE DELORME

TRANSLATED BY KIRBY CHILDRESS

Biography has proven itself to be to be a major and influential genre in the fields of history and literature alike. Margareta Jolly explains, "The writing of lives is an ancient and ubiquitous practice. Biographies have been important as genealogical, religious, and didactic forms since the start of recorded literature" (Jolly ix). From its beginning, *bande dessinée,* as an art form, has been interested in representing the lives of influential individuals, whether in a factual or romanticized mode. As Jean-Philippe Martin wrote, "Along with bas-reliefs on the lives of saints, painted portraits and films, *bande dessinée* has nearly always been associated with the genre of biography. Works such as *Dom Bosco* and *Charles de Foucauld,* as well as other celebrated works by Jigé, or even the graphic novel biography of Winston Churchill by Franck Bellamy, were all built on the model described by cartoonist Yves Chaland" (94).[1] However, as evidenced by the work of Martin and his references to works that are exclusively by male authors, biographical *bande dessinée* has predominantly focused on famous men's lives.

This was the context in which artist and illustrator Catel Muller, referred to as Catel, published her collaboration with José-Louis Bocquet, *Kiki de*

---

1. All translations are by Childress unless otherwise noted.

Montparnasse (2007), and it makes the book's publication a triple rupture in the history of *bande dessinée*. First, Catel helped institutionalize the subgenre *la biographie dessinée* ("drawn" or "graphic" biography) as she went on to publish a series of works such as *Olympe de Gouges* (2012), *Ainsi soit Benoîte Groult* (2013), *Joséphine Baker* (2016), and *Alice Guy* (2021). Second, her work has brought to light the stories of influential women who have not received their due attention. Catel and Bocquet refer to these women and this series as "The Clandestine Women of History." Third, with the success of these feminist works, Catel has paved the way for other women artists, illustrators, and authors who likewise seek to increase visibility of influential women. For example, Pénélope Bagieu has since published two volumes of *Culottées: Des femmes qui ne font que ce qu'elles veulent* [*Brazen: Rebel Ladies Who Rocked the World*] in 2016 and 2017. Camille Roelens remarked that *Culottées*, "having such a wide historical and geographical range," reveals to its readers "thirty portraits of relatively unknown women, stars, queens and even warriors—women who, from Ancient Greece to Bush's America, from imperial China to the Indian Wars, took their fates into their own hands."

To paint a portrait of Catel, we must first recognize her role in the notable and recent rise of *biographies dessinées*—especially the increase of works being created by women and about women. Then, by analyzing interviews of Catel from 2019–22, we will see her transformation as her own engagement with the feminist movement—alongside her husband, the novelist, editor, and screenwriter José-Louis Bocquet—becomes more concrete. We will discuss in detail the style and methods Catel uses in her work as we look, step by step, at the creation process of one of Catel's *biographies dessinées*.

Telling Women's Stories through *Biographies Dessinées*: A Rising Trend in France

Catel is one of few women authors to have experienced such a level of success and popularity in the field of *bande dessinée*. Her success has provided her with material and financial means to continue her work competitively in the field. Though the number of women *bande dessinée* authors is on the rise, they remain a minority in the profession and earn lower incomes than their male counterparts. In 2016, a survey conducted by the authors on the board of the États Généraux de la Bande Dessinée (EGBD) revealed that only 27 percent of authors were women. The percentage of authors under thirty is higher, with 41 percent women authors (as opposed to 23 percent for men), and higher still for authors under forty, with 80 percent women (56 percent for men). It was in light of this context that Pénélope Bagieu (who is thirty-seven) stated in January 2020 that gender does not take precedence over the personality of the author:

> There was an important awakening among BD authors from that moment on [speaking of the 2016 Angoulême incident]. We see it today through the numerous successes of women-authored works being released. No one would ask Marion Montaigne (*Tu mourras moins bête* . . .) or Emil Ferris (*My Favorite Thing Is Monsters*, winner of Best Album 2019 in Angoulême) what it's like to be a woman in the BD business. It has become insignificant. (qtd. in Potet)

Likewise in 2020, Thierry Groensteen published two articles dedicated to women authors of *bande dessinée* as well as representations of women's stories. In "Femmes (2): La creation au féminin," he estimates that the proportion of women authors of *bande dessinée*, having tripled over thirty years to reach nearly 12 percent in 2014, is now nearly 20 percent. However, he signals as well that this rate remains low in comparison with the number of women authors of children's literature—a field where women make up 66 percent of authors. Groensteen recognizes that, for a long time, *bande dessinée* did not reserve space for women. In terms of both creation and storytelling, few women cartoonists managed to break into an almost exclusively male profession. In this context, Groensteen argues:

> There is a genre being cultivated by women authors of *bande dessinée*. It is the biographies of "Great Women" who have left their mark on history. Catel's portraits of Kiki de Montparnasse, Benoîte Groult, and Olympe de Gouges—alongside Puchol's resurrection of Joan of Arc and Montellier's retracing of the destinies of Camille Claudel, Marie Curie and Christine Brisset—appear to be the expression of a feminist militancy to reassert the value of women's stories and women authors of *bande dessinée*.

Similarly, Jean-Philippe Martin notes that "the genre of biography has gained respectability since the 2000s, having proven itself capable of offering noteworthy titles" (100). It is estimated that *biographies dessinées* represent at least 10 percent of all albums published in France since the year 2010. Among them, a significant number are by women authors of *bande dessinée*. Martin adds:

> The field in which we are seeing the most innovative biographies is surely that of art. Writers, musicians, painters, and singers all benefit from the

increased attention directed toward them by authors of *bande dessinée*. Dedicating a biography to an artist is often the result of combining several intentions: to pay homage, to translate a certain aesthetic intimacy where an author immerses herself in the artistic techniques of her subject, and to attempt to understand the creation behind a work. (98)

Catel, for one, has shown primary interest in the art world. Beginning with *Kiki de Montparnasse* in 2007, which had considerable success, she continued to build the genre of women's stories in *biographies dessinées* with albums devoted to Benoîte Groult, Josephine Baker, and Alice Guy. And yet, the subject of Catel and Bocquet's upcoming album will not belong to the art world. Rather, they have chosen a timelier subject, Anita Conti, a pioneer in the field of ecology and first French female oceanographer.

To fully outline the development of *biographies dessinées*, it is necessary to establish first the characteristics of this genre. To do this, we can turn to Martin's three criteria of "traditional" drawn biographies. First, there must be a description of what Martin calls *le déroulé de carrière* [career arc], which lays out the origins of the subject—from birth, to education, to career itself. Second, the subject must also *faire bonne figure* or have made a positive mark on history or embody moral values such as a hard-work ethic or a sense of sacrifice. Lastly, the work must adopt a certain register and tone—one that is both serious and realistic. I would add a fourth criterion concerning women's *biographies dessinées* specifically: the subject must be a woman, likely famous in her time, sometimes forgotten but always remarkable. In other words, a clandestine woman of history. In this way, the work will also strongly contribute to the recognition of women's stories and shape a revisionist (corrective) view of history.

Such is the case for the work of Catel, which has brought new attention to women such as Olympe de Gouges and Alice Guy. Catel's work is far from unique, even if similar works are not of the same magnitude. Other women authors of *bande dessinée* have contributed notable works, such as *Céleste, Tome 1: "Bien sûr Monsieur Proust"* published in 2022 by Chloé Cruchaudet, which paints the portrait of the woman who was much more than Marcel Proust's irreplaceable governess. Likewise, in 2021, Virginie Ollagnier and Carole Maurel published *Nelly Bly: Dans l'antre de la folie*, an album dedicated to a pioneer of investigative journalism and clandestine reporting in the United States. This work earned them the Prix Artémisia in 2022.[2]

---

2. Created in 2008, this award recognizes comics written and/or illustrated by one or more women. Its goal is to showcase the work of women authors. Originally, only one *bande dessinée* was honored, but the Artémisia has since evolved to a total of six awards in 2020 (Grand Prix, Prix de l'environnement, etc.).

These *biographies dessinées* made by women are overwhelmingly feminist and produced almost exclusively by women. Some work alone, such as Paulina Spucches, who created the biography of American photographer Vivian Maier, *Vivian Maier: À la surface d'un miroir* (2021). There are also those who work in tandem with other women, such as Mayalen Goust and Eileen Hofer who cocreated *Alicia: Prima ballerina Assoluta* (2022), which tells the story of Alicia Alonso, the founder and director of the National Ballet of Cuba, which began in 1948. However, these works may also be the product of mixed teams, as is the case of *À mains nues* by Clément Oubrerie and Leïla Slimani. In two volumes (2020 and 2021), Oubrerie and Slimani tell the story of a forgotten heroine of the twentieth century: Suzanne Noël, the doctor and feminist who pioneered the field of facial reconstructive surgery. Rarely, but at times, women's stories are being created by teams of predominantly (or solely) men. Even more rare are those published by solo male authors. Catel was thus at the forefront of a burgeoning genre that has privileged both women's graphic biography and women graphic biographers.

A Feminist Author Committed to Recognizing "The Clandestine Women of History"

Catel defines herself as an author, or rather as someone who tells stories, whether they be written or drawn. She holds a specific place in the world of contemporary Francophone *bande dessinée*. Recognized in France and internationally, she heads a small team that assists her in these works. Her situation is quite rare: most authors, especially women, deal with much instability and lack job security, as was reported during the Angoulême festival in January 2020.[3] Olympe de Gouges, Kiki de Montparnasse, and to a smaller degree Benoîte Groult and Josephine Baker owe their resurgence to interest sparked by Catel's graphic biographies. Catel's background and training resemble that of the majority of her peers. As a child she loved drawing, and between the ages of seven and seventeen, she created hundreds of illustrations, paintings, and pages of *bandes dessinées*. From 1984 to 1989 she completed her studies before entering the École supérieure des arts décoratifs (a decorative arts academy) in Strasbourg, where she became friends with Blutch. The

---

3. On June 5, 2016, the thirty authors nominated for the Grand Prix at the Angoulême International Comics Festival were announced. The nominees were all men. In protest, many of the authors such as Riad Sattouf, Daniel Clowes, and Joann Sfar asked to be removed from the selection. A movement to boycott the voting began to spread across social media by way of the hashtag #WomenDoBD.

two of them studied under Claude Lapointe, the founder of the illustration studio and master artist in his own right. Numerous authors and illustrators hail from his studio, including Daniel Blancou, Élodie Durand, and Marjane Satrapi. In addition to Catel's decorative arts degree, she earned a master's degree of fine arts. In 1990, Catel moved to Paris and began her career doing illustrations for children's books from various publishing houses such as Hachette and Hatier. As she stated in 2018, "I made so many illustrations for children after arriving in Paris. For so long, I never even considered doing anything else" (qtd. in Peras). As of 2020, she has illustrated more than fifty works. Still, her fame rests mainly on her *bandes dessinées*.

Catel greatly admires the work of Claire Bretécher (1940–2020). A prominent author of French-language comics, Bretécher's poignant and innovative work garnered attention in the 1970s. She is most known for her work mocking bourgeois, French intellectuals—published in *Le nouvel observateur* between 1973 and 1981—which were later transformed into a full *bande dessinée* titled *Les frustrés*. She also published several notable albums dealing with themes of maternity and adolescence, such as in her successful series *Agrippine* (1988–2009). In 1982, Bretécher received the Grand Prix Spécial award at the annual festival of *bande dessinée* in Angoulême. For Catel, Bretécher possessed an art of movement, expression, pauses, and precision, which she valued over truth. It was Bretécher's work that inspired Catel to make her own *bandes dessinées*. As Catel expressed in 2016, "She was not afraid to take risks, she is passionate. She inspires us to tell our stories, to condemn, to not be afraid. Today, I am clearly a daughter of Bretécher" ("Claire Bretécher").

Benoîte Groult, Catel's second role model, was born in 1920 and died in 2016. A journalist, novelist, and militant feminist, Groult authored several best-sellers including *Ainsi soit-elle* [As She Is], an essay that recounts her feminist awakening. The essay was published in 1975 and millions of copies were sold. In 1986, she published Olympe de Gouge's 1791 *Déclaration des droits de la femme et de la citoyenne* [Declaration of the Rights of Women and of the Female Citizen] for the first time in its entirety. Catel's mother, an avid reader of Groult's work, encouraged the adolescent Catel to read *Ainsi soit-elle*: "At 15 years old, I discovered *Ainsi soit-elle* (1975), and it came as quite a shock. I learned the terrible news that women were mistreated in the world. In my small village in Alsace, I never encountered misery or suffering. This was a revelation to me. Benoîte Groult, who overcame all of the major upheavals of the twentieth century, is not only an example of emancipation, but of glamour as well" (Berkani).

Catel, having been influenced by these two great examples of feminism, followed suit both in her work and by joining the Collectif des Créatrices de

Bande Dessinée Contre le Sexisme [Women BD Authors Collective Against Sexism]—an organization created by Jul Maroh and Lisa Mandel in France in 2015.[4] The collective openly asserts its feminism and, as of January 2020, is comprised of 261 scriptwriters, illustrators, and colorists from all generations. Catel describes her participation in this collective as one of solidarity, though lacking in engagement. Other notable members, such as Florence Cestac, born in 1949, have joined alongside younger authors like Morgane Parisi, born in 1986. Even Marjane Satrapi, though she has not published any *bande dessinée* since *Poulet aux prunes* in 2004, joined the collective. The group advocates against labeling works by women as a narrative genre on its own: "'Female comics' is not a genre of storytelling. Adventure, science-fiction, thriller, romance, autobiography, humor, history, tragedy are genres of storytelling and women authors mast them without having to be reduced to their sex."[5] The members of the collective hope that their position, opinions, and testimonials will lead to an annihilation of sexism in the world of *bande dessinée* and beyond. On the collective's website, one can find this charter along with a list of the creators, a history of their actions, testimonials, a blog, and links to other resources. Recently, in 2016, members of the group joined forces to speak out against the absence of women among the thirty authors selected for the Grand Prix at the *bande dessinée* festival in Angoulême. The issue led to a cultural awakening and to the cancellation of that list. Since then, there has been an increase in diversity on the juries of various *bande dessinée* festivals. For instance, while not a single woman author of *bande dessinée* had received the Grand Prix at Angoulême since Florence Cestac in 2000, Japanese manga artist Rumiko Takahashi was awarded the prize in 2019. Then, in 2022, a *bande dessinée* author from Quebec, Julie Doucet, was likewise awarded the Grand Prix.

In this context of the lack of visibility of women authors of *bande dessinée*, Catel and Bocquet share in their commitment to pay homage to the women who served as role models of emancipation and courage for them, hoping that their works would invite their readers to reconsider the role of these women in history. As Catel has remarked:

> I must pay homage to these women who allowed me to be where I am today. I did not live through the war, through segregation, I was lucky enough to grow up in a society where I can express myself. My *bandes dessinées* are my way of giving thanks to those who came before me. (qtd. in Berkani)

---

4. Jul Maroh has since come out as transgender and nonbinary but originally published under their birth name.

5. Translation as found on the organization's official website: http://bdegalite.org/.

Catel and Bocquet's commitment to forgotten women in the history of *bande dessinée* was enthusiastically received by the publisher Casterman in a collection titled *Écritures* [Writings]. The process of making the biographies was the same each time: Bocquet writes the storyline and conducts the bibliographic research, Catel then attends to the illustration, and the two work together on the storyboard. Each book comes with a bibliography, short biography, and timeline put together by Bocquet. Additionally, there are ties linking Catel's heroines. For instance, Benoîte Groult, in 1975, dedicated her widely published feminist essay, *Ainsi soit-elle*, to Olympe de Gouges. Catel and Bocquet subsequently discovered Olympe de Gouges while reading *Ainsi soit-elle*, leading them to discuss her while working on Catel's *Ainsi soit Benoîte Groult*—which she created on her own and published with Grasset in 2013. The newspaper *Libération* had offered Catel the opportunity to produce a double-page spread on the person of her choice. Hesitating between Bretécher and Groult, she decided at last to write about the latter. We learn from the cover of Catel's book that Groult was not fond of *bande dessinée*, an opinion based on her negative memories of Bécassine, a young woman who is always depicted as speechless, and indeed, without a mouth. Despite this, Catel and Groult developed a strong friendship throughout the process. After the first interview, the two engaged in a long series of meetings. Over a five-year period, Catel drew and took notes throughout these meetings, which took place in Paris, Hyères in the Midi region, and Doëlan in Brittany, all places where Groult would live depending on the seasons. Catel recounts Groult's life, including her involvement in the fight for women's right to vote, freedom to divorce, access to abortion services, equal pay, feminization of professions, the right to assisted suicide, and so on. *Ainsi soit Benoîte Groult* won the Artémisia grand prize for *bande dessinée* by a woman author in 2014.

Kiki de Montparnasse, published in 2007, was the first joint publication by Catel and Bocquet. It is the story of Alice Prin, also known as Kiki, who became an icon in the artistic scene of Paris during the *années folles*, a period characterized by intense social, cultural, and artistic endeavors between 1920 and 1929. Alongside Man Ray, Picasso, and Cocteau, Kiki became a key figure of the avant-garde movement as a muse, painter, singer, and actress. She became a surrealist icon after being photographed by Man Ray in 1924 in *Le violon d'Ingres* [Ingres's Violin], where she posed, her back to the camera, nude, with the sound holes of a violin painted on her back. She became an example of emancipation and liberty (figure 11.1). As of January 2020, this work has been translated into over fifteen language and over 100,000 copies have been sold in France.

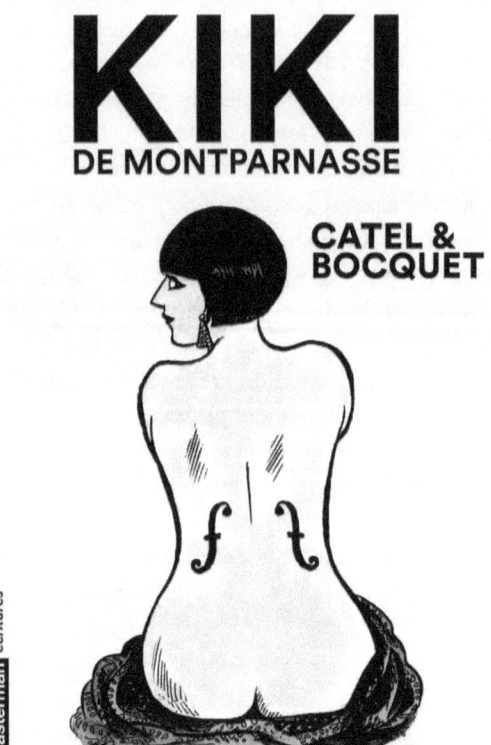

FIGURE 11.1. Catel Muller and José-Louis Bocquet, *Kiki de Montparnasse*, 2007, cover. Used with the generous permission of the authors and Editions Casterman.

Olympe de Gouges, published in 2012, tells the story of Marie Gouze, one of the first feminists in modern history. After being widowed at eighteen years old, Gouze refused to remarry. A French law at that time prohibited women from publishing any works without their husband's consent. Rather than risk her independence, she chose to raise her son on her own and began publishing under the name of Olympe de Gouges. Outraged by slavery and injustice, she wrote plays, novels, and eventually, in 1791, the *Déclaration des droits de la femme et de la citoyenne*. During the Enlightenment, and as a republican, she joined the fight for women's right to vote and to divorce as well as equality of the sexes and individuals. She died under the guillotine in Paris during the Terror in November 1793. As of 2022, this book had become the most sought after of the "Clandestine Women of History" series due to a resurgence of discussions on women's freedom of expression and their right to think and to act.

In 2016, Catel and Bocquet published *Joséphine Baker*, which brings to light the life of the African American performer, of a modest upbringing at the time of segregation, who began singing and dancing at a young age. Baker came to Paris at age nineteen in 1925 and quickly rose to fame as an icon of the *années folles*, praised by Picasso, Cocteau, and Le Corbusier. As a singer, she triumphed all over Europe, especially with her song "J'ai deux amours, mon pays et Paris" [I Have Two Loves, My Country and Paris], which propelled her to become the first woman of color to be an international star. The song was written by Géo Koger and Henri Verna, to the music of Vincent Scotto, for Josephine Baker upon her arrival in Paris in 1930. Created as part of the revue *Paris qui remue* at the Casino de Paris, the song celebrates the French empire based in Paris as part of the Paris Colonial Exposition in 1931. The book shows also lesser-known aspects of Josephine Baker's life: her involvement in the French Resistance; her fight alongside Martin Luther King Jr. against racial segregation; and her role as mother of an atypical family or the "Rainbow Tribe"—beginning in the 1950s, she adopted twelve orphans from around the world and brought them to live with her in Dordogne, in her castle in Milandes. On November 30, 2021, Josephine Baker became the seventy-seventh person (and sixth woman) inducted into the Panthéon, after Simone Veil in 2018. There, among other important French figures, Baker takes her place as a celebrated music hall performer and as an anti-racism activist.

Joining these "Clandestine Women of History" is a *bande dessinée* about Alice Guy in 2021, titled *Alice Guy* [Alice Guy: First Lady of Film], published once more with Casterman as part of the *Écritures* collection. Guy was born in 1873 in France and passed away in the United States in 1968. She became the first female director in the history of cinema in 1896 with her film *La fée aux choux* [The Fairy of the Cabbages]; then in 1910, she became the first woman to set up a production company, the Solax Film Co. In the United States, Pamela Green made a documentary about Guy in 2019 titled *Be Natural: The Untold Story of Alice Guy-Blaché*. The choice of Alice Guy as subject for their next book began with Francis Lacassin, a specialist in cinema and the first to have served as chair of the history of *bande dessinée* at the Sorbonne University in Paris. Lacassin has written widely on Alice Guy and even met her while she was still alive. Upon Lacassin's death, he left Bocquet a collection of manuscripts, documents, and photos all surrounding Guy. These archives served as the foundation of research for Bocquet and Catel as they worked.

A Versatile Author: Working in Pairs and Leading a Creative Team

Catel rarely works alone, though this was the case for *Ainsi soit Benoîte Groult* and more recently for *Le roman des Goscinny, naissance d'un gaulois* [The Goscinny Story, Birth of a Gaul], which was published in 2019. Still, these works were both the result of lengthy discussions with their subjects: Benoîte Groult and subsequently Anne Goscinny, the daughter of René Goscinny—the writer of *Astérix, Lucky Luke, Le petit Nicolas,* among others. A novelist herself, Goscinny is continuing her father's work (she is thus his literal and figurative heir). It is clear that Catel prefers working with others, especially in partnerships. Her professional relationship with author and illustrator Claire Bouilhac, with whom she shares feminist convictions, has led to the production of several works since 2009, such as *Adieu Kharkov* in 2015 and *La princesse de Clèves* in 2019. More recently, her encounter with Anne Goscinny led to not only *Roman des Goscinny* but also to a young adult series titled *Le monde de Lucrèce* [Lucretia's World], which they have been working on together since 2018 and to great success. Nevertheless, her most significant collaborative efforts remain those with Bocquet. Catel is far from the first to produce such collaborations. Désirée, the author, and Alain Frappier, the illustrator, have worked together since 2002 and have published four graphic novels together since 2012, such as *Le choix* [The Choice], an autobiographical account of the fight for women's right to contraception and abortion, or *Le temps des humbles* [The Time of Humbles], published in 2020 and set during Salvador Allende's presidency in Chile between 1970 and 1973.[6] It is significant both that Catel works in collaboration (as modeled by much feminist work either in collectives or others), but her relative fame surpasses the collaboration and thus inclines her public and critical recognition toward that of the *auteure*—a complicated model, as discussed by other contributors to this volume.[7]

Style and Color

Catel has a highly identifiable style: precise, supple, and expressive, or as she describes it, a simplified realism. She adopts Hergé's *ligne claire* but adds more spirit to her drawings. Her drawings change in order to match her subjects and their time periods. For instance, for her work on Olympe de

---

6. See chapter 8 in this volume for Catriona Macleod's discussion of *Le choix*.

7. See the introduction to this volume by Margaret C. Flinn, chapter 1 by Jessica Kohn, and chapter 2 by Sylvain Lesage.

Gouges, Catel took her inspiration from etchings, which were popular in the eighteenth century. For Josephine Baker, whose career began in Paris in the time of expressionism, Catel used a style that resembled what was being taught at the École de Paris in the 1920s. With high contrast black-and-white images, Catel brings the spirit of the era to the pages of her book. In her work on Alice Guy, her illustrations imitate the Art Nouveau movement, popular in Guy's time. As Catel stated herself, "Style plays an important role in creating ambiance, it sets the scene for the story" (Interview).

Catel's choice between black-and-white images or color depends largely on the context of the subject. As in the case of "Clandestine Women in History," the principal reason behind her decision to use only black-and-white illustration is mostly artistic. The women in these stories are historical figures, which means that the documents used by Catel and Bocquet in their research were also in black and white—such as the photos of Kiki de Montparnasse by Man Ray or the eighteenth-century etchings for Olympe de Gouges and even the silent films of Alice Guy. What is more, Catel considers her work to be graphic *novels*; therefore, it is only logical that the writing and images be black and white to resemble a novel. She elaborates, "You can read it quickly and draw it quickly. It's the same size and format as a novel" (Interview).

Additionally, using only black-and-white images is an economical decision. Each of these works is over three hundred pages long. Printing them in color would have been extremely expensive, especially on the international level. Today, printing three hundred pages in black and white is the same cost as printing forty-eight pages in color. In fact, many foreign publishers lack the means necessary to print books in color, like in Poland, for instance, where circulation and readership are limited despite ambitious efforts to put forth quality *bande dessinée*. The use of color thus depends on the context. For *Le monde de Lucrèce*, creating a universe without color for contemporary young adult readers was unthinkable for Catel. Colors give more life and sense to the narrative. Likewise, in *Le roman des Goscinny*, the colors help in differentiating the different speakers: René Goscinny's chapters are in blue while Anne's are in orange, and the trichromatic nature of the work adds to the story. Thus, even when including color, Catel adheres to a relatively lean palette, highly conditioned by narrative function, leaving the story (or novelistic) aspect of the work to dominate.

The Creative Process

Catel begins the research for each book by visiting the places that were important to her subject. The idea to travel to these locations came about while Catel and Bocquet were working on *Kiki de Montparnasse* in 2004. Until then, Catel had never undertaken a *bande dessinée* project on a real person. She wanted to be as close to the truth as possible, leading her to such places as where Kiki lived as a child. As Catel explains,

> Châtillon-sur-Seine, I had no idea what it looked like. It's a small town in Burgundy with only three pictures available on the Internet. In order to understand what Kiki knew, like her walk to school and whether it was long or not, I had to go there. Kiki says that she often skipped school, heading off on side roads—but was it a hundred meters or two kilometers? Were these little adventures dangerous? I needed to see for myself. (Interview)

Catel's approach described here illustrates her desire to depict in the most accurate way possible the life and personality of the women whose stories she tells. This research practice has evolved and become more systematic as Catel has worked on subsequent books, leading to many memorial journeys, or rather trips down the protagonist's own memory lane. Many authors use similar methods when undertaking historical *bandes dessinées*, whether it consists of retracing one's own memories (as is the case for Marjane Satrapi's *Persepolis*) or a relative's (as in Art Spiegelman's *Maus*) as it pertains to major historical events of the twentieth and twenty-first centuries (Delorme). The author documents every minute detail of the journey, which is surprisingly short and dense when compared to the lengthy production of the book itself. These journeys allow the author-researcher to gather documents, some of which appear in the final product. Often, authors will include a description of their memorial journey in the album, accompanied by sketches made and pictures taken throughout the trip to help separate their account from the rest of the narrative. The journey is thus both research practice and potential source of metadiscursive commentary through paratextual elements in the final work.

Catel's objective in these memorial journeys is twofold: she wishes to immerse herself in the places familiar to her subject and also to collect concrete tracks and archives relating to the protagonists. She states,

> For Josephine Baker, I had to go to St. Louis, in the U.S., it was different than for Kiki. . . . By going to the actual places, not only can one discover these locations in order to illustrate them from every angle, but also, one becomes familiar with the protagonist's very psyche and way of perceiving the world. We feel what they felt, the smells, the light, the atmosphere, the isolation, or the freedom. Everything that the person could have felt, we feel it. No longer connected by mere images over long-distance, we

are surrounded by this person's life. These trips are informative, despite their difficulty—like going to St. Louis in the middle of winter where the cold reaches −10 degrees Celsius. . . . It changes things, including how we perceive what has already been documented. What we learned about her childhood surpassed anything we could have imagined. (Interview)

When working on *Alice Guy*, Catel and Bocquet had planned on traveling to Chile. Guy's family was of Chilean origin, and Guy herself had spent some of her childhood there, from the ages of three to six. Relying on documents she had gathered previously, Catel had already drawn the pages concerned with that period of her subject's life but wanted to make sure they fully represented reality. Being on site in Chile would allow Catel to feel legitimate, or genuine, in her representations, having been where Guy had been. These scouting trips always include sketches and notes in the little black sketchbooks that she always has on her. As of October 2022, Catel had filled up seventy-six Moleskine notebooks. She keeps a notebook, pencil, and pen with her always. What she can't draw on the spot, she photographs for later, just as many other *bande dessinée* authors do.

The people she meets often contribute in some way to her notebooks, whether it be a drawing or a note that Catel later transfers to her blog or her books. We see this in *Ainsi soit Benoîte Groult*, where one page shows Catel boarding a train for Paris at the end of her stay in Hyères with Groult (162). The following frame shows Catel reading her notebook, the contents of which are revealed in the following frame. It is a scanned copy of a short note from Groult describing the trip: "May 24, 2010. Hyères. We spoke for 3 days. We laughed. We cried, too! Your friend, Benoîte." With the note are some of Catel's drawings that show the stairs that lead to Groult's office as well as the office itself with its view of the Mediterranean.

Once Bocquet has finished the storyline and Catel has completed the preliminary sketches, the two work together to organize the storyboard. Bocquet reads the storyline to Catel and together, they break it down into pages and frames. The illustration is done by Catel, later, in her studio in Paris, which consists of a room on the second floor of her house with three desks—one of which is a large table where Catel lays out her works in progress. Along the walls of her studio are bookshelves filled with drawings, her own and those of others, and other objects, books, materials, and her collection of notebooks. Other times, Catel works from her other studio in Fécamp on the coast of Normandy.

Before the 2000s, Catel worked primarily in watercolors. She would even stretch her own watercolor paper on a wooden board. Since then, she continues to create watercolor paintings for exhibitions and selling. With the invention of computers, everything changed: "[Computers] allow us to do magnificent things" (Interview). Catel first makes sketches in pencil on a light box before moving on to the inking process, the coloring, and finally, the scanning and retouching of the images on the computer. Though for many years she managed all of this work on her own, success has provided Catel with the opportunity to expand and delegate some of these tasks to a small team of assistants. Now, when she is producing a work in color, she provides her colorist with a sample page and sends them to finish the job digitally. She also employs an illustrator, trained at the École supérieure des arts décoratifs de Strasbourg, and a graphic designer from an art school in Belgium. They both "clean up" the scanned pages, removing any impurities and completing any drawings that were not totally finished—for example, if a fingertip was missing from a hand. A model maker also assists in the lettering: filling the speech bubbles with Bocquet's text. Lastly, Catel elicits the help of a community manager who operates her website, which offers visitors information about all of her books, her Moleskine notebooks, and her portfolio as well as a gallery and upcoming projects. The manager additionally manages Catel's schedule, blog, and social media presence when she is scouting and for book signings, speeches, exhibits, and the like. The team consists of seven people.

Conclusion

Catel's work may not seem totally unique when compared to that of other contemporary authors: her drawings are in pencil and ink, she uses brush pens and watercolors while still using modern technology such as computers, digital photos, and the internet in her creative process. Her prominence in the world of Francophone *bande dessinée*, however, and the representative (if grander scale) nature of her process makes her exemplary: she essentially presides over and provides artistic vision for a studio of collaborators. Over the past few years, she has proven to be a forerunner among women authors, boldly venturing into the representation of these clandestine women who changed history. It was a choice not without risk on her part to take on such a limited specialization. Her success can be attributed to several factors, including her competence as an artist, her supple style, and her ability to alter her work to match different styles. Her ability to delegate, manage, and collaborate with other artists and authors, most notably Bocquet—with whom she shares both her feminist ideals and her taste for history—is another invaluable skill. Lastly, the current political climate with its focus on women's rights—even though there remains progress to be made—has helped increase the circulation of Catel's work.

Alongside Bocquet, Catel has helped legitimize the *biographies dessinées* genre by producing high-quality albums. Her work sets the bar regarding narrative, illustration, and historical accuracy. Providing readers with documentation and research has become a standard practice in the world of historical *bande dessinée*. Additionally, Catel's work on "The Clandestine Women of History" has been enormously successful. Not only has she sold over 100,000 copies of each album, her work is also frequently on display in a wide range of exhibits, and she has been the recipient of several awards since 2007.

As the head of her own studio, she is able to work simultaneously on multiple projects that feature important historical women. Catel has shown that one can be a woman dedicated to a cause, namely feminism, and be highly successful in the field of *bande dessinée*. She has likewise become a role model, inspiring other young artists and authors. Through her work on "The Clandestine Women of History," she has brought to light and to life the forgotten stories of so many women, demonstrating that women's stories are just as interesting as those of men.[8]

Works Cited

Berkani, Véronique. "Catel Muller et les clandestines de l'histoire." *L'Alsace,* 29 Dec. 2014, https://www.lalsace.fr/actualite/2014/12/29/catel-muller-et-les-clandestines-de-l-histoire#.

Bouilhac, Claire, and Catel Muller. *La princesse de Clèves.* Dargaud, 2019.

Bouilhac, Claire, Emmanuelle Polack, and Catel Muller. *Rose Valland, capitaine beaux-arts.* Dupuis, 2009.

Bouilhac, Claire, Mylène Demongeot, and Catel Muller. *Adieu Kharkov.* Dupuis, 2015.

Delorme, Isabelle. *Quand la bande dessinée fait mémoire du XXe siècle: Les récits mémoriels historiques en bande dessinée.* Les Presses du Réel, 2019.

Dupin, Louise. *Des femmes: Observations du préjugé commun sur la différence des sexes.* Edited by Frédéric Marty, Classiques Garnier, 2022.

Frappier, Désirée, and Alain Frappier. *Le choix.* La Ville Brûle, 2015.

Groensteen, Thierry. "Femme (2): La création feminine." *NeuviemeArt2.0,* 2014, http://neuviemeart.citebd.org/spip.php?article727.

Groult, Benoîte. *Ainsi soit-elle.* Grasset, 1975.

---

8. A recent example of the forgotten women who are now being brought to light is that of Louise Dupin. A pioneer of the feminist movement during the Enlightenment, Dupin wrote *Des femmes: Observations du préjugé commun sur la différence des sexes,* which was just published in 2022, nearly three centuries later, thanks to Frédéric Marty.

Jolly, Margareta. *Biography and Autobiography*. Oxford UP, 2012.

Martin, Jean-Philippe. "Biographie." *Le bouquin de la bande dessinée: Dictionnaire esthétique et thématique*. Edited by Thierry Groensteen, Robert Laffont, 2020, pp. 94–100.

Muller, Catel. *Ainsi soit Benoîte Groult*. Grasset, 2013.

———. "Claire Bretécher." *Catel Muller*, 15 Dec. 2015, http://catel-m.com/CATEL.muller/claire-bretecher/.

———. Interview. Conducted by Isabelle Delorme, 23 Jan. 2020.

———. *Kiki de Montparnasse*. Casterman, 2007.

———. *Le roman des Goscinny, naissance d'un gaulois*. Grasset, 2019.

Muller, Catel, and José-Louis Bocquet. *Alice Guy*. Casterman, 2021.

———. *Joséphine Baker*. Casterman, 2016.

———. *Olympe de Gouges*. Casterman, 2012.

Peras, Delphine. "Dans le bureau de . . . Catel." *L'express*, 22 July 2018, https://www.lexpress.fr/culture/livre/dans-le-bureau-de-catel_2026112.html.

Potet, Frédéric. "Pénélope Bagieu: 'Dans le monde de la BD, pour certains, je reste un malentendu.'" *Le monde*, 12 Jan. 2020, https://www.lemonde.fr/culture/article/2020/01/12/penelope-bagieu-l-habitude-de-l-echec-a-fait-de-moi-un-roc_6025580_3246.html.

Roelens, Camille. "Féminismes d'ici et d'ailleurs, d'hier et d'aujourd'hui." *Neuvieme-Art*2.0, 2019, http://neuviemeart.citebd.org/spip.php?article1230.

CHAPTER 12

The Women behind the Woman behind the Man

Women Drawing Plural Collective Voices onto the Page in Emilie Plateau's *Noire*

VÉRONIQUE BRAGARD

Women artists' works like Julie Doucet's *My New York Diary* (1999), Marjane Satrapi's *Persepolis* (2003), or Alison Bechdel's *Fun Home* (2006) have entered the graphic narrative scene via autobiography and intimate storytelling. In her groundbreaking analysis *Graphic Women* (2010), Hilary Chute highlights how graphic narratives by women are drawn from an embodied perspective. Attendant to Chute's discussion of trauma and bodily intimacy in the gutters of graphic narratives is the fact that these artists share an investment in both telling and showing intimate bodily and traumatic experiences, merging past and present onto the same panel. Comics visualize what cannot be said or attempt to put in words/images what cannot or can no longer be visualized. Comics is a haptic form often about bodies, Chute argues, and about "locating them in space and time" ("Comics" 112). In her analysis of shame, Kristen Radtke observes that comics allow for the sexualized body to be present every time it is drawn, since the medium involves dense replication, illustrating comics' possibility to create a corporeal repetition and presence. In turn, this "has allowed many female illustrators to confront how they see their bodies and how their bodies are seen by the men around them" (Radtke). What also plays a role in this embodied experience, according to Eszter Szép, is the form of lines. In *Comics and the Body: Drawing, Reading and Vulnerability* (2020), drawn lines and physicality are read as the drawer's bodily trace and haptic charge that generate relationship and rethinking.

The comics medium, as Frederick Aldama's contribution in *The Routledge Companion to Gender and Sexuality in Comic Book Studies* posits, has been dominated by male writers and heteronormative values. However, since the underground comix movement in the 1970s, the field has been witness to a blossoming of diverse approaches and progressive images, leaving behind a predominantly male representation of gender roles and readership. Besides the pedagogical and psychological orientation of many women's comics, numerous recent female comics artists have also offered more epic and biographical/historical stories addressing feminist as well as political issues. Liv Strömquist's famous volumes are cases in point as they engage with gender theories, using the carnivalesque to expose the taboo representation of female sexual organs, for instance. In this way, comics, like feminist perspectives, participate in debunking normalized versions of social organization, offering alternative readings of exploitative systems and hierarchies as well as alternative appropriations of the comics medium.

Many female artists like Liv Strömquist and Pénélope Bagieu revisit and explore the history of famous historical female figures who played a role in diversifying or emancipating women's roles. They use the medium to foreground historical figures and alternative values. Within these alter-narratives, female characters do not appear as superheroes but as transmitters of super values. Instead of the usual quest narrative of fame and individual success, they render visible small people, small acts, and slow change in the midst of hard activist struggles. Such narratives thereby show how the history of women's emancipation has not been an abrupt revolution per se but a slow ongoing process. And despite all the financial problems comics artists face to get published and acknowledged, theirs is a struggle that entails the wish to represent their peers struggling. In many ways, their metafictional work emerges as a mise en abyme of their own precarious situations and their heroic artistic endeavors to gain visibility themselves.

This goes hand in hand with Golnar Nabizadeh's observations. In *Representation and Memory in Graphic Novels*, Nabizadeh argues that varied forms in comics help generate diverse representations of identities, alternate ways of giving voice to groups or individuals that have been dismissed. As mentioned above, female authors participate in rendering visible female acts and figures to counter their dismissal. In *Culottées* (2016),[1] Bagieu revisits some

---

1. The US release and translation of Bagieu's book, *Brazen: Rebel Ladies Who Rocked the World*, won an Eisner Award in 2019.

thirty women's stories, which cover diverse time periods and cultural and geographical backgrounds, and points to how many creative and determined women dared move away from traditional roles and expectations: from the resistant dancer Josephine Baker to the bearded lady Clementine Delait to the Apache fighter and shaman Lozen to the athlete and bathing suit inventor Annette Kellerman. In a similar vein, Brimant and Meurisse's *Drôle de femmes* (2010) looks at how women have struggled to have their humor heard.

Emilie Plateau's *Noire: La vie méconnue de Claudette Colvin* (2015), inspired by Tania de Montaigne's essay and subsequent play (2020), addresses a more collective and yet specific aspect of the Civil Rights Movement that led to the recognition of African American citizenship. Moving away from epic superheroes or trauma aesthetics often associated with comics, Plateau's work attempts to portray militant acts of boycott with minimalist drawings pointing to both racial discrimination and systemic intersectionality issues in image form. The graphic novel is based on documented research and tells the marginalized story of one of the first rebellious figures of the Civil Rights Era, retrieving her name from forgotten archives. Claudette Colvin's unknown story is here conveyed in minimalist style, a style that, I will argue, enables both individualization as well as an engagement with collective aspects of the multifaceted Civil Rights Movement she embodies.

This chapter focuses on how Plateau's *Noire* adapts Tania de Montaigne's original essay with the possibilities of comics, foregrounding small acts and slow and collective change via original visual comics strategies. Plateau's graphic novel not only moves away from the epic monologic idea of emancipation centered on one individual and radical change but engages with slow and collective change initiated by several women, who have often been made invisible in male-centered historiographies. I first consider how the creative piece employs several multimodal strategies to address the role but also the limitations of female actors in this collective struggle. More specifically, I examine the visual possibilities explored by Plateau in *Noire*. I first tackle the ambivalence of the brown color the artist plays with to question racial discrimination and absurdity. Drawing on Szép's study of comics' engagement with vulnerability in *Comics and the Body: Drawing, Reading, and Vulnerability*, I analyze how Plateau's small characters as well as backgrounds foster empathy with the vulnerability of the protesters' bodies. The figurative minimalism (close to children's literature/drawings) of the vulnerable body enables both an individual and collective identification. A third section addresses the symbolic image of the seat, which is explored to highlight how women have occupied space or been denied seats in the larger context of the Civil Rights Movement. A new collective memory is here created, one that is made possible beyond the gutter. New cognitive and visual gaps allow Plateau to address racism and intersectionality in oblique ways.

Plateau's Rewriting of Tania de Montaigne's *Noire*

Tania de Montaigne's book-length essay *Noire: La vie méconnue de Claudette Colvin* was published in 2015[2] and revolves around the story of the civil rights activist Claudette Colvin as part of a series of "nos heroines" that explores women's forgotten struggles. De Montaigne, a French journalist and writer, turned her book into a play in 2020. Of Caribbean origins, she discovered racial discrimination when she grew up in Paris and decided to speak up and take the stage in Paris as a storyteller addressing the audience.

Noire directly addresses the contemporary reader who is invited to "take a deep breath" and immerse themselves in 1950s Alabama to learn about Claudette Colvin's life in that tense political period. The reader learns that, left to be raised by her aunt, who died when she was thirteen, Claudette Colvin grew up in a segregated state. On March 2, 1955, aged fifteen, she refused to give her seat to a white man on the bus. This gesture, which may seem so trivial today, marked a real position at the time: by refusing to comply with a dehumanizing and humiliating law, she would be arrested, insulted, and assaulted by the police. Out of police custody, she decided to plead not guilty and to sue the city of Montgomery, supported by the Women's Political Council and the National Association for the Advancement of Colored People (NAACP). Claudette is portrayed in this essay as a fragile, silent yet brave woman. She pled not guilty and, with the help of women like Ann Gibson Robinson, started boycotts. During her trial, she was found guilty of three counts: disturbance of public order, violation of the law, and assault on law enforcement officials. This decision destroyed her life and dreams. Later, becoming pregnant by a married man, she was forced to leave Montgomery, and her political action was forgotten. Replaced by Rosa Parks, her name fell into oblivion for a number of reasons that De Montaigne explores. Claudette Colvin is still alive and currently resides in New York.

De Montaigne's essay recounts how Claudette's action, and other women's refusal to give their seats, led to the Supreme Court's decision to ban bus segregation yet their contribution was ignored by the media. As de Montaigne denounces, male circles took over and decided the actions

---

2. In the year of its release, Tania de Montaigne's work won le Prix littéraire Simone Veil.

they would take. The essay makes clear that Claudette Colvin, because she was too dark-skinned, too poor, and pregnant, was excluded from history. She actually became pregnant when she was fifteen, a socially unacceptable, shameful situation. By contrast, Rosa Parks was the small, fragile, well-dressed seamstress who would not defy the male world and was chosen to represent this female protest movement. She also refused to give up her seat on a bus. But the author reminds us of the common biases that favored Parks over Colvin: Rosa Parks was light-skinned and had straightened hair. It was her name and not Claudette's that was therefore foregrounded. As boycotts were organized, a leaflet mentioned Claudette . . . Colbert, not Colvin. Claudette Colbert is the name of an actress, after whom Colvin was named. This first act of erasure epitomizes her very invisibilization. Martin Luther King Jr. (MLK) would subsequently become the spokesperson for this movement, his figure would go so far as to almost rub out these strong and courageous acts initiated by women, his "male charisma" placing him above them in the collective imagination and the male-centered media.

Plateau's graphic novel, published in 2019, closely follows de Montaigne's book and mode of address, making use of minimalist drawings and unframed panels that strip the story of any aesthetic weight. This minimalist style, which mostly depicts small childish characters and sketchy landscapes, keeps the essence of the acts Plateau wants to highlight in focus. The apostrophe that opens both the essay and the comic book with "take a deep breath" leads to an empathy process also present at the visual level in small streets and figures.

Because of their unframed drawings, the sequences challenge the central role of the gutter in stimulating the reader's participation. Jan Baetens considers that the gutter has been overestimated as it can have different functions or go unnoticed (216). In Plateau's unframed panels, gutters serve a specific visual function, which goes beyond filling narrative gaps to concentrate on bodily language, voice, or nonviolence, for instance. But color and empty spaces fill the narrative-cognitive function as well. In line with and extending Baetens's observation, this paper looks at how the effects created by *Noire* result from very specific aspects: color, character drawing, and symbolism in seats. Shades of orange/brown, for instance, play a decisive role as they offer a cognitive question to be pondered by the reader. The use of color moves beyond interpretations related to economic costs to gain a very symbolic meaning, especially in a comic that addresses racism and intersectionality. It urges one to expand traditional analyses of the symbolic uses of chromatic structures in graphic storytelling. The unabashed minimalist style also slows down reading and puts emphasis on symbolic moments and places (trials, public spaces, violence, fear) rather than actions. Dwellings and haptic surfaces, Szép reminds us, are both places and processes that here speak to the experience of vulnerability in public spaces.

Shades of Brown as New Gutters

Plateau's *Noire* opens with landscapes, brown-leaved trees and buildings that are foregrounded as the narrator addresses us and zooms from the North to South to reach Alabama. These first colored images emerge as natural: they are associated with a forest, woods, or the sky. It is with page 5 that the reader comes to understand that colors can be coupled with negative elements to construct and engender discrimination: "white only" signs haunt segregated Montgomery streets. The reader is involved and invited to enter the shoes of an African American citizen in the 1950s. Brown and white characters in brown and white environments are brought to dialogue and take interest in each other's experience. Yet, small "whites only" signs point to how colors become associated with exclusion and discrimination. When no separation existed in shops, people of color were to stay outside (a practice shown on page 7). Later in the graphic novel, even New York becomes brown and warm, further destabilizing the color symbolism.

This alternation of colors enables Plateau to emphasize racialized politics: when race plays a role, characters are of different colors, put aside, more visible. When we see Claudette for the first time, she is drawn in white in a small rural wooden house. The year is 1939, the date of her birth. She is neutral, as the artist argues, because she is like others when away from public spaces. The brown color used until then to emphasize wooden materials, leaves or clothes, warmth, conviviality—not skin—becomes associated with difference. As soon as she is with white people, Claudette becomes brown and different. She turns brown because people see her this way. On many other panels, when she is at home or at school, she is represented in white. But Claudette is this tiny woman with glasses, vulnerably drawn yet strongly determined to defend her rights.

This color tension culminates in an explanation regarding the segregation rules in buses. Claudette is fifteen when she refuses to give her seat (see figure 12.1). The use of white and shades of brown clearly brings discrimination and segregation to the fore. Claudette is eventually arrested. The drawings in these panels make bus segregation most palpable in the use of shades of orange/brown that show how Black people were forced to give their seats to white people. The reader here needs to pay more attention to color than to

Vous vous installez à une place réservée aux noirs.

Mais si un blanc est contraint de rester debout,

vous devrez lui céder votre siège.

FIGURE 12.1. Emilie Plateau, *Noire: La vie méconnue de Claudette Colvin*, 2019, p. 10.

the transition gaps of the gutter. It is color that builds tabular relationships. In many ways Claudette's almost invisible and passive act tells a lot about her socially and racially vulnerable status.

The double page that follows her arrest is almost completely black: the color of violence, humiliation, police force. When she is freed, black becomes the color of police brutality and insults (24–25) later associated with the fear of KKK violence (31). She is then helped by the NAACP (Ann Gibson Robinson and Rosa Parks) who want to organize a boycott and for her to plead not guilty. After her trial where she is found guilty, Claudette falls into despair but keeps participating in the NAACP gatherings. Black is again used in the next four pages with short sentences in white: "You won't tell anyone"; "I'm a married man"; "You got it, you'll shut up"; and we see Claudette running away. She crosses the page, in tears, her face tormented, hands on her belly until we see her telling her parents about her pregnancy. These dark pages announce that she will be further marginalized and will lose her chance to become a lawyer (which was her dream). The black pages evoke a traumatic experience.

Plateau alternates between these symbolic uses of black and the brown-orange color making sure they do not become essentialized. While brownish orange remains the color of warm rural homes, it is also the color of violent attacks, of piss on shop windows, cars destroyed by acid, stones thrown into their windows, and other brutal, racist acts. Spot color is used through the book to highlight the eruption of violence, such as when two broken windows on a small house are the only brown-orange in a panel, or a damaged car is the only color in another panel (99). It is the color of warm large fields of the South but also of cemeteries.

Reading transitions in color here expand on the role of the gutter-as-gap, which is a space where readers interpret and connect elements. Readers have to animate the gutter but also ponder the actions behind the colors and the changes in color. The symbolism of the color, which viewers are invited to connect here in the broken windows and brown, damaged car, reveals itself to be a construction that speaks to the brutality of African American history.

Toward the end, during the rallies of activists, brown becomes the color of large groups of African Americans getting organized and united to resist. Color takes here a very political meaning and a dimension that is fundamental to the language and ethics foregrounded in the piece. It is collectivity that is valorized in the numerous brown characters united in boycott becoming one single brown figure of defiance. A contrast is then created between the large meetings of activists and the small silhouette of Claudette in the middle of a blank page, a direct allusion to her vulnerability and marginalization from these collective gatherings. She progressively disappears and is excluded from the movement.

Last, but not least, the many almost empty white pages of the book draw the reader's attention to the subtle details and bodily gestures that convey Claudette Colvin's socially vulnerable body and position. The nonmovement of the characters, almost somewhat frozen on the page, reinforce both the symbolic act of passive resistance and the role of nonviolence in the Civil Rights Movement. Space is given to testifying, voicing one's experience in front of the judges as Claudette, despite her marginalization, accepted to be among the five plaintiffs in the court case of *Browder v. Gayle*.

Collective versus Individuation: Strength and Vulnerability

Claudette is drawn as a small fragile character, who has a physical identity of her own in Plateau's book: glasses and curly hair distinguish her from Rosa Parks or tall Joan Robinson. She is in many ways individualized and recognizable.

The apostrophe in the text "You are Claudette Colvin" as well as the personal handwriting of the text add to this individualized and intimate relationship with one unique and special woman. Chute highlights how handwriting emphasizes a bodily mark (*Graphic Women*, 11). In Plateau's work, two types of handwriting underline the witness-listener relationship that is established. Later we see two colors for handwriting, one being that of the omniscient narrator, the other, the personal voice of individual characters.

However, thanks to the book's minimalism, Claudette Colvin's external appearance is made to resemble that of her friends in many ways. The female boycotters and activists have similar physical traits, positions, and clothes. These similarities strengthen a shared experience and collective force that reinforces solidarity in vulnerability. The collective is further graphically conveyed by the numerous figures in buses, in churches, and in the streets as they boycott public transportation. In her discussion of lines and haptic elements in comics, Szép highlights how these are also interpreted by the reader's body, which can apprehend the trace of the drawer's hand and personality (2). Plateau's characteristic style with small, frozen, calm characters emphasizes similar bodies and clothes whether they are Black or white. Her minimalist and orderly body lines urge toward an embodied engagement with vulnerability, which Judith Butler reminds us is a universal condition (Szép 9). In this case, it reinforces a common experience beyond racial constructions and a fragile position that applies to both men and women.

The graphic novel looks at Claudette Colvin's life but more broadly at the women behind Rosa Parks and behind the male leaders with MLK at its center. It enables polyphony while foregrounding collectivity in the numerous characters, in the images and the "you" that keeps addressing the reader. The Civil Rights Movement, as Plateau shows, started with a few women and their simple small acts, as well as with numerous meetings. In many ways her almost invisible act tells a lot about her vulnerable status. The drawings of *Noire* condense narrative fragments to force the reader to zoom in on gesture and the physical relationship that stands for the values of the characters. Their personalities lie in the ways in which Plateau shows them in action but also in a minimalist perspective to emphasize the symbolic and subversive nature of their actions. Via the direct address to "you," the reader is largely positioned as listener but also potentially as an actor facing a similar experience, filling Claudette's shoes and engaging with her vulnerability.

Equally important are the details of the backgrounds behind Plateau's figures. Wooden shacks in bad shape surrounded by material pieces, broken or repaired windows, shops under the rain, but also trees and grass create pauses and surfaces with haptic details that emphasize the lower income housing of families of color as well as solidarity (in blues music, reunions, church meetings). Plateau's drawings are anything but simplistic as they create haptically charged backgrounds that highlight the "temporality of dwelling" as Szép puts it (112), physical details that invite readers to situate characters. The book repeatedly features the tiny houses they inhabit and that are twice or thrice their size only. These elements point to the vulnerability of a whole community.

Seats: Occupying Public Space

Perhaps the most original aspect of *Noire* is the ways in which Plateau conveys self-assertion but also the tensions within collectivities via a diverse representation of seats. The image of the seat, central to the story of Claudette Colvin and Rosa Parks, emerges as the embodiment of the act of taking one's place in society despite laws, separations, absences, segregation, and exclusions. Sitting is something we do every day, and yet we do not realize how this trivial act can be political. While giving your seat to other people evokes benevolence, occupying a throne or an important seat is a sign of power. Seats are thus familiar objects, but they can speak to serious issues. The seat is a physical reminder of the human occupation of space, a proxy for humans trying to be in a certain position or role. On the one hand, Plateau uses the seat to suggest discrimination but also political agency, and on the other hand, the seat further conveys family values and intersectionality.

First, the image of the empty seat foregrounded by Plateau enables the viewer to visualize segregation and discrimination. The graphic novel denounces the fact that four people needed to leave their seats to give room to white people. Seats become empty because of racism, they separate human beings because of segregation laws. But the line is crossed, and Claudette remains seated. Her act becomes associated with political assertion and the reappropriation of social/political power. The allusion to future sit-ins where sitting gains political power and where public space is reappropriated is most obvious. Empty seats are later associated with the boycotts that led to emptying the seats of buses. At the end of the story, as civil rights have been obtained, we see buses filled with seated people of color. These 1956 boycotts (by five women) will lead to the *Browder v. Gayle* ruling that declared segregation in public transports unconstitutional. Seats are also associated with police interrogation, jail conditions, discussions with the mayor, and the court judges listening and eventually condemning Claudette (85).

But sitting is also used by Plateau to emphasize moments of discussion, reflection, or confession. Several times Claudette is portrayed sitting and discussing her actions and emotions with her family and friends (45, 59, 71). She is sitting in between her uncle and aunt, who comfort her, when she announces she is pregnant. Sitting gains new meaning as it sheds light on the different possibilities it offers: silence as well as a comfortable position from which to debate, dialogue, and participate in rallies. It also offers the possibility to gather in unity before action in churches or large auditoriums. The power of the group is highlighted with large auditoriums filled with sitting participants, engaged in the organizing of boycotts (87).

However, as the following vignette highlights, Plateau uses the empty seat to also address issues related to sexism, which operated within the Civil Rights Movement. Intersectionality and how women within the Civil Rights Movement had their seats stolen by men is made palpable through a brief series of panels in which men are portrayed as making decisions while the empty seats that surround them represent the women who have been marginalized from the movement (see figure 12.2). After the first boycotts, women were no longer invited to participate in the discussion on future actions. The church's pastor as well as MLK are shown discussing the image of Claudette Colvin (they consider her psychologically unstable and shameful because she is pregnant). Male Black leaders, who here become privileged, are shown alone, a sign that reinforces the fact that they refused to publicize Colvin's pioneering effort. Systems of oppression are shown as overlapping, intersecting: race, patriarchy, and class play a role in Claudette Colvin's experience of marginalization. Kimberlé Crenshaw, who coined the term intersectionality in the 1980s, writes that "when we talk about intersectionality, we are talking about people who are marginal within the movements that represented them" (218). Colvin's is a case in point.

The book ends with an image of Claudette sitting on a bench in New York, unacknowledged and yet more visible and self-assertive (122). Her resistance has been recognized as a street has her name, which the text highlights. Again, there is no real movement, because she is sitting, but remaining seated, one is reminded, has clearly become an act of resistance, a political gesture. Sitting means occupying public space and embodying

FIGURE 12.2. Emilie Plateau, *Noire: La vie méconnue de Claudette Colvin*, 2019, p. 75.

a political voice. In a similar way, drawing the one seating also becomes a political act. Plateau's address, "You are Claudette Colvin," further engages with the power of art to create empathy and a proactive role.

The blank spaces as well as the frozen positions of the characters reinforce a nonviolent approach to the civil rights struggle, leaving room to emphasize Claudette's voice and zoom in on details of bodily expression. In comics, space can represent time, yet here space is not there to move forward but to anchor present voices in the moment of acknowledgement.

Conclusion

Building on Tania de Montaigne's essay, Plateau's visual narrative makes visually accessible what an activist scholarship has sought to correct. The fact that Rosa Parks, as a historical figure, was deliberately chosen as being strategically viable has been a more broadly known story in recent years as critical light has been shed on the erasure of women's contributions to the Civil Rights Movement. The 2000s have seen the publication of a number of critical pieces that re-examine these omissions, including *Want to Start a Revolution? Radical Women in the Black Freedom Struggle* (2009), *Gender and the Civil Rights Movement* (2004), and *Claudette Colvin: Twice Toward Justice* (2009). Comics have also participated in this memory process, focusing on more marginal characters and standpoints, as Jorge Santos highlights in his reading of the *March* trilogy in *Graphic Memories of the Civil Rights Movement: Reframing History in Comics*. Tania de Montaigne and Emilie Plateau make these recent findings accessible to a Francophone audience who may not be familiar with such critical re-examinations of the Civil Rights Movement. *Noire* is made to resonate within a Francophone context where racism and discrimination operate in other ways (as de Montaigne testifies in interviews) but where outcries paralleling those of the Black Lives Matter movement have erupted in recent years, such as in the protests following the death of Adama Traoré while in police custody.

The English-translation title of Emilie Plateau's graphic novel *Colored: The Unsung Life of Claudette Colvin* (2019) clearly highlights how the graphic tritone adaptation challenges constructions of race. As I have shown, Plateau's creative and ambivalent use of shades of brown/orange enable her to expand on the graphic novel possibilities to convey and reflect on issues of invisibility and racial marginalization via the ambivalence of colors, the ability of lines to convey vulnerability, the emptiness of seats, and a minimalistic style that challenges usual gutter-centered comics reading. More importantly, while she underlines the collective and feminine side of the struggle, she makes creative use of the very sites that were central to the Civil Rights Movement: namely color, collectivity, and resistance (in sittings or defiantly refusing to give one's seat). Her work declines the possibilities of the visual, complicating these aspects to highlight the roles of resistance and openness in the medium.

Works Cited

Aldama, Frederick Luis. "Gender and Sexuality in Comics: The Told, Untold Stories." *The Routledge Companion to Gender and Sexuality in Comic Book Studies,* edited by Frederick Luis Aldama, Routledge, 2020.

Baetens, Jan. "Gap or Gag: On the Myth of the Gutter in Comics Scholarship." *Etudes francophones,* vol. 32, 2020, pp. 213–17.

Bagieu, Pénélope. *Culottées.* Gallimard Jeunesse, 2016.

Birmant, Julie, and Chatherine Meurisse. *Drôles de femmes*. Dargaud, 2016.

Chute, Hillary. "Comics Form and Narrating Lives." *Profession*, 2011, pp. 107–17.

———. *Graphic Women: Life and Narrative in Contemporary Comics*. Columbia UP, 2010.

Crenshaw, Kimberlé, and Patricia Schulz. "Intersectionality in Promoting Equality." *Equal Rights Review*, vol. 16, 2016, pp. 205–19.

De Montaigne, Tania. *Noire: La vie méconnue de Claudette Colvin*. Grasset, 2015.

Nabizadeh, Golnar. *Representation and Memory in Graphic Novels*. Routledge, 2020.

Plateau, Émilie. *Noire: La vie méconnue de Claudette Colvin*. Dargaud, 2019.

Radtke, Kristen. "Body of Work: How the Graphic Novel Became an Outlet for Female Shame." *The Guardian*, 29 Aug. 2019, https://www.theguardian.com/books/2019/aug/28/body-of-work-how-the-graphic-novel-became-an-outlet-for-female-shame.

Santos, Jorje, Jr. *Graphic Memories of the Civil Rights Movement: Reframing History in Comics*. U of Texas P, 2019.

Szép, Eszter. *Comics and the Body: Drawing, Reading, and Vulnerability*. Ohio State UP, 2020.

CONTRIBUTORS

ARMELLE BLIN-ROLLAND is a Lecturer in French and Francophone studies at Bangor University, Wales, UK. Her research specialties include French and Francophone environmental humanities, *bande dessinée* and text/image studies, and adaptation and intermediality. She has published widely on these topics, including in *European Comic Art, Studies in Comics, Modern Languages Open*, and *Modern and Contemporary France*. Her first monograph, *Adapted Voices*, was published by Legenda in 2015. Her current research project investigates the relationship between narrative, space, and the environment in contemporary France from multispecies, ecofeminist, and eco-decolonial perspectives. She is review coeditor for *European Comic Art*.

Assistant Professor of French at Florida State University, **MICHELLE BUMATAY** specializes in African Francophone and diasporic cultural production focusing primarily on *bandes dessinées*. Interested in questions of representation, migration, transcolonial violence, and historiography, she has published in *Contemporary French Civilization, Francosphères, Études francophones, European Comic Art, Research in African Literatures*, and *Alternative Francophone*, and she has contributed chapters to several anthologies on comics. She is also currently on the editorial boards of *European Comic Art, Imaginaries: Films, Fictions, and Other Representations of the French-Speaking Worlds*, and *New Archipelagoes: World Writing in French*.

253

VÉRONIQUE BRAGARD is Associate Professor in English and Francophone studies at the Université catholique de Louvain (Belgium), where she teaches classes on u/dystopian literatures and a research seminar on comics and the postcolonial. Her current projects focus on the Belgian colonial past as well as Belgo-Congolese literatures, artistic expressions, and decolonialization praxis in comics. She has published numerous articles and book chapters on comics adaptations, coloniality, and colonial monuments in comics (*Memory Studies, Literature Compass, European Comic Art*).

BENOÎT CRUCIFIX is Assistant Professor in cultural studies at KU Leuven and researcher at the Royal Library of Belgium (KBR), where he leads the FED-tWIN project "Popular Heritage Lost & Found." His monograph *Drawing from the Archives: Comics Memory in the Contemporary Graphic Novel* was published through Cambridge University Press in 2023. He is currently coeditor in chief of the open-access, peer-reviewed journal *Comicalités*.

ISABELLE DELORME is an Associate Researcher in the Centre d'Histoire at Sciences Po-Paris. She received her PhD in history on graphic memoirs in 2016. She is the author of *Quand la bande dessinée fait mémoire du 20e siècle: Les récits mémoriels historiques en bande dessinée* (les Presses du réel, 2019). Her research focuses on the representation of memory in comics and on the traumatic memory, individual and collective, of contemporary historical events (wars, genocides, attacks, etc.). Recently, she has been researching female biographies and the work of Catel. Since 2018, she also oversees a refugee access program at Sciences Po.

JACQUES DÜRRENMATT is Professor of stylistics and poetics at Sorbonne University (Paris). He has published several works on the questions raised by the division and fragmentation of literary or audiovisual objects and on the aesthetic uses of punctuation, typography, and montage but also on everything that concerns eccentricity in the arts. For several years, he has been interested in what comics bring to the field of literature, notably with a book on the subject published by Classiques Garnier in 2013: *Bande dessinée et littérature*.

MARGARET C. FLINN is Associate Professor in the Department of French and Italian and the Department of Theatre, Film, and Media Arts at The Ohio State University. She is the author of *The Social Architecture of French Cinema, 1929–39* (Liverpool UP, 2014) as well as articles, book chapters, and translations on French and Francophone cinema, *bande dessinée*, film theory, and new media art. Her essays on *bande dessinée* have appeared in journals such as *Inks, European Comic Art,* and *The Journal of Graphic Novels and Comics*. In addition to this book, she is the editor or coeditor of numerous special journal issues and currently serves on the editorial boards of *Comicalités* and *Film Matters*.

ALEXANDRA GUEYDAN-TUREK is Associate Professor of French at Swarthmore College. She examines Francophone cultural productions from the MENA region and their sociopolitical transformative potential. Her articles focusing on graphic works, from autographics to underground comix and locally produced manga, have been published in *ImageText, Journal of Graphic*

Novels and Comics, European Comic Art, French Cultural Studies, International Journal of Francophone Studies, and *Nottingham French Studies*. In 2019, she and Carla Calargé coedited a special issue of *Nouvelles études francophones* on *bande dessinée*. Since 2022, she has served as editor in chief of *Nouvelles études francophones*.

JENNIFER HOWELL is an Associate Professor of French and Francophone studies at Illinois State University. Her research focuses on the Francophone literatures and cultures of North Africa and the Vietnamese diaspora and specifically on how political trauma is historicized and remembered in popular culture and the visual arts. Her articles have appeared in such journals as *Contemporary French and Francophone Studies, Journal of North African Studies, European Comic Art,* and *French Review*. She is the author of *The Algerian War in French-Language Comics: Postcolonial Memory, History, and Subjectivity* (Lexington Books, 2015).

JESSICA KOHN holds a PhD in history, the subject she teaches in a French international high school. She is the author of *Dessiner des petits Mickeys: Une histoire sociale de la bande dessinée en France et en Belgique, 1945–1968* (Éditions de la Sorbonne, 2022). Her research focuses on the sociohistorical construction of the cartoonists' profession in the twentieth century.

SYLVAIN LESAGE is Associate Professor of history at the University of Lille and specializes in book history and media studies. He is the author of *Publier la bande dessinée: Les éditeurs Franco-Belges et l'album* (Presses de l'ENSSIB, 2018); *L'effet livre: Métamorphoses de la bande dessinée* (Presses universitaires François-Rabelais, 2019); and *Ninth Art: Bande dessinée, Book Publishing and the Gentrification of Mass Culture, 1964–1975* (Palgrave Macmillan, 2022).

CATRIONA MACLEOD is Senior Lecturer in French studies at the University of London Institute in Paris. Her research interests concern representations of women in *bandes dessinées* and narratives of trauma and migration in visual forms. She is the author of *Invisible Presence: The Representation of Women in French-Language Comics* (Intellect, 2021) and has published in journals such as *L'esprit créateur, Contemporary French Civilisation,* and *European Comic Art*. Her current research project focuses on contemporary female artists' use of the *bande dessinée* as a form of political and social activism aiming to break entrenched female bodily "taboos."

MARK MCKINNEY is Professor of French at Miami University (Ohio). With Alec G. Hargreaves, he coedited *Post-Colonial Cultures in France* (Routledge, 1997). He also edited *History and Politics in French-Language Comics and Graphic Novels* (UP of Mississippi, 2008). He authored *The Colonial Heritage of French Comics* (Liverpool UP, 2011), *Redrawing French Empire in Comics* (The Ohio State UP, 2013), and *Postcolonialism and Migration in French Comics* (Leuven UP, 2021). With Laurence Grove and Ann Miller, he founded and coedited (2008–16) the journal *European Comic Art*. He has also published articles and book chapters on postcolonialism in comics and prose fiction.

INDEX

abortion: access, 168, 170, 229; anti-, 161, 163, 171; experience, 161–63, 166, 170, 173, 175–76; legality, 79, 161–64, 166, 168–70, 176; narratives, 162, 165–66, 175; pro-, 168; procedure, 172, 175; pro-choice, 161–65, 168–71, 173, 175–76; pro-life, 161–65, 170–71, 175–76; rights, 160–61, 232; stigma, 161. *See also* feminism; United States

Abouet, Marguerite, 8, 124–29, 132, 136–40, 215

activism, 16, 76, 81–85, 91, 110 fig. 5.2, 112, 155–56, 158. *See also* feminism

Adèle Blanc-Sec (Tardi), 42

Adventures of Lieutenant Blueberry, The (Charlier and Giraud), 47

Africa: *Kubuni* exhibition, 140; pre-independence, 131; Western stereotypes about, 125, 128, 133, 135. *See also* North Africa; South Africa; West Africa

African: artists, 137; authors, 132n5; BD, 139; cartoonists, 138–39, 199, 215; colonialism, 211–12, 214, 216, 218–19;

history, 217; magazines, 130 fig. 6.1, 136; slave trade, 206; Western stereotypes about, 125, 200, 202, 205; women, 125–26, 128–29, 131, 132n5, 136, 140, 199–200, 207–8, 214–16, 218. *See also* feminism; stereotypes

African American, 241, 244, 246

Afrobul (Fuillu), 216

"Ahed wa Karīm" (Fakhouri), 151

Ah! Nana (Delobel), 10, 42, 56–60, 62, 70. *See also* sexuality

Ainsi soit Benoîte Groult (Catel), 229, 232, 235

Ainsi soit-elle (Groult), 227, 229

Algues vertes, l'histoire interdite (Léraud and Van Hove), 117

Allen, Mallary, 161–62, 164–65, 168, 170, 175–76

Alice Guy (Catel), 231, 235

Alonso, Alicia, 226

Amazons, 198–200, 201 fig. 10.1, 202–3, 204 fig. 10.2, 205–7, 210–19

America. *See* North America

257

American: academia, 8; cinema, 127, 129, 193; comics, 5–6, 9, 22, 39–40, 43, 45, 47–49, 56, 69, 85, 136, 173; people, 70, 187; pop culture, 131, 135
Americanized, 22, 33 tables 1.5–1.6
Amoco Cadiz oil spill, 109, 110 fig. 5.2. *See also* Breton
Angoulême: Anne Simon, 189; *bande dessinée* museum, 189; controversy, 14, 39, 143n1, 224, 226n3; International Comics Festival, 7, 38–39, 48, 53–55, 135, 139–40, 226–27; *Kubuni* exhibition, 140; Nicole Claveloux, 53, 71
Anjela (Le Guen), 98, 114–19
Arab, 16, 85–86, 142, 143n1, 145, 149, 154
Arab Spring, 75, 83, 86
Arabic, 75, 81, 85, 87, 89, 145, 148–49, 151n7, 155. *See also* Darija
"Ar c'hleuz" (Duval, Anjela), 116–17
Assigned Male. *See Assignée garçon* (Labelle)
Assignée garçon (Labelle), 1–2
Astérix (character), 185, 187
Astérix (comic) (Goscinny and Uderzo), 100
auteur, 12–14, 39–40, 43, 47, 49–50, 232
auteure. *See* auteur
autobiographical, 10–11, 14–15, 23–24, 59, 137, 156, 170, 228, 232, 239
autobiography. *See* autobiographical
autodidact myth, 23–24, 29
avortement, 160n1. *See also* abortion
Aya de Yopougon (Abouet), 124–26, 129, 136, 137n9, 140
Ayouch, Nabil, 79–80

Baartman, Saartjie, 208–9, 218
Bagieu, Pénélope, 7–8, 223–24, 240
"Baignade de nègres" (Lumière), 209
Baker, Josephine, 225–26, 231, 233–34
bande dessinées adultes, 55, 57
Bandit! See Brigande! (Rouxel and Michon)
"Barzhonegoù-noz—Barzhonegoù-deiz," 115
Bécassine, 99–100, 102, 184, 185n8, 229

Béhanzin, King, 200, 203, 204 fig. 10.2, 205, 207, 217n14
Benacquista, Tonino, 162, 164, 166, 175
Bernadette (Forster), 22, 26, 32–33
Bingo, 131
biographic. *See* biography
biography, 23–24, 31, 98, 114, 155, 216, 222–26, 229, 237, 240
bluestocking, 186–87, 194
Bocquet, José-Louis, 222–23, 225, 228–29, 231–37
Bonaparte, Roland, 203, 206–7, 110
Bourgeon, François, 199, 206–7, 218
boycott, 241–43, 245–47, 249
Brazen. See Culottées (Bagieu)
Brétecher, Claire, 10, 25, 29, 31–32, 227
Breton: Amoco Cadiz oil spill, 109, 110 fig. 5.2, 111; comics, 98, 119; language, 107–8, 114–15; women, 98–100, 109, 113. *See also* feminism; representation; stereotypes
Brigande! (Rouxel and Michon), 101–3, 106
Brittany, 97, 99, 101–2, 107–9, 114–15, 118–19. *See also* representation
Browder v. Gayle, 246, 249

Ça restera entre nous / Kalf al-bab (Samadal and Baqi), 143–45, 151, 154, 158. *See also* Lebanese
canon, 21–23, 39. *See also* stereotypes
caricature, 182–84, 187, 191
Casini, Stefano, 199, 207–9, 211
Casterman, 42–44
Catel, 222–29, 231–37. *See also* feminism
Catholic *illustrés. See* Catholic magazines
Catholic magazines, 22, 26, 29, 31–33, 35
Cestac, Florence, 163–64, 166, 175
Cham, 185–89, 191–92, 195
Charlie Hebdo, 37, 164
Charlier, Jean-Michel, 46–47
children's books: illustrated magazines, 31–32; Nicole Claveloux, 55–56, 60, 62, 68, 71; and women, 22, 30, 32, 34, 54, 224. *See also* publishing
Civil Rights Movement, 241, 246–47, 249, 251

"Clandestine Women of History, The" (Catel), 237
Claveloux, Nicole, 53, 55–56, 58–64, 66, 68–70. *See also* Angoulême; children's books; feminism
Cœurs vaillants, 31
Colbert, Claudette, 243
Collectif des Créatrices de Bande Dessinée Contre le Sexisme, 227
colonialism: in art, 206, 209, 211, 217–18; biases of, 135; critiques of, 207, 211, 214; and exoticization, 199–200, 201 fig. 10.1, 205, 210–11, 214–15, 218; in Morocco, 87; post-, 126, 199, 218–19; and slave trade, 216; and violence, 213. *See also* eroticism; representation
Colored. *See Noire* (Montaigne)
colorist, 11, 15, 37–50
Colvin, Claudette, 241–43, 246, 249
comics writer, dominance of, 39, 45–47
Constant, Nicole, 28
Conti, Anita, 225
Coryn, Laetitia, 79–80, 90
Couao-Zotti, Florent, 215–16
Culliford, Nine, 40–41
Culottées (Bagieu), 223, 240–41

Dahomey: Amazons of, 198–200, 203, 207, 211–12, 215; colonization of, 199, 205, 218; Franco-Dahomean War, 200, 203; slave trade in, 216. *See also* representation
Dallas, 129, 132
Darija, 81, 87–88, 90
de Gouges, Olympe, 229–30. *See also* feminism
Déclaration des droits de la femme et de la citoyenne (de Gouges), 5, 227
Delicices d'Afrique (Abouet), 132
Delobel, Anne, 42–43
Delporte, Yvan, 46
Des-agréments d'un voyage d'agrément (Doré), 193
Des salopes et des anges (Benacquista and Cestac), 163–65, 169, 176
Deux vieilles filles vaccinées à marier (Cham), 185–89
diaspora, 126, 133, 136, 138, 140

Dictionnaire des idées reçues (Flaubert), 185
Dionnet, Jean-Pierre, 57, 60
Doré, Gustave, 188, 193, 195
du Faouët, Marion, 101–3, 106–7. *See also* feminism
Duval, Anjela, 98, 114–19
Duval, Marie, 182, 185

ecographics, 97, 118–20
ecosystem, 116–17
education: sexual, 81, 83–84, 89; men's, 29; women's, 27–29
Elyon's, 2, 125, 133, 135–40
Emsav, 99
environment, 99, 102, 106–9, 110 fig. 5.2, 112–15, 119–20
eroticism: colonial, 199–200, 201 fig. 10.1, 203, 204 fig. 10.2, 205–11, 215, 218; and female body, 82, 103, 148, 152; queer, 151; and sexuality, 153

Fakhouri, Nour Hifaoui, 151–53
Fantômette (Chaulet), 189
Fasiki, Zainab, 77–91
February 20 Movement, 76, 83, 85. *See also* Morocco
feminism: and abortion, 164, 168; and activism, 16, 82; African, 129; and *bandes dessinées*, 7, 9, 56, 223–24, 226, 228, 240; Benoîte Groult, 227; Breton, 99–100, 107; Catel, 236–37; eco-, 97–98, 100–101, 103, 108, 109n11, 118–19; inclusive, 154, 158; Marion du Faouët, 102; Moroccan, 76, 82–83, 85, 89, 91; Nicole Claveloux, 58–60, 62; Olympe de Gouges, 230; Second Wave, 55; and universalism, 5. *See also* Lebanese
Filles d'albums (Gagne), 11
Forest, Judith, 14–15
Forster, Nadine, 25
Francophone, 2, 7–8, 98, 124, 128, 132n5, 149, 173, 195, 251
Frappier, Alain, 162, 166, 232
Frappier, Desirée, 162, 166, 170, 232

Galandon, Laurent, 208–9, 211
Gallimard, 125, 139

Gasmi, Abir, 149–51
Gbéhanzin (Couao-Zotti and Adadja), 216–18
gender: binary, 112; discrimination, 77, 87; distribution in comics, 39, 44, 55; diversity, 98; divisions, 182; and education, 27; equality, 14, 76, 81–82, 99, 152, 155; expectations, 58–59, 100; experience, 16; fluidity, 4, 60, 115, 150–51; genderqueer, 2n2, 3; history, 22; identity, 83–85, 87, 108–9, 131, 143–44; and nature, 98, 103, 108, 115, 119; performativity, 109, 131, 146; reversals, 192–93; roles, 41, 136–37, 184, 240; stereotypes, 77, 154; violence, 75–76, 79, 83, 89. *See also* identity; Morocco; representation; stereotypes; victim
Ghezo, King, 216
Giraud, Jean. *See* Moebius
Glele, King, 200, 215
Go, Go, Go, Grabote!, 68
Goscinny, Anne, 232
Goscinny, René, 29, 46, 233
Gousse and Gigot (characters), 190–91
Gousse & Gigot (Simon), 189
Gouze, Marie. *See* de Gouges, Olympe
Grabote (character), 64, 66, 68–69
Grabote (comic) (Claveloux), 64, 66, 69
Grand Prix, 7, 38, 54, 226n3, 228
graphic novel, 6, 12, 14, 48, 251
Great Outdoors, The. *See Les grands espaces* (Meurisse)
Groult, Benoîte, 227, 229, 235. *See also* feminism
Guen, Christelle Le, 98, 114
Guillerez, Janic, 57
Guy, Alice, 231, 233, 235

Habaieb, Noha, 149–51
hammam, 84
Harlin Quist, 60–61
HBO, 126
Heavy Metal, 69
Henriot, 203, 205
Hergé, 23, 44–45, 195
heteronormativity, 59–60, 81, 240
heterosexual, 115, 187
homosexuality, 58, 79–80

Horellou, Alexis, 107, 114
hshouma, 75–76, 80–81, 86–87, 89, 91. *See also* Morocco
Hshouma (Fasiki), 76, 78, 80–87, 90–91
Hunna (Fakhouri and Feyrouz), 155

identity: collective, 34; cultural, 15; feminine, 131, 185; gender, 83–85, 87, 108; intersectionality, 83; national, 202; and nature, 100, 119; sexual, 88; and technology, 136. *See also* gender
Il fallait que je vous dise (Mermilliod), 162, 170, 172, 175–76
Ingres's Violin. *See Le violon d'Ingres* (Man Ray)
intersectionality, 82–83, 126n2, 241, 243, 248–49. *See also* identity
Islam, 83, 85
Ivory Coast, 125–26, 129, 132, 127

"Je mène les loups" (Guilcher), 103
Jewish, 169
Joséphine Baker (Catel and Bocquet), 231
"Journée à la campagne" (Claveloux), 70

Kahina, 86
Kechiche, Abdellatif, 208–9
Keleck, 57–58
Khalil, Samira, 155n8
Kiki de Montparnasse (Catel and Bocquet), 225, 229, 234
King, Martin Luther, Jr. (MLK), 231, 243
Kobaissy, Farah, 155
Kpengla, King, 206
Kubuni exposition, 140. *See also* Africa

La Brèche, 8–9
la Castafiore, 195
La légèreté (Meurisse), 37
La main verte (Claveloux), 53–54, 69
La Vénus du Dahomey (Casini and Galandon), 199, 206–9, 213–14, 216, 218
La vie d'Ebène Duta (Abouet), 125–26
Labelle, Sophie, 1–4. *See also* United States
Lacassin, Francis, 231

Lanfeust de Troy (Guth), 49
Lapointe, Claude, 227
Lay, Delphine Le, 98, 107, 114
Le choix (Frappier and Frappier), 166, 169–70, 176
"Le corps de l'autre" (Gasmi and Habaieb), 149
Le Docteur Festus (Töpffer), 192
Le monde de Lucrèce (Catel), 233
Le roman des Goscinny, naissance d'un gaulois (Catel), 232–33
Le temps des humbles (Frappier and Frappier), 232
Le transperceneige (Rochette), 48
Le violon d'Ingres (Man Ray), 229
Lebanese: *Ça restera entre nous / Kalf al-bab*, 144; comics (general), 143, 145; feminism, 16; LGBTQ+ rights, 156
Lebanon, 142–44, 151
L'éducation sentimentale (Flaubert), 186
Lefèvre, Lucien, 200, 201 fig. 10.1
Léonnec, Paul, 203, 205
Les Bréchoises, 9
"Les couleurs de la mémoire" (Sonon and Couau-Zotti), 215–16
Les femmes ont toujours travaillé (Schweitzer), 41n7
Les femmes soldats du Dahomey (Serbin and Masioni), 216–18
Les grands espaces (Meurisse), 37
Les Humanoïdes Associés, 57, 62
Les passagers du vent (Bourgeon), 199, 206, 218
Les schtroumpfs. See *Smurfs, The* (Peyo)
letterer, 40, 46–47
Libération, 14, 229
Lightness. See *La légèreté* (Meurisse)
"L'insupportable Grabote et le lion Léonidas" (Claveloux), 64
"Little Vegetable Who Dreamed He Was a Panther, The" (Claveloux), 59
Louise XIV (Claveloux), 69
Lucky Luke, 46

Macaron, Raphaelle, 156–57
Maigrot, Henri. See Henriot
Mandengue, Joëlle Epée. See Elyon's
manga, 3, 5–6, 133

Marche pour la vie, 160
marginalized, 10–11, 54, 143, 156, 181, 214, 241, 246, 249
Maroh, Jul, 2n3, 228n4
Masioni, Pat, 217
maternal, 108–9, 112
MENA (Middle East and North Africa), 75–76, 82–83, 85–87, 142, 144–45, 148, 154. See also Africa; Middle East
Merhej, Lena, 145–49
Merlet, Isabelle, 37–38, 48
Mermilliod, Aude, 170–73, 175–76
Métal hurlant, 57, 69
Meurisse, Catherine, 7n9, 37–38
Mézières, Jean-Claude, 29
Michon, Roland, 101
Middle East, 76, 142, 149. See also MENA (Middle East and North Africa)
Middle Passage, 206
Mireille, 33
Mitterrand, François, 107–8, 114
Moebius, 47, 70
Mohammed VI, King, 76
Molière, 192
Monsieur Pencil (Töpffer), 192
Montaigne, Tania de, 242, 251
Montellier, Chantal, 58, 224
Montparnasse, Kiki de, 229
Morocco: February 20 Movement, 76; gender-based violence, 76, 79, 83; gender discrimination, 83, 85; hshouma, 75–76; language, 81, 87, 90; women, 79, 80–81, 84, 86–87, 89, 91; Women Power Collective, 81, 83. See also sexuality
Morte saison (Claveloux), 69
mother, 54, 100, 108–9, 118, 164, 171
Moudawana, 76
Much Loved (Ayouch), 79
Muller, Catel. See Catel
Musset, Alfred de, 183–84, 191–92

NAACP, 242, 245
nature, 97–98, 100–103, 104 fig. 5.1, 106–7, 110 fig. 5.2, 112–16, 118–20. See also gender; identity
Nelly Bly (Ollagnier and Maurel), 225
Noire (Montaigne), 242

nonbinary, 2
Noomin, Diane, 175n10
North Africa, 75–76, 85–86
North America, 203, 206, 223
North American. *See* American
nuclear: anti-, 107–8, 112, 114; energy, 112, 114; power, 112; power plant, 98, 107, 113

Okapi, 64, 66, 68–69
Olympe de Gouges (Catel), 230
Oubrerie, Clément, 124–27, 226
Oxfam (Oxford Committee of Famine Relief), 155

Panthéon, 168, 231
parité, 5, 9
parity. *See parité*
Parks, Rosa, 242–43, 247–48, 251
Paroles d'honneur (Slimani and Coryn), 79–80, 89–91
Passengers of the Wind, The. *See Les passagers du vent* (Bourgeon)
patriarchal, 76, 81, 85–86, 143, 148, 249
Peale, Raphaelle, 187, 189
penciller, 46
Pennelle, Renaud, 209
Personal Status Code. *See* Moudawana
Peyo, 40–41
Pezron, Henry, 106
picture book, 55–56, 61–62, 71
Pilote, 26, 31, 33, 46, 57
Plateau, Emilie, 241–44, 246–51
Plogoff (Lay and Horellou), 98, 107–8, 114
Plogoff (place), 98, 107–9, 110 fig. 5.2, 112, 114
pornographic. *See* pornography
pornography, 58, 80, 148, 151–53, 209–10
postcolonialism. *See* colonialism
Poucette (Turin), 62
Prin, Alice. *See* Montparnasse, Kiki de
pro-choice. *See* abortion
pro-life. *See* abortion
publishing: children's, 55–56, 60, 62, 68; collective, 12; Franco-Belgian, 7; Francophone, 6; industry, 5, 11, 16; process, 38

queer, 2–3, 60, 144–45, 149–51, 156

race, 82, 202, 244, 249, 251
racism, 133, 135, 207, 218, 243, 248, 251
representation: of Breton women, 98; of Brittany, 99; colonial, 199–200, 209, 211; of Dahomean Amazons, 200, 202–3, 205, 207, 215; gender, 101, 143; of women (general), 41, 148–49, 171, 184, 187, 224, 236, 240; of women *bédéistes*, 5, 7, 9, 11, 15, 16
Robin Hood, 101, 106
Rochette, Jean-Marc, 48
Roe v. Wade, 160, 168
Ronsard, Pierre de, 102–3, 106
Rouxel, Laëtitia, 98, 101–2, 120
rural, 99, 102, 107, 113, 119
Ruy-Vidal, François, 60–61

Samandal, 12, 16, 143–45, 149–50, 154–58
Sand, George, 183–84, 186, 191–92
Satrapi, Marjane, 14
Sex and the City, 126–27, 132, 136
sexism, 2n3, 5, 7, 207, 228, 249
sexual harassment, 76–77, 79, 84, 87, 156
sexuality: *Ah! Nana*, 58; critique of, 153; expressions of, 85, 90, 146, 151–52, 153; female, 79, 80–82, 88, 90–91, 148–50; in Morocco, 79–87, 89–91. *See also* heterosexual; homosexuality
Simon, Anne, 189, 191. *See also* Angoulême
slave trade, 199, 205–6, 219
Slimani, Leïla, 79–80, 87, 89–91
Smurfs, The (Peyo), 40–41, 46
Sonon, Héctor, 215
South Africa, 135, 205
Spirou, 22, 30–31
"Steak" (Macaron), 156
stereotypes: of Africans, 125, 128, 140, 210; and BD canon, 23, 25; Belgian, 135; of Breton women, 100, 119; gender, 49, 77, 154, 164

Strömquist, Liv, 240
Syrian, 142, 155–56

Tardi, Jacques, 42–43
This Will Stay Between Us. See *Ça restera entre nous / Ḳalf al-bab* (Samadal and Baqi)
Time of Humbles, The. See *Le temps des humbles* (Frappier and Frappier)
Tintin (character), 185
Tintin (Hergé), 22, 44, 195
Töpffer, Rodolphe, 181–83, 185, 188, 190–91, 193, 195
trans. *See* transgender
transgender, 2n3, 84
tressage effects, 101, 109, 112–14

Uderzo, Albert, 30, 43
Un cœur simple (Flaubert), 184
Une gamine dans la lune (Claveloux), 59
Union Démocratique Bretonne, 99
United States: abortion in, 160, 168, 175n8; comics industry, 49; Sophie Labelle, 4

universalism, 4–5

Vaillant, 31
Veil, Simone, 163, 166, 168–69, 172
Vénus noire (Kechiche), 208, 218
Viardot, 183
victims: of gender-based violence, 77–79, 85, 154, 157; of patriarchy, 148
Vlamynck, Fanny, 45

West Africa, 124, 136, 139–40, 200, 206
Wimmen's Comix, 58n10
Women BD Authors Collective Against Sexism. *See* Collectif des Créatrices de Bande Dessinée Contre le Sexisme
Women Power Collective, 81, 83. *See also* Morocco
Women Soldiers of Dahomey, The. See *Les femmes soldats du Dahomey* (Serbin and Masioni)

Zha, Edith, 69
Zoos humains, 209

STUDIES IN COMICS AND CARTOONS

Jared Gardner, Charles Hatfield, and Rebecca Wanzo, Series Editors
Lucy Shelton Caswell, Founding Editor Emerita

Books published in Studies in Comics and Cartoons focus exclusively on comics and graphic literature, highlighting their relation to literary studies. The series includes monographs and edited collections that cover the history of comics and cartoons from the editorial cartoon and early sequential comics of the nineteenth century through webcomics of the twenty-first. Studies that focus on international comics are also considered.

Drawing (in) the Feminine: Bande Dessinée and Women
    EDITED BY MARGARET C. FLINN

Lost Literacies: Experiments in the Nineteenth-Century US Comic Strip
    ALEX BERINGER

Growing Up Graphic: The Comics of Children in Crisis
    ALISON HALSALL

Muslim Comics and Warscape Witnessing
    ESRA MIRZE SANTESSO

Beyond the Icon: Asian American Graphic Narratives
    EDITED BY ELEANOR TY

Comics and Nation: Power, Pop Culture, and Political Transformation in Poland
    EWA STAŃCZYK

How Comics Travel: Publication, Translation, Radical Literacies
    KATHERINE KELP-STEBBINS

Resurrection: Comics in Post-Soviet Russia
    JOSÉ ALANIZ

Authorizing Superhero Comics: On the Evolution of a Popular Serial Genre
    DANIEL STEIN

Typical Girls: The Rhetoric of Womanhood in Comic Strips
    SUSAN E. KIRTLEY

Comics and the Body: Drawing, Reading, and Vulnerability
    ESZTER SZÉP

Producing Mass Entertainment: The Serial Life of the Yellow Kid
    CHRISTINA MEYER

The Goat-Getters: Jack Johnson, the Fight of the Century, and How a Bunch of Raucous Cartoonists Reinvented Comics
    EDDIE CAMPBELL

Between Pen and Pixel: Comics, Materiality, and the Book of the Future
    AARON KASHTAN

Ethics in the Gutter: Empathy and Historical Fiction in Comics
    KATE POLAK

Drawing the Line: Comics Studies and INKS, *1994–1997*
    EDITED BY LUCY SHELTON CASWELL AND JARED GARDNER

The Humours of Parliament: Harry Furniss's View of Late-Victorian Political Culture
    EDITED AND WITH AN INTRODUCTION BY GARETH CORDERY AND JOSEPH S. MEISEL

Redrawing French Empire in Comics
    MARK MCKINNEY

www.ingramcontent.com/pod-product-compliance
Lightning Source LLC
Chambersburg PA
CBHW030131240426
43672CB00005B/106